ON TOUR

ON TOUR

The British Traveller in Europe

EDITED BY

Michael Foss

MICHAEL O'MARA BOOKS LIMITED

First published in Great Britain by
Michael O'Mara Books Limited
Lion Yard, 11–13 Tremadoc Road,
London SW4 7NF

On Tour: The British Traveller in Europe

A CIP catalogue record for this book is available from
the British Library

ISBN 0–948397–89–6

Editors: Anne Forsyth and Diana Vowles

Phototypeset by Input Typesetting Limited, Wimbledon, London
Printed and bound by Redwood Burn Limited,
Trowbridge, Wiltshire

Frontispiece 'They "do" Cologne Cathedral' from
The Foreign Tour of Messrs Brown, Jones and Robinson
by Richard Doyle, 1855 (Bradbury & Evans)

CONTENTS

Introduction

Mr V. S. Pritchett, a wise visitor to many lands, once stigmatized himself as 'an offensive traveller'. There is no need for surprise. All records of travel are, to a certain degree, exercises in offensiveness. A person (usually male) takes a swing through a tract of country not his own and about which he knows little. Though depending on the natives for all the necessities of life, he is a bundle of complaints. At the drop of a hat he will browbeat the poor, insult the bourgeois, bad-mouth institutions, and ridicule authority. Returning in perfect safety, but at the cost of some inconvenience and loss of dignity, he relieves his spleen in a picturesque but irascible book, and gives himself the satisfaction of having produced a work of perceptive, trenchant criticism. Life abroad continues exactly as before.

The British on the Continent of Europe, travellers whom this anthology follows through four and a half centuries of wandering, have always been very good at a sort of grumbling, blinkered prejudice. In 1785 a Frenchman watched their progress: 'To cover leagues on land or on water; to take punch and tea at the inns; to speak ill of all the other nations, and to boast without ceasing of their own; that is what the crowd of English call travelling.' Insular, energetic, conventional, smug, and completely maddening. Of course, there is wonderful entertainment in the clash of national antipathies. Who can resist the 'offensiveness' of Fynes Moryson and Dr Burney on Germany, of Giles Fletcher and J. F. Fraser on Russia, of Lady Montagu on Bohemia and Vienna, of Arthur Young and Hazlitt on France, of Roger Ascham and Dickens and nearly everyone else on Italy and in particular of Tobias Smollett on everywhere he went? These travellers were rich in opinion and prejudice, and wrote before the 20th-century Great Nervousness as to identity and values made modern wanderers more circumspect and sympathetic towards foreigners.

But the long parade of British continental travellers, trailing clouds of ill-temper and disgust, offers us today not only amusement but also a good deal of historical instruction. We should not forget that it was the feeling of our own insularity and cultural backwardness that drew British citizens onto the Continent in the first place. Dr Johnson put the matter in his usual blunt way: 'A man who has not been in Italy is always conscious of an inferiority.' And most

7

old travellers, even the most crotchetty, had to admit that a large part of the European mainland showed marks of superior civilization. To counter-balance this intellectual shock (half-feared, half-expected), English travellers carried a conviction, generally confirmed by experience, of the superiority of English government. English criticism, setting aside the too-frequent occasions of local irritation, was fundamentally of governments not peoples. A close look at the accounts of travel bears this out.

The travellers almost always have kind words for peasants, labourers and the unfortunate poor. Richard Ford in Spain, Young and Hazlitt and Robert Louis Stevenson in France, Edward Lear in Italy, Boswell in Corsica, Alexander Kinglake and Lear in Greece (and many others), all had an affectionate respect for the value and integrity of peasant life, crushed though it was almost everywhere by appalling burdens. And the more they saw of these burdens, the more they railed at the forces that imposed the burdens: social injustice, absentee landlords, administrative incompetence and corruption, cynical and chaotic government. From the long view of history, the October Revolution of 1917 is implicit in Giles Fletcher's 16th-century account of Russia; the collapse of the Austro-Hungarian Empire flows almost inevitably from the Vienna witnessed by Lady Wortley Montagu; Horace Walpole, Smollett and Arthur Young teach us to expect the French Revolution; the Italian revival of the Risorgimento is no surprise after the peculiar squalor described by Smollett and Dickens, by Edward Lear and George Gissing.

So despite their load of insular prejudice, the works of British travellers in Europe, far from being collections of mere condescension and back-biting, constitute on the whole an honourable, humane, democratic tradition. They are valuable historical witnesses. In retrospect, the eccentric and grumpy travellers' record assumes importance. It is wise to listen; and that remains the case with our modern travellers. As there were hidden prophecies in the older tales, so there are surely warnings among those who still write today in the old honourable tradition. What do V. S. Pritchett and Penelope Chetwode have to say about the changing face of Spain? Take heed when Patrick Leigh Fermor describes the modern disintegration of Aegean life. Reading these accounts, we may have good reason to fear other revolutions.

On the subject of travels, a 17th-century author modestly wrote: 'The flowers of this large garden will not upon the sudden be knit up into one nosegay.' The field is so big, the varieties of the blooms too many. But here, at least, is a representative bunch from the garden, blazing with the colours of a very mixed experience and giving off robust British aromas.

CHAPTER 1

Setting Out

*Travel is a necessary footnote to all history. But this universal fact
of public and private life goes largely unremarked by historians; the
stolen letter in the story by Edgar Allan Poe escaped notice by being
too obvious. Nomads, soldiers, sailors, traders, envoys and pilgrims
have been taking hard roads, or trusting themselves uneasily to the
water, since the dawn of society. Around 1200 BC Ulysses was a
notoriously footloose wanderer. He has become the archetype of the
traveller. Abraham and Buddha, Alexander and Julius Caesar,
though remembered for other reasons, were also famous for their
journeys. Indeed, a person can hardly get a name in history without
many busy travels or a grand and perilous expedition.*

*If early travellers had been consulted, private curiosity would have
rated rather low as a reason for travelling. Ulysses himself was a lost
soldier trying to return home, driven round and about by incompetent
seamanship and the unpleasantness of the gods. But at a certain
point, as a measure of developing civilization, man began to wonder
at the strangeness of neighbours, and soon he had the energy and
wealth to jump over the wall and take a look in his neighbours'
grounds.*

*Observers set out, armed with courage and notebooks. Certain
lands beckoned. Long ago, the Chinese were going to India. Arabs
went to Africa and, to complete the circle, Italians set out for China.
Within Europe, local currents of movement swirled here and there,
revealing no general pattern except that Italy seemed to be at the
epicentre of the flow. Ancient Greece had been eclipsed and the Italians were now the European pacemakers. Most things that were bold,
revolutionary and naughty had a beginning in Italy, and once the
other Europeans had roused themselves from dogmatic slumber, at
about the start of the 16th century, Italy became the source, guide
and goal for all who thought and all who wondered:*

THE SCHOOLMASTER CAUTIONS YOUNG ENGLISHMEN
TO BEWARE OF ITALY: 1570

I know divers noble personages, and many worthy gentlemen of
England, whom all the Siren songs of Italy could never untwine

from the mast of God's Word, nor no enchantment of vanity overturn them from the fear of God and love of honesty.

But I know as many, or mo[re], and some sometime my dear friends (for whose sake I hate going into that country the more), who parting out of England fervent in the love of Christ's doctrine, and well furnished with the fear of God, returned out of Italy worse transformed than ever was any in Circe's court. I know divers, that went out of England, men of innocent life, men of excellent learning, who returned out of Italy, not only with worse manners, but also with less learning; neither so willing to live orderly, nor yet so able to speak learnedly, as they were at home, before they went abroad.

Roger Ascham
The Scholemaster: Book 1
1570

TRAVEL TEACHES THE SCIENCE OF THE WORLD

Divers dedicate themselves to the knowledge of sciences, not knowing that they forget the most necessary, to wit, the science of the world.

This is it above all things that preferreth men to honors, and the charges that make great houses and Reipublicks to flourish; and render the actions and words of them who possesse it, agreeable both to great and small. This science is onely acquisted by conversation: by divers discourses, and in the judicious consideration of the fashion of the living one with another. And above all, and principally by Travellers, and Voyagers in divers Regions, and remote places, whose experience confirmeth the true Science thereof; and can best draw the anatomy of humane condition. Wherein touching my particular, whether discontent or curiosity drove me to this second perambulation, it is best reserved to my owne knowledge: As for the opinion of others, I little care either for their sweetest temper, or their sowrest censure; for they that hunt after other mens fancies, goe rather to the market to sell than to buy, and love better to paint the bare fashion and outsides of themselves, then to rectify or repaire their owne defects and errours; wherewith I leave them.

William Lithgow
Rare Adventures and Painful Peregrinations
1632

THE NEED FOR ISLANDERS TO TRAVEL ABROAD

Amongst other people of the Earth, *Islanders* seeme to stand in
most need of Forraine *Travell*, for they being cut off (as it were)
from the rest of the Citizens of the World, have not those obvious
accesses, and contiguity of situation, and with other advantages of
society, to mingle with those more refined Nations, whom Learning
and Knowledge did first Urbanize and polish. And as all other
things by a kind of secret instinct of Nature follow the motion of
the Sun, so it is observed that the *Arts* and *Sciences* which are the
greatest helps to Civility, and all *Morall* endowments as well as
Intellectuall, have wheel'd about and travell'd in a kind of concomi-
tant motion with that great Luminary of Heaven: They *budded*
first amongst the *Brachmans* and *Gymnosophists* in *India*, then
they *blossom'd* amongst the Chaldeans and Priests of *Egypt* whence
they came down the *Nile*, and crossed over to *Greece*, and there
where they may bee said to have *borne ripe fruit*, having taken
such firme rooting, and making so long a *Plantation* in *Athens* and
else where: Afterwards they found the way to *Italy*, and thence
they clammer'd over the Alpian hills to visit *Germany* and *France*,
whence the *Britaines* with other North-west Nations of the lower
World fetch'd them over and it is not improbable that the next
Flight they will make, will bee to the Savages of the new discovered
World [*in America*], and so turne round, and by this circular perambulation visit the *Levantines* again.

To have been always transported with a desire of *Travell*, and
not to be bounded, or confined within the shoares and narrow circumference of an *Island*, without ever-treading any peece of the
Continent; whereas on the other side, meane and vulgar spirits,
whose *Soules* sore no higher than their *Sense*, love to hover ever
about home, lying still as it were at dead anchor, moving no further
than the length of the cable, whereunto they are tyed, not daring
to lance out into the maine, to see the wonders of the deep: Such a
one was hee of whom *Claudian* speakes, to have had his *birth,
breeding*, and *buriall* in one Parish; (whence he never had sallied
out the whole course of his life:) such slow and sluggish spirits may
be said to bee like Snailes or Tortuises in their shels, crawling
always about their own home, or like the *Cynique*, shut up always
in a Tub.

Amongst other Nations of the World the *English* are observed to
have gained much, and improved themselfes infinitely by voyaging
both by Land and Sea.

James Howell
Instructions for Forraine Travell, 1642

Foreign travel was within reach and had become intellectually respectable. Many Englishmen were eager to set out and there was no shortage of advice and admonition to help them on their way. Problems had to be faced. There was the question of language. Then attention had to be given to diet, health and the bewildering behaviour of other peoples. Authorities must be consulted and prejudices re-organized. And in the last resort a gift of cigars might be worth a world of expertise:

HOW TO MAKE YOURSELF UNDERSTOOD ABROAD

Those who wish to make themselves understood by a foreigner in his own language should speak with much noise and vociferation, opening their mouths wide. Is it surprising that the English are, in general, the worst linguists in the world, seeing that they pursue a system diametrically opposite? For example, when they attempt to speak Spanish – the most sonorous tongue in existence - they scarcely open their lips, and, putting their hands in their pockets, fumble lazily, instead of applying them to the indispensable office of gesticulation. Well may the poor Spaniards exclaim, *These English talk so crabbedly, that Satan himself would not be able to understand them.*

George Borrow
The Bible in Spain
1843

PITFALLS OF FRENCH. MR BOSWELL IS SOMEWHAT TONGUE-TIED

When I do not understand words perfectly, I look them up in the dictionary, and I write them down with their meanings. Every Wednesday I have the pleasure of passing the evening in a literary society where it is not permitted to speak a word of anything but French; and I dine at Mr. Brown's, where there are two ladies who do not speak English, and where for that reason it is always necessary to speak French. Yet I cannot observe that I am making rapid progress. In writing, I am slow and clumsy, and in speaking I have great difficulty in expressing myself and often make terrible blunders. Instead of saying, 'Would you like to play at shuttlecock?' (*volant*), I said, 'Would you like to play at robber?' (*voleur*); and instead of, 'Mademoiselle, I am entirely at your service' (*tout ce qu'il vous plaira*), I said, 'Mademoiselle, I am something (*quelque chose*) that will please you.' Such blunders make a man very ridicu-

lous. But I must not be downhearted. Very soon I hope to acquire
propriety of language. I confess that we do not speak French at Mr.
Brown's as assiduously as we ought. Laziness disposes us to speak
English and sometimes barbarous Latin. But after today (Monday
31 October) I am determined never to speak except in French. Let
us see if I have any resolution.

James Boswell
Boswell in Holland
1763

A MUDDLE OF FOXES AND CHEESE: LEARNING
SPANISH BY EAR

Discourse in any case was limited by ignorance of one another's
languages. On the first evening at dinner (excellent *gazpacho* followed by a very good curry, his cook having spent two years with
an Indian family) I attempted to talk about foxhunting. Antonio
made, or rather I thought that he made, the astonishing remark
that in this part of Spain vixen were milked and their milk was
made into cheese. What he actually said was that poisoned cheese
was put out on the hills to kill foxes. I tried to warn him against
indulging in such practices when he went to work in the Cottesmore
Hunt Kennels where he had arranged to go during winter in order
to learn English. Do foxes really eat cheese?

When Max Beerbohm imperfectly understood a French literary
lady at a dinner party in London, he simply said '*C'est vrai*' when
she had finished launching at him 'a particularly swift flight of
winged words'. I found the magic Spanish word '*claro*' (clearly) far
more reliable. For whereas Max Beerbohm was badly caught out,
'*claro*' never once let me down, being a suitable comment on a
positive, negative or interrogative sentence.

Penelope Chetwode
Two Middle-Aged Ladies in Andalusia
1963

PRECEPTS FOR ENGLISH TRAVELLERS

Nothing is a more certaine signe of sicknesse growing, then the
obstruction of the body, against which in Italy I tooke each morning,
while I was so disposed, a spoonefull of the sirrop of Corinthian
Currants. Damasco Prunes boyled, and other moist things, as
Butter and Honey, are good for this purpose, as a German Phisitian
writes, whom I follow in this point. My experience hath taught
mee, that it is most dangerous to stop the Flux of the body, which

experience I dearely bought, by the losse of my foresaid Brother, and there is no better remedy for it, then rest. But if it continue many daies, and too much weaken the body, Rice well boyled, hard Egges, Water tempered with Steele, red and sowrish Wines, and Marmalate, are good to bind the body.

Touching exercise, since it must be gentle, and onely till we raise colour in our faces, not til we sweate, it may seeme ridiculous to prescribe the same to Travellers, who are almost continually in motion. Therefore I will only admonish the Traveller, to avoide extremity therein, and that he neither drinke when he is hot, nor suddenly expose himselfe to cold, and that when he is extremely cold, hee likewise warme himselfe by little and little, not suddenly at a great fier, or in a hot stove, and that after dinner he rest a while.

Touching sleepe, breeding by excesse raw humours, and watching that dries the body, they are happy who keepe the meane, and they are the Phisitians friends, who delight in extremes, and to their counsell I commend them.

Surely a Traveller must live after other mens fashion not his owne, alwaies avoiding extremities by discourse according to the Italian Proverb,

> *Paese dove vai, usa comme truovi.*
>
> The Country where thou goest,
>
> Use thou as doe the most.

Now in this so great varietie of fashions in all Nations, it seemes unpossible to give any set rules, since the French say well,

> *Tant de payis, tant' de guises.*
>
> As many Nations, So many fashions.

And since no man is able to number these divers events, first, I advise the Traveller in generall to be so wary, as he adventure not to doe any new thing, till the example of others give him confidence. Let him reprove nothing in another mans house, much lesse in a strange Commonwealth, in which kind it is not amisse to seeme dumb or tongue-tied, so he diligently imploy his eyes and eares, to observe al profitable things. Let him be curteous, even somewhat towards the vice of curtesie, to his Host, the children, and his fellow sojourners in the house. I doe not advise him to imitate them, who will put off their hat to a very Dog; for in all actions basenesse must bee shunned, and decency embraced, but it is veniall somewhat to offend in the better part, applying our selves to the divers natures of men. If hee shall apply himselfe to their manners, tongue, appar-

14

rell and diet with whom he lives, hee shall catch their loves as it
were with a fish-hooke. For diet, he needes lesse care, but for apparrell he must fit it to their liking; for it is a good precept aswell at
home as abroad, to eate according to our owne appetite, but to bee
apparrelled to other mens liking. I have observed the Germans and
French in Italy, to live and converse most with their owne
Countrimen, disdaining to apply themselves to the Italians language, apparrell, and diet, and the English above all others, to subject themselves to the Lawes, customes, language, and apparrell of
other Nations.

Perhaps severe and froward censors may judge it an apish vice
thus to imitate other nations, but in my opinion, this obsequiousnes
of conversation, making us become all things to all men, deserves
the opinion of a wise man, and one that is not subject to pride: but
he must alwaies shunne extremity, lest while he affects to be aff-
able, hee incurre the infamy of a flatterer.

Fynes Moryson
Itinerary
1617

THE TRAVELLER'S LAST RESORT IN SPAIN

However, avoid all superfluous luggage, especially prejudices and
foregone conclusions, for *en largo camino paja pesa*, a straw is heavy
on a long journey, and the last feather breaks the horse's back. A
store of cigars, however, must always be excepted; take plenty and
give them freely; it always opens a conversation well with a Spaniard, to offer him one of these little delicate marks of attention.
Good snuff is acceptable to the curates and to monks (though there
are none just now). English needles, thread, and pairs of scissors
take no room, and are all keys to the good graces of the fair sex.
There is a charm about a present, *backshish*, in most European as
well as Oriental countries, and still more if it is given with tact,
and at the proper time; Spaniards, if unable to make any equivalent
return, will always try to repay by civilities and attentions.

Richard Ford
Gatherings from Spain
1846

At last, the English were on their way. Europe was a strange place, no doubt; but not so strange that a person of sense would go off the road entirely. Practical and dour, the English went on doggedly. And a sanguine disposition helped to make the way lighter:

THE SENSIBLE TRAVELLER GETS UNDER WAY

MAY 26TH. So short a time had I passed before in France, that the scene is totally new to me. Till we have been accustomed to travelling, we have a propensity to stare at and admire everything and to be on the search for novelty, even in circumstances in which it is ridiculous to look for it. I have been upon the full silly gape to find out things that I had not found before, as if a street in Paris could be composed of anything but houses, or houses formed of anything but brick or stone, or that the people in them, not being English, would be walking on their heads. I shall shake off this folly as fast as I can, and bend my attention to mark the character and disposition of the nation. Such views naturally lead us to catch the little circumstances which sometimes express them; not an easy task, but subject to many errors.

Arthur Young
Travels in France
1787

JAMES BOSWELL WORKS OUT A VIRTUOUS REGIMEN

SUNDAY 9 OCTOBER. If the day is good, put on your scarlet clothes and behave with decency before fair lady at French church. Home till half an hour after twelve at journal, and then go to Brown and dine and be cheerful and happy. After church, journal all evening, to bring it up once clear. Then you'll be quite regular. Indulge not whims but form into a man.

TUESDAY 11 OCTOBER. From this day follow Mr. Locke's prescription of going to stool every day regularly after breakfast. It will do your health good, and it is highly necessary to take care of your health. This morning read from breakfast till college. Be temperate and rise at seven each morning. Take some negus at night to prevent damps. It is necessary. Take constant exercise.

I like exceedingly to wash my feet in warm water. It gives me a kind of tranquillity. I am not joking; I speak from experience. I have often done it merely for pleasure. But if I receive so much delight from washing my feet, how great must have been the luxury of the Romans, who solaced thus their entire bodies. The warm

The British family abroad, 1816

baths which they had everywhere contributed greatly to felicity . . . Truly, without exaggeration, one cannot imagine anything more consoling than after a day of annoyance and fatigue to undress and stretch one's self out at full length in fluid warmth, to have one's nerves gently relaxed, to enjoy indolent ease and forget all one's cares.

James Boswell
Boswell in Holland
1763

A CHALLENGE FOR THE BOLD: TRAVEL IN
19TH CENTURY SPAIN

Spain abounds with wide tracts which are perfectly unknown to the Geographical Society. Here, indeed, is fresh ground open to all who aspire in these threadbare days to book something new; here is scenery enough for a score of quartos. How many flowers pine unbotanised, how many rocks harden ungeologised; what views are dying to be sketched; what bears and deer to be stalked; what trout to be caught and eaten; what valleys expand their bosoms, longing to embrace their visitor; what virgin beauties hitherto unseen await the happy member of the Travellers' Club, who in ten days can exchange the bore of eternal Pall Mall for these untrodden sites; and then what an accession of dignity in thus discovering a terra incognita, and rivalling Mr. Mungo Park!

Those who have endurance and curiosity enough to face a tour in Sicily, may readily set out for Spain; rails and post-horses certainly get quicker over the country; but the pleasure of the remembrance and the benefits derived by travel are commonly in an inverse ratio to the ease and rapidity with which the journey is performed. In addition to the accurate knowledge which is thus acquired of the country (for there is no map like this mode of surveying), and an acquaintance with a considerable, and by no means the worst portion of its population, a riding expedition to a civilian is almost equivalent to serving a campaign. It imparts a new life, which is adopted on the spot, and which soon appears quite natural, from being in perfect harmony and fitness with everything around, however strange to all previous habits and notions; it takes the conceit out of a man for the rest of his life – it makes him bear and forbear. It is a capital practical school of moral discipline, just as the hardiest mariners are nurtured in the roughest seas. Then and there will be learnt golden rules of patience, perseverance, good temper, and good fellowship: the individual man must come out, for better or worse.

Then and there, when up, about, and abroad, will be shaken off dull sloth; action – Demosthenic action – will be the watchword. The traveller will blot out from his dictionary the fatal Spanish phrase of procrastination *by and by*, a street which leads to the house of *never*, for '*por la calle de despues, se va a la casa de nunca.*' Reduced to shift for himself, he will see the evil of waste – the folly of improvidence and want of order. He will whistle to the winds the paltry excuse of idleness, the Spanish '*no se puede*', '*it is impossible*'. He will soon learn, by grappling with difficulties, how surely they are overcome, – how soft as silk becomes the nettle when it is

18

sternly grasped, which would sting the tender-handed touch, – how powerful a principle of realizing the object proposed, is the moral conviction that we can and will accomplish it. He will never be scared by shadows thin as air, for when one door shuts another opens, and he who pushes on arrives. And after all, a dash of hardship may be endured by those accustomed to loll in easy britzskas, if only for the sake of novelty; what a new relish is given to the palled appetite by a little unknown privation! – hunger being, as Cervantes says, the best of sauces, which, as it never is wanting to the poor, is the reason why eating is their huge delight.

Richard Ford
Gatherings from Spain
1846

GETTING BY WITH INGENUITY AND A DONKEY

It was already hard upon October before I was ready to set forth, and at the high altitudes over which my road lay there was no Indian summer to be looked for. A tent, above all for a solitary traveller, is troublesome to pitch, and troublesome to strike again; and even on the march it forms a conspicuous feature in your baggage. A sleeping-sack, on the other hand, is always ready – you have only to get into it; it serves a double purpose – a bed by night, a portmanteau by day; and it does not advertise your intention of camping out to every curious passer-by. This is a huge point. If the camp is not secret, it is but a troubled resting-place; you become a public character; the convivial rustic visits your bedside after an early supper; and you must sleep with one eye open, and be up before the day. I decided on a sleeping-sack; and after repeated visits to Le Puy, and a deal of high living for myself and my advisers, a sleeping-sack was designed, constructed, and triumphantly brought home.

This child of my invention was nearly six feet square, exclusive of two triangular flaps to serve as a pillow by night and as the top and bottom of the sack by day. I call it 'the sack', but it was never a sack by more than courtesy: only a sort of long roll or sausage, green water-proof cart cloth without, a blue sheep's fur within. It was commodious as a valise, warm and dry for a bed. There was luxurious turning room for one; and at a pinch the thing might serve for two. I could bury myself in it up to the neck; for my head I trusted to a fur cap, with a hood to fold down over my ears and a band to pass under my nose like a respirator; and in case of heavy rain I proposed to make myself a little tent, or tentlet, with my water-proof coat, three stones, and a bent branch.

19

It will readily be conceived that I could not carry this huge package on my own, merely human, shoulders. It remained to choose a beast of burden. Now, a horse is a fine lady among animals, flighty, timid, delicate in eating, of tender health; he is too valuable and too restive to be left alone, so that you are chained to your brute as to a fellow galley-slave; a dangerous road puts him out of his wits; in short, he's an uncertain and exacting ally, and adds thirtyfold to the troubles of the voyager. What I required was something cheap and small and hardy, and of a stolid and peaceful temper; and all these requisites pointed to a donkey.

There dwelt an old man in Monastier, of rather unsound intellect according to some, much followed by street-boys and known to fame as Father Adam. Father Adam had a cart, and to draw the cart a diminutive she-ass, not much bigger than a dog, the colour of a mouse, with a kindly eye and a determined under-jaw. There was something neat and high-bred, a quakerish elegance, about the rogue that hit my fancy on the spot. Our first interview was in Monastier market-place. To prove her good temper, one child after another was set upon her back to ride, and one after another went head over heels into the air; until a want of confidence began to reign in youthful bosoms, and the experiment was discontinued from a dearth of subjects. I was already backed by a deputation of my friends; but as if this were not enough, all the buyers and sellers came round and helped me in the bargain; and the ass and I and Father Adam were the centre of a hubbub for near half an hour. At length she passed into my service for the consideration of sixty-five francs and a glass of brandy. The sack had already cost eighty francs and two glasses of beer; so that Modestine, as I instantly baptised her, was upon all accounts the cheaper article. Indeed, that was as it should be; for she was only an appurtenance of my mattress, or self-acting bedstead on four castors.

By the advice of a fallacious local saddler, a leather pad was made for me with rings to fasten on my bundle; and I thoughtfully completed my kit and arranged my toilette. By way of armoury and utensils, I took a revolver, a little spirit-lamp and pan, a lantern and some halfpenny candles, a jack-knife and a large leather flask. The main cargo consisted of two entire changes of warm clothing – besides my travelling wear of country velveteen, pilot-coat, and knitted spencer – some books, and my railway-rug, which, being also in the form of a bag, made me a double castle for cold nights. The permanent larder was represented by cakes of chocolate and tins of Bologna sausage. All this, except what I carried about my person, was easily stowed into the sheepskin bag; and by good fortune I threw in my empty knapsack, rather for convenience of carriage than from any thought that I should want it on my journey. For more immediate needs, I took a leg of cold mutton, a bottle of Beaujolais, an empty bottle to carry milk, an egg-beater, and a considerable quantity of black bread and white, like Father Adam, for myself and donkey, only in my scheme of things the destinations were reversed.

R. L. Stevenson
Travels with a Donkey
1879

MAKING THE BEST OF A BAD JOB

Evans and I bought some stores the other day at the co-operative society in the Haymarket: they were to pack them in two cases and send them to us, as they did; but the day after came a message to say they had made a mistake, and put a parcel not ours in one of the cases, instead of some bologna sausage we had ordered, and which they then delivered. I asked them to unpack the case and take their property away; they said they would send the next day to do it; I agreed to that, but told them that if they didn't come that day, to Iceland their case would go with all that was in it, and that there we would eat their parcel if it was good to eat, or otherwise treat it as it deserved. Well, they never came, and here was the case with the hidden and mysterious parcel in its bowels: many were the speculations as to what it was, on the way; and most true it is that I suggested (as the wildest possible idea) fragrant Floriline and hair-brushes – now in went the chisel, and off came the lid: there was the side of bacon; there were the tins of preserved meat; there was the Liebig, the soup-squares, the cocoa, the preserved carrots and the peas and sage and onions – and here IT was – wrapped up first in shavings – then in brown paper, then in waterproof paper, then in more ditto, then in whitey-brown – and here IT is – four (was it) boxes of FRAGRANT FLORILINE, and two dozen bottles of Atkinson of Bond Street his scents, white violet, Frangipanni, Guard's Bouquet – what do I know? yea and moreover the scents were stowed in little boxes that had hair-brushes printed on them.

We looked at each other to see if we were drunk or dreaming, and then – to say we laughed – how does that describe the row we made; we were on the edge of the hayfield at the back of the house; the haymakers ran up and leaned on their rakes and looked at us amazed and half-frightened; man, woman and child ran out from

21

their houses, to see what was toward; but all shame or care had left us and there we rolled about and roared, till nature refused to help us any longer.

William Morris
Journal of Travel in Iceland
1871

Early enthusiasts had seen travel as a national virtue which the educated classes ought to take up. Protestant writers, such as Roger Ascham, stressed that knowledge of Europe was a serviceable commodity which rebounded to the security of an England beset by wily Catholics. So for a long time the active pursuit of knowledge was as much a part of travel as curiosity or pleasure. Continental peoples were specimens to be studied. But gradually a slight wilful perversity began to elbow out the virtuous enquiries. Travellers still had notebooks in hand, and gave respectful attention to antiquities, art and culture. But Europe was becoming a playroom rather than a schoolroom. A leisurely chase after diversion was less arduous and more fun than looking at ruins, churches, fortifications and places of government.

Already, there was something of this attitude in Fynes Moryson, who began his travels in 1605. Journeys were to be enjoyed – and to write books about afterwards. In the course of time the literary gents (and a few ladies) embarked in stately manner for their continental ramble, often cluttered with wives and babies, and returned with solid volumes for the bookseller's list. These literary heavyweights – indulgent wanderers, chroniclers of foibles, follies and colourful foreigners – were (dare we say it?) the first tourists:

THE WRITER SETS OUT IN THE PROPER SPIRIT: 1780

I strayed about the choir and chapels, till they grew so dark and dismal, that I was half inclined to be frightened; looked over my shoulder; thought of spectres that have an awkward trick of syllabling men's names in dreary places; and fancied a sepulchral voice exclaiming: 'Worship my toe at Ghent, my ribs at Florence; my skull at Bologna, Sienna, and Rome. Beware how you neglect this order; for my bones, as well as my spirit, have the miraculous property of being here, there, and everywhere.' These injunctions, you may suppose, were received in a becoming manner, and noted all down in my pocket-book by inspiration (for I could not see) and, hurrying into the open air, I whirled away in the dark to Margate.

William Beckford
Dreams, Waking Thoughts and Incidents
1783

THE NEW SENTIMENTAL TRAVELLER
OF THE 18TH CENTURY

The balance of sentimental commerce is always against the expatriated adventurer: he must buy what he has little occasion for, at their own price – his conversation will seldom be taken in exchange for theirs without a large discount – and this, by the bye, eternally driving him into the hands of more equitable brokers, for such conversation as he can find, it requires no great spirit of divination to guess at his party –

This brings me to my point; and naturally leads me (if the see-saw of this *Desobligeant** will but let me get on) into the efficient as well as final causes of travelling –

Your idle people that leave their native country, and go abroad for some reason or reasons which may be derived from one of these general causes –

Infirmity of body,

Imbecility of the mind, or

Inevitable necessity.

The two first include all those who travel by land or by water, labouring with pride, curiosity, vanity, or spleen, subdivided and combined *in infinitum.*

The third class includes the whole army of peregrine martyrs; more especially those travellers who set out upon their travels with the benefit of the clergy, either as delinquents travelling under the direction of governors recommended by the magistrate – or young gentlemen transported by the cruelty of parents and guardians, and travelling under the direction of governors recommended by Oxford, Aberdeen, and Glasgow.

There is a fourth class, but their number is so small, that they would not deserve a distinction, was it not necessary in a work of this nature to observe the greatest precision and nicety, to avoid a confusion of character. And these men I speak of, are such as cross the seas and sojourn in a land of strangers, with a view of saving money for various reasons and upon various pretences: but as they might also save themselves and others a great deal of unnecessary

---

* A carriage with room for only one passenger.

trouble by saving their money at home – and as their reasons for travelling are the least complex of any other species of emigrants, I shall distinguish these gentlemen by the name of

Simple Travellers

Thus the whole circle of travellers may be reduced to the following *heads*:

Idle Travellers
Inquisitive Travellers
Lying Travellers
Proud Travellers
Vain Travellers
Splenetic Travellers

Then follow

The Travellers of Necessity
The delinquent and felonious Traveller
The unfortunate and innocent Traveller
The simple Traveller

And last of all (if you please) The Sentimental Traveller (meaning thereby myself), who have travell'd, and of which I am now sitting down to give an account – as much out of *Necessity*, and the *besoin de Voyager*, as any one in the class.

Knowledge and improvements are to be got by sailing and post-ing for that purpose; but whether useful knowledge and real improve-ments, is all a lottery – and even where the adventurer is suc-cessful, the acquired stock must be used with caution and sobriety, to turn to any profit – but as the chances run prodigiously the other way, both as to the acquisition and application, I am of opinion, That a man would act as wisely, if he could prevail upon himself to live contented without foreign knowledge or foreign improvements, especially if he lives in a country that has no absolute want of either – and indeed, much grief of heart has it oft and many a time cost me, when I have observed how many a foul step the inquisitive Traveller has measured to see sights and look into discoveries; all which, as Sancho Pança said to Don Quixote, they might have seen dry-shod at home. It is an age so full of light, that there is scarce a country or corner of Europe, whose beams are not crossed and interchanged with others – Knowledge in most of its branches, and in most affairs, is like music in an Italian street, whereof those may partake, who pay nothing – But there is no nation under heaven –

– We are only looking at this chaise, said they – Your most

obedient servant, said I, skipping out of it, and pulling off my hat – We were wondering, said one of them, who, I found, was an *inquisitive Traveller*, – what could occasion its motion. – Twas the agitation, said I coolly, of writing a preface. – I never heard, said the other, who was a *simple Traveller*, of a preface wrote in a *Desobligeant*. – It would have been better, said I, in a *Vis à Vis*.

As an Englishman does not travel to see Englishmen, I retired to my room.

Laurence Sterne
A Sentimental Journey
1768

CHAPTER 2

Along the Way

The Journey
Travellers set out with their expectations high; the road soon taught
them a more sober wisdom. For if the people were ready and eager,
the lands beneath their feet were not. The highroads of Europe were
tedious, uncomfortable places; those moving along them were subject
to delay, pains, insult and danger, interspersed with a few good
moments. For some three hundred years, roughly until the beginning
of this century, the litany of complaint remained constant:

TRAVELLING IN POLAND
IN THE EARLY 17TH CENTURY

In Villages and small Cities, by the high way a passenger shall
find no bed, but he may carry a bed in his Coach, and sit upon it
conveniently. Others use to sleepe upon straw, lapped with a furred
horsemans coate, which they use to weare, and if they have no such
coate, they must be content to sleepe upon cleane straw: And all
the passengers lie together in the warme stoave, with those of the
Family, both Men and Weomen. Neither shall they find in such
places any Wine or choice meates, which they use to bring from
Cities in their Coaches. For the Innes in such places are poore
naked houses, having nothing to sell, but close by them are the
shambles, the Bakers & Brewers houses, where the passengers buy
beere & such meat as they like, and bring it to the Inne, which a
poore Hostesse will dresse, affoording them onely fier, and a course
Tablecloth. And it seemed to me, that the Lord of the place useth
to impose upon some vassall this charge to entertaine strangers:
for the Hostesse will give her labour for nothing, except in curtesie
you desire her to eate with you, and if you freely give her a small
reward, as three pence for the whole Company, shee will thinke
you deale bountifully with her, but shee will aske you nothing. Also
you may freelie carrie away in your Coach, flesh, bread, wine, or
anie thing that remaines, which I have seene done many times. No
Countrey in Europe affoordes victuals at a lower rate. My selfe and

a Companion, did in a Countrey Towne invite two Guests, and our dinner for foure persons came but to foure Grosh and a halfe.

Fynes Moryson
Itinerary
1617

THE LADY TRAVELLER TAKES HER OWN BED THROUGH BOHEMIA AND SAXONY IN 1716

The kingdom of Bohemia is the most desert of any I have seen in Germany. The villages are so poor, and the post-houses so miserable, that clean straw and fair water are blessings not always to be met with, and better accommodation not to be hoped for. Though I carried my own bed with me, I could not sometimes find a place to set it up in; and I rather chose to travel all night, as cold as it is, wrapped up in my furs, than go into the common stoves, which are filled with a mixture of all sorts of ill scents.

You may imagine how heartily I was tired with twenty-four hours' post-travelling, without sleep or refreshment (for I can never sleep in a coach, however fatigued). We passed, by moonshine, the frightful precipices that divide Bohemia from Saxony, at the bottom of which runs the River Elbe; but I cannot say, that I had reason to fear drowning in it, being perfectly convinced, that, in case of a tumble, it was utterly impossible to come alive to the bottom. In many places, the road is so narrow, that I could not discern an inch of space between the wheels and the precipice. Yet I was so good a wife, as not to wake Mr. Wortley, who was fast asleep by my side, to make him share in my fears, since the danger was unavoidable, till I perceived, by the bright light of the moon, our postilions nodding on horseback, while the horses were on a full gallop. Then indeed I thought it very convenient to call out to desire them to look where they were going. My calling waked Mr. Wortley, and he was much more surprised than myself at the situation we were in, and assured me, that he passed the Alps five times in different places, without ever having gone a road so dangerous. I have been told since, that it is common to find the bodies of travellers in the Elbe; but, thank God, that was not our destiny; and we came safe to Dresden, so much tired with fear and fatigue, it was not possible for me to compose myself to write.

Lady Mary Wortley Montagu
Travel Letters
1763

BOSWELL COMES TO TERMS WITH GERMAN ROADS, AND WRITES A POEM

After sleeping all night in a thick mist on the post-wagon, I awaked much out of order. My blood was quite stagnated, and my teeth were loose. I was alarmed. When we came to a *station*, I got down and danced with much vigour, which by degrees brought me to myself. I must really take care on these wagons. I now wrap myself up, head and all, in a great cloak. But even thus the cold gets at me. Besides, when so wrapped up, I am quite an Egyptian mummy and have no use of my arms, so that if the wagon were overturned, I should be quite helpless, and probably be bruised and broken. Let me then take care.

At one I set out for Frankfurt. The wagon was covered with leather, but it was a monstrous machine. One could see nothing from its little openings, for it had no glasses. It jolted most horridly, and as it was constructed with iron bars, when I attempted to sleep, I received most severe raps and was really in danger of having my head broke. In short, it was a trying machine, worse than my good friends the open post-wagons, for upon them I could see the country, feed on the fresh air, and sleep like a mariner on the top of a mast.

I am surprised how I neglected to mention that one of my chairmen at Kassel had been in the Hessian troops who were in Scotland in 1745. He talked of *Bart*, by which he meant to say Perth. I had with me in the wagon a French servant, a blackguard, impudent dog. Yet at night I supped with him and my servant. Such is my hardy plan on my German travels. I also lay down with them on the straw. It was terrible. The heat of an iron stove rendered the straw musty and the air hot, and this, joined to the breaths of a good many people by no means of the most clean race, rendered the room most abominable. I could not sleep. One sad circumstance in the *Stube*, or common room of a German inn, is being obliged to sleep with a tallow candle or a coarse lamp a-burning. I had recourse to the *Stall Knecht** and got a place in the hayloft, where I slept sound though cold.

> Here am I, sitting in a German inn,
> Where I may penance do for many a sin,
> For I am pester'd with a thousand flies,
> Who flap and buzz about my nose and eyes.
> A lumpish landlord has the easy chair;
> Hardly he speaks, but wildly does he stare.

* Stableman

28

In haste to get away, I did not dine,
And now I've had cold beef and cursed wine,
And in five minutes, or a little more,
I shall be stretch'd on musty straw to snore.

SUNDAY 28 OCTOBER. In the afternoon we got rid of the Frenchman, and I and Jacob came to Marburg, a large city. I was out of
order. I knew not what to make of my existence. I lay down between
two feather beds and resigned myself to my fate.

James Boswell
On the Grand Tour
1764

BAD ROADS AND SELF-RELIANT TRAVELLERS

This scanty condition of the Peninsular roads accounts for the very
limited portions of the country which are usually visited by foreigners, who – the French especially – keep to one beaten track, the
high road, and follow each other like wild geese; a visit to Burgos,
Madrid, and Seville, and then a steam trip from Cadiz to Valencia
and Barcelona, is considered to be making the grand tour of Spain;
thus the world is favoured with volumes that reflect and repeat
each other, which tell us what we know already, while the rich and
rare, the untrodden, unchanged, and truly Moro-Hispanic portions
are altogether neglected, except by the exceptional few, who venture
forth like Don Quixote on their horses, in search of adventures and
the picturesque.

The other roads of Spain are bad, but not much more so than in
other parts of the Continent, and serve tolerably well in dry weather. They are divided into those which are practicable for wheel-
carriages, and those which are only bridle-roads, or as they call
them, 'of horseshoe', on which all thought of going with a carriage
is out of the question; when these horse or mule tracks are very
bad, especially among the mountains, they compare them to roads
for partridges. The cross roads are seldom tolerable; it is safest to
keep the highroad – or, as we have it in English, the furthest way
round is the nearest way home – for there is no short cut without
hard work, says the Spanish proverb, '*ho hay atajo, sin trabajo*'.

All this sounds very unpromising, but those who adopt the customs of the country will never find much practical difficulty in
getting to their journey's end; slowly, it is true, for where leagues
and hours are convertible terms – the Spanish *hora* being the heavy
German *stunde* – the distance is regulated by the day-light. Bridle-
roads and travelling on horseback, the former systems of Europe,

29

are very Spanish and Oriental; and where people journey on horse and mule back, the road is of minor importance. In the remoter provinces of Spain the population is agricultural and poverty-stricken, unvisiting and unvisited, not going much beyond their chimney's smoke. Each family provides for its simple habits and few wants; having but little money to buy foreign commodities, they are clad and fed, like the Bedouins, with the productions of their own fields and flocks. There is little circulation of persons; a neighbouring fair is the mart where they obtain the annual supply of whatever luxury they can indulge in, or it is brought to their cottages by wandering muleteers, or by the smuggler, who is the type and channel of the really active principle of trade in three-fourths of the Peninsula. It is wonderful how soon a well-mounted traveller becomes attached to travelling on horseback, and how quickly he becomes reconciled to a state of roads which, startling at first to those accustomed to carriage highways, are found to answer perfectly for all the purposes of the place and people where they are found.

Richard Ford
Gatherings from Spain
1846

A HIGH-SPIRITED DICKENS LEAVES PARIS BEHIND

There was, of course, very little in the aspect of Paris – as we rattled near the dismal Morgue and over the Pont Neuf – to reproach us for our Sunday travelling. The wine-shops (every second house) were driving a roaring trade; awnings were spreading, and chairs and tables arranging, outside the cafés, preparatory to the eating of ices, and drinking of cool liquids, later in the day; shoe-blacks were busy on the bridges; shops were open; carts and waggons clattered to and fro; the narrow, up-hill, funnel-like streets across the River, were so many dense perspectives of crowd and bustle, parti-coloured night-caps, tobacco-pipes, blouses, large boots, and shaggy heads of hair; nothing at that hour denoted a day of rest, unless it were the appearance, here and there, of a family pleasure-party, crammed into a bulky old lumbering cab; or of some contemplative holiday maker in the freest and easiest dishabille, leaning out of a low garret window, watching the drying of his newly polished shoes on the little parapet outside (if a gentleman), or the airing of her stockings in the sun (if a lady), with a calm anticipation.

Once clear of the never-to-be-forgotten-or-forgiven pavement which surrounds Paris, the first three days of travelling towards

Marseilles, are quiet and monotonous enough. To Sens. To Avallon.
To Chalons. A sketch of one day's proceedings is a sketch of all
three; and here it is.

We have four horses, and one postilion, who has a very long
whip, and drives his team, something like the Courier of Saint
Petersburgh in the circle at Astley's or Franconi's: only he sits his
own horse instead of standing on him. The immense jack-boots worn
by these postilions, are sometimes a century or two old; and are so
ludicrously disproportionate to the wearer's foot, that the spur,
which is put where his own heel comes, is generally halfway up the
leg of the boots. The man often comes out of the stable-yard, with
his whip in his hand and his shoes on, and brings out, in both
hands, one boot at a time, which he plants on the ground by the
side of his horse, with great gravity, until everything is ready.
When it is – and oh Heaven! the noise they make about it! – he
gets into the boots, shoes and all, or is hoisted into them by a couple
of friends; adjusts the rope-harness, embossed by the labours of
innumerable pigeons in the stables; makes all the horses kick and
plunge; cracks his whip like a madman; shouts 'En route – Hi!' and
away we go. He is sure to have a contest with his horse before we
have gone very far; and then he calls him a Thief, and a Brigand,
and a Pig, and what not; and beats him about the head as if he
were made of wood.

Charles Dickens
Pictures from Italy
1846

*And out of this grumbling undercurrent of discontent arose from
time to time more vigorous protests at discomfort or danger:*

DEATH AND MONSTROSITY ON THE WAY TO ORLEANS

The way from Paris to this city, as indeed most of the roads in
France, is paved with a small square freestone, so that the country
does not much molest the traveller with dirt and ill way, as in
England, only 'tis somewhat hard to the poor horses' feet, which
causes them to ride more temperately, seldom going out of the trot,
or *grand pas*, as they call it. We passed divers walled towns, or
villages; amongst others of note, Chartres and Etampes, where we
lay the first night. This has a fair church. The next day, we had an
excellent road; but had like to come short home: for no sooner were
we entered two or three leagues into the Forest of Orleans (which

extends itself many miles), but the company behind us were set on
by rogues, who, shooting from the hedges and frequent covert, slew
four upon the spot. Amongst the slain was a captain of Swiss, of
the regiment of Picardy, a person much lamented. This disaster
made such an alarm in Orleans at our arrival, that the Prévôt
Marshal, with his assistants, going in pursuit, brought in two whom
they had shot, and exposed them in the great market-place, to see
if any would take cognisance of them. I had great cause to give God
thanks for this escape; when coming to Orleans and lying at the
White Cross, I found Mr. John Nicholas, eldest son to Mr. Secretary.
In the night a cat kittened on my bed, and left on it a young one
having six ears, eight legs, two bodies from the middle downwards,
and two tails. I found it dead, but warm, in the morning when I
awaked.

John Evelyn
Diary
1644

A MALODOROUS STAGE-COACH

I took my seat in the *fourth place* of the Diligence. Here I met with
every thing to annoy an Englishman. There was a Frenchman in
the coach, who had a dog and a little boy with him, the last having
a doll in his hands, which he insisted on playing with; or cried and
screamed furiously if it was taken from him. It was a true French
child; that is, a little old man, like Leonardo da Vinci's *Laughing
Boy*, with eyes glittering like the glass ones of his favourite doll,
with flaxen ringlets like her's, with cheeks as smooth and
unhealthy, and a premature expression of cunning and self-com-
placency. A disagreeable or ill-behaved child in a stage coach is a
common accident, and to be endured. But who but a Frenchman
would think of carrying his dog? He might as well drag his horse
into the coach after him. A Frenchman (with leave be it spoken)
has no need to take a dog with him to ventilate the air of a coach,
in which there are three other Frenchmen. It was impossible to
suffer more from heat, from pressure, or from the periodical 'exha-
lation of rich-distilled perfumes'. If the French have lost the sense
of smell, they should reflect (as they are a reflecting people) that
others have not. Really, I do not see how they have a right in a
public vehicle to assault one in this way by proxy, any more than
to take one literally by the nose. One does not expect from the
most refined and polished people in Europe grossnesses that an
Esquimaux Indian would have too much sense and modesty to be
guilty of. If the presence of their dogs is a nuisance, the conversation

of their masters is often no less offensive to another sense – both
are suffocating to every body but themselves, and worthy of each
other. Midas whispered his secret to the reeds, that whispered it
again. The French, if they are wise, ought not to commit the
national character on certain delicate points in the manner they
do. While they were triumphant, less caution might be necessary:
but no people can afford at the same time to be odious as well as
contemptible in the eyes of their enemies.

William Hazlitt
Notes of a Journey through France and Italy
1826

*The journeys on the plains were bad enough. But mountain travel
was a far worse business altogether. For centuries it remained a
matter for fear and a cause for wonder:*

COLD COMFORT IN THE SWISS ALPS

This night, through almost inaccessible heights, we came in prospect of Mons Sempronius, now Mount Sampion, which has on its
summit a few huts and a chapel. Approaching this, Captain Wray's
water-spaniel (a huge filthy cur that had followed him out of
England) hunted a herd of goats down the rocks into a river made
by the melting of the snow. Arrived at our cold harbour (though
the house had a stove in every room) and supping on cheese and
milk with wretched wine, we went to bed in cupboards so high from
the floor, that we climbed them by a ladder; we were covered with
feathers, that is, we lay between two ticks stuffed with them, and
all little enough to keep one warm. The ceilings of the rooms are
strangely low for those tall people. The house was now (in September) half covered with snow, nor is there a tree, or a bush,
growing within many miles.

From this uncomfortable place, we prepared to hasten away the
next morning; but, as we were getting on our mules, comes a huge
young fellow demanding money for a goat which he affirmed that
Captain Wray's dog had killed; expostulating the matter, and
impatient of staying in the cold, we set spurs and endeavoured to
ride away, when a multitude of people being by this time gotten
together about us (for it being Sunday morning and attending for
the priest to say mass), they stopped our mules, beat us off our
saddles, and, disarming us of our carbines, drew us into one of the
rooms of our lodging, and set a guard upon us. Thus we continued

Travelling the mountain road

prisoners till mass was ended, and then came half a score grim Swiss, who, taking on them to be magistrates, sate down on the table, and condemned us to pay a pistole for the goat, and ten more for attempting to ride away, threatening that if we did not pay it speedily, they would send us to prison, and keep us to a day of public justice, where, as they perhaps would have exaggerated the crime, for they pretended we had primed our carbines and would have shot some of them (as indeed the Captain was about to do), we might have had our heads cut off, as we were told afterwards, for that amongst these rude people a very small misdemeanour does often meet that sentence. Though the proceedings appeared highly unjust, on consultation among ourselves we thought it safer to rid ourselves out of their hands, and the trouble we were brought into; and therefore we patiently laid down the money, and with fierce countenances had our mules and arms delivered to us, and glad we were to escape as we did. This was cold entertainment, but our journey after was colder, the rest of the way having been (as they told us) covered with snow since the Creation; no man remembered it to be without; and because, by the frequent snowing, the tracts are continually filled up, we passed by several tall masts set up to guide travellers, so as for many miles they stand in ken of one another, like to our beacons. In some places, where there is a cleft between two mountains the snow fills it up, whilst the bottom, being thawed, leaves as it were a frozen arch of snow, and that so hard as to bear the greatest weight; for as it snows often, so it perpetually freezes, of which I was so sensible that it flawed the very skin of my face.

John Evelyn
Diary
1646

A DEATH IN MOUNTAIN SUNSHINE

We were eight days in coming hither from Lyons; the four last in crossing the Alps. Such uncouth rocks, and such uncomely inhabitants! My dear West, I hope I shall never see them again! At the foot of Mount Cenis we were obliged to quit our chaise, which was taken all to pieces and loaded on mules; and we were carried in low arm-chairs on poles, swathed in beaver bonnets, beaver gloves, beaver stockings, muffs, and bear-skins. When we came to the top, behold the snows fallen! and such quantities, and conducted by such heavy clouds that hung glouting, that I thought we could never have waded through them. The descent is two leagues, but steep and rough as O**** father's face, over which, you know, the devil

35

walked with hobnails in his shoes. But the dexterity and nimbleness of the mountaineers are inconceivable: they run with you down steeps and frozen precipices, where no man, as men are now, could possibly walk. We had twelve men and nine mules to carry us, our servants, and baggage, and were above five hours in this agreeable jaunt! The day before, I had a cruel accident, and so extraordinary an one, that it seems to touch upon the traveller. I had brought with me a little black spaniel of King Charles's breed; but the prettiest, fattest, dearest creature! I had let it out of the chaise for the air, and it was waddling along close to the head of the horses, on the top of the highest Alps, by the side of a wood of firs. There darted out a young wolf, seized poor dear Toby by the throat, and, before we could possibly prevent it, sprung up the side of the rock and carried him off. The postilion jumped off and struck at him with his whip, but in vain. I saw it and screamed, but in vain; for the road was so narrow, that the servants that were behind could not get by the chaise to shoot him. What is the extraordinary part is, that it was but two o'clock, and broad sunshine. It was shocking to see anything one loved run away with to so horrid a death.

Horace Walpole
Letters
1739

In the midst of many trials, there was an excitement to early travel which grew less and less as roads became smoother and passages more secure. Old journeys were a rare adventure. The apprehension of departure, the expectation of arrival! At the end of the day, even though tortured by circumstance, with bones shaken and the heart in the mouth, one had accomplished something:

THE JOY OF A SAFE ARRIVAL

Paris, Aug. 20, 1775

I have been sea-sick to death; I have been poisoned by dirt and vermin; I have been stifled by heat, choked by dust, and starved for want of anything I could touch: and yet, Madam, here I am, perfectly well, not in the least fatigued; and, thanks to the rivelled parchments, formerly faces, which I have seen by hundreds, I find myself almost as young as when I came hither first in the last century. In spite of my whims, and delicacy, and laziness, none of my grievances have been mortal: I have borne them as well as if I had set up for a philosopher, like the sages of this town.

Horace Walpole
Letters
1775

TO BERLIN IN MISERY

I quitted Schwarmuth at seven o'clock in the evening, in hopes of getting to Berlin before midnight. The weather was now extremely disagreeable; rain was coming on, with a cold and furious north wind full in my face. The wagon with which I had been furnished, at the last post-house, was the worst and most defenceless that I had hitherto mounted; before nine o'clock, it rained violently, and became so dark, that the postilion lost his way, and descended from his place, in the front of the wagon, in order to feel for it with his hands; but being unable to distinguish any track of a carriage, he mounted again, and, in driving on, at a venture, got into a bog, on a bleak and barren heath, where we were stuck fast, and obliged to remain from eleven o'clock at night, till near six the next morning; when daylight enabled us to disentangle the horses and carriage, and discover the road to the capital of Brandenburg. It had never ceased raining and blowing the whole night; the cold was intense; and nothing could be more forlorn than my condition.

Charles Burney
Continental Travels
1770–72

AT REST ON THE SPANISH ROADS

In general the order of the course is as follows: the breakfast consists at early dawn of a cup of good stiff chocolate, which being the favourite drink of the church and allowable even on fast days, is as nutritious as delicious. It is accompanied by a bit of roasted or fried bread, and is followed by a glass of cold water, to drink which is an axiom with all wise men who respect the efficient condition of their livers. After rumbling on, over a given number of leagues, when the passengers get well shaken together and hungry, a regular knife and fork breakfast is provided that closely resembles the dinner or supper which is served up later in the evening; the table is plentiful, and the cookery to those who like oil and garlic excellent. Those who do not, can always fall back on the bread and eggs, which are capital; the wine is occasionally like purple blacking, and sometimes serves also as vinegar for the salad, as the oil is said to be used indifferently for lamps or stews; a bad dinner, especially if the bill be long, and the wine sour, does not sweeten the passengers' tempers; they become quarrelsome, and if they have the good luck, a little robber skirmish gives vent to ill-humour.

At nightfall after supper, a few hours are allowed on your part to steal whatever rest the *mayoral* and certain *voltigeurs*, creeping and winged, will permit; the beds are plain and clean; sometimes the mattresses may be compared to sacks of walnuts, but there is no pillow so soft as fatigue; the beds are generally arranged in twos, threes, and fours, according to the size of the room. The traveller should immediately on arriving secure his, and see that it is comfortable, for those who neglect to get a good one must sleep in a bad. Generally speaking, by a little management, he may get a room to himself, or at least select his companions. There is, moreover, a real civility and politeness shown by all classes of Spaniards, on all occasions, towards strangers and ladies; and that even failing, a small tip, *una gratificacioncita*, given beforehand to the maid, or the waiter, seldom fails to smooth all difficulties. On these, as on all occasions in Spain, most things may be obtained by good humour, a smile, a joke, a proverb, a cigar, or a bribe.

Richard Ford
Gatherings from Spain
1846

A SUSPICIOUS STRANGER ARRIVES

April 19. – At 5.30 a.m. I walk down the hill, and drawing more or less by the way, gradually reach my farthest point, the bridge over the Tavaria, a distance of some eleven *kilomètres*, or seven miles. Such a walk here, at early morning, is unboundedly full of pleasant items; the whistle and warble of countless blackbirds, and the frequent cuckoo's note; flowers everywhere, especially the red cyclamen, blue vetch, yellow broom, tall white heath, pink cranesbill, and tiny blue veronica; the great rocks – at this hour in deep shadow – overgrown with ivy, moss, and a beautiful red lichen; the slopes of fern and cystus; all these are on each side, and below there is ever the grand valley scene. I must linger yet another day at Sarténé; indeed, a week would be a short stay in these parts for an artist who really wished to study this fine order of Corsican landscape.

About the seventh *kilomètre* the road is lively by groups of peasants going up to the town on the fête day – lively, that is by movement, not by colour, for all are gloomily black, caps, beards, and dresses – trotting on little ponies, many of which carry two riders. While I sit drawing above the Tavaria bridge, a shepherd leaves his large flock of black sheep and stands by me. At length he says, 'Why are you drawing our mountains?' 'Per fantasia e piacere,' I reply, 'for fun, and because it gives me pleasure to draw such beautiful places.' 'Puole,' quoth he, 'ma cosa siggriffica?' – 'That may be, but what is the meaning of it?' – 'da qualche parte d'Italia venite certo' – 'You come, it is plain, from some part of Italy; do you go about mapping all our country?' – 'facendo tutta la Corsica nostra dentr' una carta geografica?' But I, who cannot work and talk at the same time, tell him so, on which he says, with an air of wisdom, 'Si capisce - I understand,' – and goes away apparently in the belief that I am constructing a political survey of the island.

Edward Lear
Journal of a Landscape Painter in Corsica
1868

THE MEDITERRANEAN IN THE MORNING

It was a Sunday morning when we woke and found that the rain had gone, the sun was shining brightly on the sea, and a clear north wind was blowing cloud and mist away. Out upon the hills we went, not caring much what path we took; for everything was beautiful, and hill and vale were full of garden walks. Through lemon-groves, – pale, golden-tender trees, – and olives, stretching their grey boughs against the lonely cottage tiles, we climbed, until we reached the pines and heath above. Then I knew the meaning of Theocritus for the first time. We found a well, broad, deep, and clear, with green herbs growing at the bottom, a runlet flowing from it down the rocky steps, maidenhair, black adiantum, and blue violets, hanging from the brink and mirrored in the water. It is impossible to go wrong in these valleys. They are cultivated to the height of about five hundred feet above the sea, in terraces laboriously built up with walls, earthed and manured, and irrigated by means of tanks and aqueducts. Above this level, where the virgin soil has not been yet reclaimed, or where the winds of winter bring down freezing currents from the mountains through a gap or gully of the lower hills, a tangled growth of heaths and arbutus, and pines, and rosemarys, and myrtles, continue the vegetation, till it finally ends in bare grey rocks and peaks some thousand feet in height. Far above all signs of cultivation on these arid peaks, you still may see villages and ruined castles, built centuries ago for a protection from the Moorish pirates. To these mountain fastnesses the people of the coast retreated when they descried the sails of their foes on the horizon. In Mentone, not very long ago, old men

The Mediterranean

might be seen who in their youth were said to have been taken captive by the Moors; and many Arabic words have found their way into the patois of the people.

J. A. Symonds
Sketches and Studies in Italy and Greece
1898

For Englishmen, travel by land was the usual, and also the preferred, way to see Europe. Naturally, many parts of Europe were not in touch with the sea, and those that were might be best approached from another angle. For the sea, nearly all travellers agreed, was unpleasant at the best of times and terrifying at the worst. Few sane people embarked upon it without an overwhelming compulsion, and then they went sadly, expecting trouble:

GREEK SAILORS

The first care of Greeks (Greek Rayahs) when they undertake a shipping enterprise, is to procure for their vessel the protection of some European power. This is easily managed by a little intriguing with the dragoman of one of the embassies at Constantinople, and the craft soon glories in the ensign of Russia, or the dazzling Tricolour, or the Union Jack. Thus, to the great delight of her crew, she enters upon the ocean world with a flaring lie at her peak; but the appearance of the vessel does no discredit to the borrowed flag: she is frail, indeed, but is gracefully built, and smartly rigged; she always carries guns, and, in short, gives good promise of mischief and speed.

The privileges attached to the vessel and her crew by virtue of the borrowed flag are so great as to imply a liberty wider even than that which is often enjoyed in our more strictly civilized countries, so that there is no good ground for saying that the development of the true character belonging to Greek mariners is prevented by the dominion of the Ottoman. These men are free, too, from the power of the great Capitalist – a power more withering than despotism itself to the enterprises of humble venturers. The capital employed is supplied by those whose labour is to render it productive; the crew receive no wages, but have all a share in the venture, and in general, I believe, they are the owners of the whole freight; they choose a captain, to whom they intrust just power enough to keep the vessel on her course in fine weather, but not quite enough for a gale of wind; they also elect a cook and a mate. The cook whom we had on board was particularly careful about the ship's reckoning, and, when, under the influence of the keen sea-breezes, we grew fondly expectant of an instant dinner, the great author of pilafs would be standing on deck with an ancient quadrant in his hands, calmly affecting to take an observation. But then, to make up for this, the captain would be exercising a controlling influence over the soup, so that all in the end went well. Our mate was a Hydriot, a native of that island rock which grows nothing but mariners and mariners' wives. His character seemed to be exactly that which is generally attributed to the Hydriot race; he was fierce, and gloomy, and lonely in his ways. One of his principal duties seemed to be that of acting as counter-captain, or leader of the opposition, denouncing the first symptoms of tyranny, and protecting even the cabin-boy from oppression. Besides this, when things went smoothly, he would begin to prognosticate evil, in order that his more light-hearted comrades might not be puffed up with the seeming good fortune of the moment.

These seamen, like their forefathers, rely upon no winds unless they are right astern, or on the quarter; they rarely go *on* a wind if it blows at all fresh, and if the adverse breeze approaches to a gale, they at once fumigate St. Nicholas, and put up the helm. The consequence of course is, that under the ever-varying winds of the Ægean they are blown about in the most whimsical manner. I used to think that Ulysses with his ten years' voyage had taken his time in making Ithaca, but my experience in Greek navigation soon made me understand that he had had, in point of fact, a pretty good 'average passage'.

Alexander Kinglake
Eothen
1844

AT PEACE IN THE BAY OF NAPLES

We were not more than an hour after time in starting. Perfect weather. I sang to myself with joy upon the sunny deck as we steamed along the Bay, past Portici, and Torre del Greco, and into the harbour of Torre Annunziata, where we had to take in cargo. I was the only cabin passenger, and solitude suits me. All through the warm and cloudless afternoon I sat looking at the mountains, trying not to see that cluster of factory chimneys which rolled black fumes above the many-coloured houses. They reminded me of the same abomination on a shore more sacred; from the harbour of Piræus one looks to Athens through trails of coal-smoke. By a contrast pleasant enough, Vesuvius to-day sent forth vapours of a delicate rose-tint, floating far and breaking seaward into soft little fleeces of cirrus. The cone, covered with sulphur, gleamed bright yellow against cloudless blue.

The voyage was resumed at dinner-time; when I came upon deck again, night had fallen. We were somewhere near Sorrento; behind us lay the long curve of faint-glimmering lights on the Naples shore; ahead was Capri. In profound gloom, though under a sky all set with stars, we passed between the island and Cape Minerva; the haven of Capri showed but a faint glimmer; over it towered mighty crags, an awful blackness, a void amid constellations. From my seat near the stern of the vessel I could discern no human form; it was as though I voyaged quite alone in the silence of this magic sea. Silence so all-possessing that the sound of the ship's engine could not reach my ear, but was blended with the water-splash into a lulling murmur. The stillness of a dead world laid its spell on all that lived. To-day seemed an unreality, an idle impertinence; the real was that long-buried past which gave its meaning to all about

Bay of Naples

me, touching the night with infinite pathos. Best of all, one's own being became lost to consciousness; the mind knew only the phantasmal forms it shaped, and was at peace in vision.

George Gissing
By the Ionian Sea
1901

A sea-journey was not the only way to travel by water. There were canals and rivers also. And as the sea was nearly always nasty, inland waterways were (despite some trouble at river crossings) generally pleasant. Historically, if there was an idyllic way to travel in Europe it was inland, by boat:

LIFE ON THE RIVER BARGE

I kept a respectful distance whenever I left my carriage, and walked on the banks of the river. Just before we came to Andernach, an antiquated town with strange morisco-looking towers, I spied a raft, at least three hundred feet in length, on which ten or twelve cottages were erected, and a great many people employed in sawing wood. The women sat spinning at their doors, whilst their children played among the water-lilies, that bloomed in abundance on the edge of the stream. A smoke, rising from one of these aquatic

habitations, partially obscured the mountains beyond, and added
not a little to their effect. Altogether, the scene was so novel and
amusing, that I sat half an hour contemplating it, from an eminence
under the shade of some leafy walnuts; and should like extremely
to build a moveable village, people it with my friends, and so go
floating about from island to island, and from one woody coast of
the Rhine to another. Would you dislike such a party?

William Beckford
Dreams, Waking Thoughts and Incidents
1783

FROM MUNICH TO PASSAU BY WATER, 1772

The Isar, upon which the city of Munich is situated, and which
empties itself into the Danube, about a hundred miles below, though
very rapid, is too much spread and scattered into different channels,
to be sufficiently deep for a bark or any kind of passage-boat, that
has a bottom to float upon it. The current of this river is even too
rapid for anything to be brought back against it; but Bavaria being a
country abounding with wood, particularly fir, rafts, or floats made
of those trees, lashed together, are carried down the stream, at the
rate of seventy or eighty miles a day. Upon these rafts, a booth is
built for passengers in common; but if anyone chooses to have a cabin
to himself, he may have it built for about four florins. I preferred
this, not only to avoid bad company and heat, but to get an opportunity of writing and digesting my thoughts and memorandums,
being at this time very much in arrears with my musical journal.

I quitted Munich at two o'clock in the afternoon. The weather
was intensely hot, and I was furnished with no means of tempering
it; a clear sky and burning sun, reflected from the water, having
rendered my fir cabin as insupportable as the open air. It was
constructed of green boards, which exuded as much turpentine as
would have vanquished all the aromatics of Arabia.

As I was utterly ignorant of the country, through which I was to
pass, and the accommodations it would afford, all that my foresight
had suggested to me, in the way of furniture and provisions, were
a mattress, blanket, and sheets; some cold meat, with bread, and a
bottle of wine; there was water in plenty always at hand. But I
soon found myself in want of many other things; and, if I were ever
to perform this voyage again, which I hope will never happen,
experience would enable me to render the cabin a tolerable residence, for a week or ten days.

There had been no rain in these parts of Germany for six weeks;
but, when we arrived at Freising, I saw a little black cloud to the

westward, which, in less than half an hour, produced the most violent storm of thunder, lightning, rain, and wind, that I ever remember to have seen. I really expected every moment, that the lightning would have set fire to my cabin; it continued all night with prodigious fury, so that my man could not get back, and I was left on the water, sole inhabitant of the float, which was secured by a hawser to a wooden bridge.

Two square holes were cut in the boards of my cabin, one on each side, by way of window; the pieces were to serve as casements, one of these was lost, so that I was forced to fasten with pins, a handkerchief against the hole, to keep out wind and rain; but it answered the purpose very ill, and moreover, it rained in, at a hundred different places; drop, drip, drop, throughout my little habitation, sometimes on my face, sometimes on my legs, and always somewhere or other. This, with the violent flashes of lightning and bursts of thunder, kept off drowsiness; luckily, perhaps, for I might have caught cold, sleeping in the wet. I had been told, that the people of Bavaria were, at least, three hundred years behind the rest of Europe in philosophy, and useful knowledge. Nothing can cure them of the folly of ringing bells whenever it thunders, or persuade them to put up conductors to their public buildings; though the lightning here is so mischievous, that last year, no less than thirteen churches were destroyed by it, in the electorate of Bavaria. The recollection of this, had not the effect of an opiate upon me; the bells in the town of Freising were jingling the whole night, to remind me of their fears, and the real danger I was in. I lay on the mattress, as far as I could from my sword, pistols, watch-chain, and everything that might serve as a conductor. I never was much frightened by lightning before, but now I wished for one of Dr. Franklin's beds, suspended by silk cords in the middle of a large room. I weathered it out till morning, without a wink of sleep; my servant told me, that the inn on shore was miserable; it rained into every room of the house, and no provisions could be found for these fifty people, but black bread and beer, boiled up with two or three eggs.

At three in the morning, the passengers were called, and soon after the float was in motion; it was now a huge and unwieldy machine, a quarter of a mile long, and loaded with deals, hogsheads, and lumber of all kinds. The sun rose very bright; but at six there was a strong easterly wind, full in our teeth, and so great a fog, that not a single object could be seen on either side of the river.

Charles Burney
Continental Travels
1770–72

45

A CROSSING OF THE TAGUS

As I saw small boats which can push off at any time lying near in abundance, I determined upon hiring one of them for the passage, though the expense would be thus considerably increased. I soon agreed with a wild-looking lad, who told me that he was in part owner of one of the boats, to take me over. I was not aware of the danger in crossing the Tagus at its broadest part, which is opposite Aldea Gallega, at any time, but especially at close of day in the winter season, or I should certainly not have ventured. The lad and his comrade, a miserable-looking object, whose only clothing, notwithstanding the season, was a tattered jerkin and trousers, rowed until we had advanced about half a mile from the land; they then set up a large sail, and the lad, who seemed to direct every-thing, and to be the principal, took the helm and steered. The evening was now setting in; the sun was not far from its bourne in the horizon; the air was very cold, the wind was rising, and the waves of the noble Tagus began to be crested with foam. I told the boy that it was scarcely possible for the boat to carry so much sail without upsetting, upon which he laughed, and began to gabble in a most incoherent manner. He had the most harsh and rapid articulation that has ever come under my observation in any human being; it was the scream of the hyena blended with the bark of the terrier, though it was by no means an index of his disposition, which I soon found to be light, merry, and anything but malevolent; for when I, in order to show him that I cared little about him, began to hum '*Eu que sou contrabandista*', 'I, who am a smuggler', he laughed heartily, and said, clapping me on the shoulder, that he would not drown us if he could help it. The other poor fellow seemed by no means averse to go to the bottom: he sat at the fore part of the boat, looking the image of famine, and only smiled when the waters broke over the weather side and soaked his scanty habili-ments. In a little time I had made up my mind that our last hour was come; the wind was getting higher, the short dangerous waves were more foamy, the boat was frequently on its beam, and the water came over the lee side in torrents. But still the wild lad at the helm held on, laughing and chattering, and occasionally yelling out part of the Miguelite air, '*Quando el Rey chegou*', 'When the king arrived', the singing of which in Lisbon is imprisonment.

George Borrow
The Bible in Spain
1842

AMONG THE BARGEES OF FLANDERS

The canal was busy enough. Every now and then we met or overtook a long string of boats, with great green tillers; high sterns with a window on either side of the rudder, and perhaps a jug or a flower-pot in one of the windows; a dingy following behind; a woman busied about the day's dinner, and a handful of children. These barges were all tied one behind the other with tow ropes, to the number of twenty-five or thirty; and the line was headed and kept in motion by a steamer of strange construction. It had neither paddle-wheel nor screw; but by some gear not rightly comprehensible to the unmechanical mind, it fetched up over its bow a small bright chain which lay along the bottom of the canal, and paying it out again over the stern, dragged itself forward, link by link, with its whole retinue of loaded scows. Until one had found out the key to the enigma, there was something solemn and uncomfortable in the progress of one of these trains, as it moved gently along the water with nothing to mark its advance but an eddy alongside dying away into the wake.

Of all the creatures of commercial enterprise, a canal barge is by far the most delightful to consider. It may spread its sails, and then you see it sailing high above the tree-tops and the windmill, sailing on the aqueduct, sailing through the green corn-lands: the most picturesque of things amphibious. Or the horse plods along at a foot-pace as if there were no such thing as business in the world; and the man dreaming at the tiller sees the same spire on the horizon all day long. It is a mystery how things ever get to their destination at this rate; and to see the barges waiting their turn at a lock, affords a fine lesson of how easily the world may be taken. There should be many contented spirits on board, for such a life is both to travel and to stay at home.

The chimney smokes for dinner as you go along; the banks of the canal slowly unroll their scenery to contemplative eyes; the barge floats by great forests and through great cities with their public buildings and their lamps at night; and for the bargee, in his float-ing home, 'travelling abed', it is merely as if he were listening to another man's story or turning the leaves of a picture book in which he had no concern. He may take his afternoon walk in some foreign country on the banks of the canal, and then come home to dinner at his own fireside.

There is not enough exercise in such a life for any high measure of health; but a high measure of health is only necessary for unhealthy people. The slug of a fellow, who is never ill nor well, has a quiet time of it in life, and dies all the easier.

I am sure I would rather be a bargee than occupy any position under Heaven that required attendance at an office. There are few callings, I should say, where a man gives up less of his liberty in return for regular meals. The bargee is on shipboard; he is master in his own ship; he can land whenever he will; he can never be kept beating off a lee-shore a whole frosty night when the sheets are as hard as iron; and so far as I can make out, time stands as nearly still with him as is compatible with the return of bedtime or the dinner-hour. It is not easy to see why a bargee should ever die.

R. L. Stevenson
An Inland Voyage
1873

BOATMEN OF THE VENETIAN LAGOON

Now we are well lost in the lagoons – Venice no longer visible behind; the Alps and Euganeans shrouded in a noon-day haze; the lowlands at the mouth of Brenta marked by clumps of trees ephemerally faint in silver silhouette against the filmy, shimmering horizon. Form and colour have disappeared in light-irradiated vapour of an opal hue. And yet instinctively we know that we are not at sea; the different quality of the water, the piles emerging here and there above the surface, the suggestion of coast-lines scarcely felt in this infinity of lustre, all remind us that our voyage is confined to the charmed limits of an inland lake. At length the jutting headland of Pelestrina was reached. We broke across the Porto di Chioggia, and saw Chioggia itself ahead – a huddled mass of houses low upon the water. One by one, as we rowed steadily, the fishing-boats passed by, emerging from their harbour for a twelve hours' cruise upon the open sea. In a long line they came, with variegated sails of orange, red, and saffron, curiously chequered at the corners, and cantled with devices in contrasted tints. A little land-breeze carried them forward. The lagoon reflected their deep colours till they reached the port. Then, slightly swerving eastward on their course, but still in single file, they took the sea and scattered, like beautiful bright-plumated birds, who from a streamlet float into a lake, and find their way at large according as each wills.

That afternoon the gondola and sandolo were lashed together side by side. Two sails were raised, and in this lazy fashion we stole homewards, faster or slower according as the breeze freshened or slackened, landing now and then on islands, sauntering along the sea-walls which bulwark Venice from the Adriatic, and singing – those at least of us who had the power to sing. Four of our Venetians

had trained voices and memories of inexhaustible music. Over the
level water, with the ripple plashing at our keel, their songs went
abroad, and mingled with the failing day.

The sun sank, not splendidly, but quietly in banks of clouds above
the Alps. Stars came out, uncertainly at first, and then in strength,
reflected on the sea. The men of the Dogana watch-boat challenged
us and let us pass. Madonna's lamp was twinkling from her shrine
upon the harbour-pile. The city grew before us. Stealing into Venice
in that calm – stealing silently and shadowlike, with scarce a ruffle
of the water, the masses of the town emerging out of darkness into
twilight, till San Giorgio's gun boomed with a flash athwart our
stern, and the gas-lamps of the Piazzetta swam into sight; all this
was like a long enchanted chapter of romance. And now the music
of our men had sunk to one faint whistling from Eustace of tunes
in harmony with whispers at the prow.

Then came the steps of the Palazzo Venier and the deep-scented
darkness of the garden. As we passed through to supper, I plucked
a spray of yellow Banksia rose, and put it in my buttonhole. The
dew was on its burnished leaves, and evening had drawn forth its
perfume.

J. A. Symonds
Sketches and Studies in Italy and Greece
1898

Road and water have always been the universal broad highways of
travel. But there were still those, even in the 20th century, who
harked back, through eccentricity or necessity, to the rugged individ-
uality of the saddle and pack-animal. And there were those, too,
who witnessed the coming of the railway train and the transform-
ation of the traveller into the undifferentiated group-beast, homo
touristicus. *It was a development not done without certain pains:*

A NERVOUS RIDE INTO THE LAVA-FIELDS OF ICELAND

Meantime we got off our horses, and sat down in a pretty grassy
hollow, and the Icelanders brought out champagne and glasses to
drink the stirrup-cup, for they were going back here: so in half an
hour's time we said good-bye for six weeks, and they mounted and
turned back west, and we rode away east into a barren plain, where
the road had vanished into the scantiest of tracks, and which was
on the edge of the lava: soon we came on to the lava itself, grown
over here with thick soft moss, grey like hoar-frost: this ended

suddenly in a deep gully, on the other side of which all was changed as if by magic, for we were on a plain of short flowery grass as smooth as a lawn, a steep green bank bordering it all round, which on the south ran up into higher green slopes, and these into a great black rocky mountain: we rode on over the east side of the bank, and then again a change: a waste of loose large-grained black sand without a blade of grass on it, that changed in its turn into a grass plain again but not smooth this time; all ridged and thrown up into hummocks as so much of the grass land in Iceland is, I don't know why: this got worse and worse till at last it grew boggy as it got near another spur of the lava-field, and then we were off it on to the naked lava, which was here like the cooled eddies of a molten stream: it was dreadful riding to me unused; but still I stumbled along, as nervous as might be; I saw the guides galloping about over it as they drove the train along, with hard work, at a smart trot: for me, I didn't understand it at all, and hung behind a good way in company of Faulkner: but we were getting near our camping ground now, and the peaked mountain-wall lay before us, falling back into a flat curve just above our resting place: streams of lava tumbled down the mountain-sides here and there; notably on one to our north, Hengill by name; on whose flank its tossed-up waves looked most strangely like a great town in the twilight we were riding through now. Well, Faulkner and I pushed on as well as we could, and at last saw the lava end in the first green slopes of the hill-spurs, where Magnússon stood by his horse waiting for us; we rode gladly enough on to the grass, and, turning a little, cantered along the slope and down into a plain that lay in the bight under the hills, in the middle of which I saw the train come to a stand: so riding through a moss at the slope's end we came into a soft grassy meadow bordered by a little clear stream and jumped off our horses after a ride of six hours and a half.

William Morris
Journal of Travel in Iceland
1871

BY DONKEY THROUGH RURAL FRANCE

On Tuesday, 1st October, we left Florac late in the afternoon, a tired donkey and tired donkey-driver. A little way up the Tarnon, a covered bridge of wood introduced us into the valley of the Mimente. Steep rocky red mountains overhung the stream: great oaks and chestnuts grew upon the slopes or in stony terraces: here and there was a red field of millet or a few apple-trees studded with red

apples; and the road passed hard by two black hamlets, one with
an old castle atop to please the heart of the tourist.

It was difficult here again to find a spot fit for my encampment.
Even under the oaks and chestnuts the ground had not only a very
rapid slope, but was heaped with loose stones; and where there was
no timber the hills descended to the stream in a red precipice tufted
with heather. The sun had left the highest peak in front of me, and
the valley was full of the lowing sound of herdsmen's horns as they
recalled the flocks into the stable, when I spied a bight of meadow
some way below the roadway in an angle of the river.

A hollow underneath the oak was my bed. Before I had fed Modestine and arranged my sack, three stars were already brightly
shining, and the others were beginning dimly to appear. I slipped
down to the river, which looked very black among its rocks, to fill
my can; and dined with a good appetite in the dark, for I scrupled
to light a lantern while so near a house. The moon, which I had
seen, a pallid crescent, all afternoon, faintly illuminated the summit
of the hills, but not a ray fell into the bottom of the glen where I
was lying. The oak rose before me like a pillar of darkness; and
overhead the heartsome stars were set in the face of the night. No
one knows the stars who has not slept, as the French happily put
it, *à la belle étoile*. He may know all their names and distances and
magnitudes, and yet be ignorant of what alone concerns mankind,
their serene and gladsome influence on the mind. The greater part
of poetry is about the stars; and very justly, for they are themselves
the most classical of poets.

> R. L. Stevenson
> *Travels with a Donkey*
> 1879

Accommodation

*As, for centuries, the roads of Europe were generally unfit for smooth
progress, so for the traveller the evening's inn was usually a wild
lottery erring on the side of unrest and squalor. The major cities of
France and Italy could sometimes produce a hotel which made up
in elegance and grandeur for a lack of bodily comforts. And the
inns of Switzerland or Germany often contrived a decent bourgeois
homeliness. But nothing could be taken for granted. 'Last night we
slept in a blood-stained hovel,' Anna Jameson lamented from Florence, in 1826, 'and tonight we are lodged in a palace. So much for
the vicissitudes of travelling.' It was wise to be prepared for the
worst:*

Along the Way

PRECAUTIONS AT THE INN

Let him enquire after the best Innes, especially in Germany, and also at night in Italy; for he may take a short dinner in any Inne of Italy, so hee lodge safely at night. In the best Innes, with moderate and ordinary expences, he shall avoid the frauds and injuries of knaves, and shall sleepe safely, both for his person and the goods hee hath with him. In all Innes, but especially in suspected places, let him bolt or locke the doore of his chamber: let him take heed of his chamber fellowes, and alwayes have his Sword by his side, or by his bed side; let him lay his purse under his pillow, but alwayes foulded with his garters, or some thing hee first useth in the morning, lest hee forget to put it up before hee goe out of his chamber: And to the end he may leave nothing behind him in his Innes, let the visiting of his chamber, and gathering his things together, be the last thing he doth, before hee put his foote into the stirrup.

Fynes Moryson
Itinerary
1605–17

Nearly everywhere, the fears of the English traveller were likely to be confirmed within the hotels and inns of Europe. One could take it as a proof of insular prejudice or, entering into the spirit of the road, accept it as a lively entertainment that enriched experience:

GERMAN INNS OF THE EARLY 17TH CENTURY

Now something must be said of Innes by the high way. Erasmus Roterodamus saith, that the Inne keepers of Germany are sordide, that is, base or slovenly: but I would rather say, they are churlish and rudely proud, or rather grave and surley. When you come in, you must salute the Hoste, and happy you if he salute you againe. You must drinke with him, and observe him in all things. For your carriage, you must lay it in the common eating roome, yet there it shall be most safe; and if you will put off your bootes, you must doe it in the same roome, and there lay them aside. You must expect the hower of eating, for they nothing regard him that desires either to hasten or protract it. You must take in good part what is set before you, demanding nothing for your owne appetite. The shot demanded, must be paid without expostulation, for the Hostes seldom deceive strangers or others, and never remit one halfe penny of that they demand. Above the table hangs a bell (especially through all lower Germany), by sounding whereof they call the

52

The Inn

servants to attend. And at Nurnberg there hangs such a little bell
under the table, which they sound if any man speake immodestly
of love matters or any like subject, and though it bee done in
sport, yet it serves to remember a wise man of his errour. In lower
Germany after supper, they leade the guests into a chamber of
many beds, and if any man have no companion, they give him a
bed-fellow. Lastly, all things must be desired and intreated, as if
the guests were intertained of free cost, for the Host thinkes you
beholden to him for your intertainement, without any obligation
on his part.

Through all Germany they lodge betweene two fetherbeds
(excepting Sweitzerland, where they use one bed under them, and
are covered with woollen blankets) and these fetherbeds for soft-
nesse and lightnesse are very commodious, for every winter night
the servants are called into the warme stove, whereof such fethers
as are reserved, they pull the fethers from the quill, using onely
the softest of them for making of beds. The bed lying under is great
and large, and that above is narrow and more soft, betweene which
they sleepe aswell in Summer as Winter. This kind of lodging were
not incommodious in Winter, if a man did lie alone: but since by
the high way they force men to have bedfellowes, one side lies open
to the cold, by reason that the upper bed is narrow, so as it cannot
fall round about two, but leaves one side of them both open to the
wind and weather. But in Summer time this kind of lodging is
unpleasant, keeping a man in a continuall sweat from head to foote.
Yet in Country Villages, and many parts of Saxony, passengers
have no cause to complaine of this annoyance, since all without

exception, rich and poore, drunken and sober, take up their lodging among the Cowes in straw, where sometimes it happens, that hee who lying downe had a pillow of straw under his head, when hee awaketh finds the same either scattered or eaten by the Cowes: yea; where they have beds, I would advise the passenger to weare his owne linnen breeches, for their sheets are seldome or never cleane.

Fynes Moryson
Itinerary
1605–17

A GERMAN INN IN THE 18TH CENTURY

We came at night to an inn in the territory of Hanover. Thus was I laid. In the middle of a great German *salle*, upon straw spread on the floor, was a sheet laid; here 'great Boswell lay'. I had another sheet and a coverlet. On one side of me were eight or ten horses; on the other, four or five cows. A little way from me sat on high a cock and many hens; and before I went to sleep the cock made my ears ring with his shrill voice, so that I admired the wisdom of the Sybarites, who slew all those noisy birds. What frightened me not a little was an immense mastiff chained pretty near the head of my bed. He growled most horribly, and rattled his chain. I called for a piece of bread and made a friendship with him. Before me were two great folding doors wide open, so that I could see the beauties of the evening sky. In this way, however, did I sleep with much contentment, and much health.

James Boswell
On the Grand Tour
1764

THE ENGLISHMAN ILL-RECEIVED IN FRANCE

I have one thing very extraordinary to observe of the French *auberges*, which seems to be a remarkable deviation from the general character of the nation. The landlords, hostesses, and servants of the inns upon the road, have not the least dash of complaisance in their behaviour to strangers. Instead of coming to the door to receive you, as in England, they take no manner of notice of you; but leave you to find or inquire your way into the kitchen, and there you must ask several times for a chamber, before they seem willing to conduct you upstairs. In general, you are served with the appearance of the most mortifying indifference at the very time they are laying schemes for fleecing you of your money. It is a very odd contrast between France and England. In the former, all the people are complaisant, but the publicans; in the latter, there is hardly any complaisance, but among the publicans.

Tobias Smollett
Travels through France and Italy
1766

FURTHER DISCOMFORT IN THE FRENCH INN

The common cookery of the French gives great advantage; it is true, they roast everything to a chip, if they are not cautioned, but they give such a number and variety of dishes, that if you do not like some, there are others to please your palate. The dessert at a French inn has no rival at an English one; nor are the liqueurs to be despised. We sometimes have met with bad wine, but upon the whole, far better than such port as English inns give. Beds are better in France; in England they are good only at good inns; and we have none of that torment, which is so perplexing in England, to have the sheets aired; for we never trouble our heads about them, doubtless on account of the climate. After these two points, all is a blank. You have no parlour to eat in; only a room with two, three, or four beds. Apartments badly fitted up; the walls white-washed; or paper of different sorts in the same room; or tapestry so old, as to be a fit nidus for moths and spiders; and the furniture such, that an English innkeeper would light his fire with it. For a table, you have everywhere a board laid on cross bars, which are so conveniently contrived, as to leave room for your legs only at the end. Oak chairs with rush bottoms, and the back universally a direct perpendicular, that defies all idea of rest after fatigue. Doors give music as well as entrance; the wind whistles through their chinks; and hinges grate discord. Windows admit rain as well as light; when shut they are not easy to open; and when open not easy to shut. Mops, brooms, and scrubbing-brushes are not in the catalogue of the necessaries of a French inn. Bells there are none; the *fille* must always be bawled for; and when she appears, is neither neat, well-dressed, nor handsome. The kitchen is black with smoke; the master commonly the cook, and the less you see of the cooking, the more likely you are to have a stomach to your dinner; but this is not peculiar to France. Copper utensils always in great plenty, but not always well-tinned. The mistress rarely classes civility or attention to her guests among the requisites of her trade.

Arthur Young
Travels in France
1787

THE TEEMING LIFE OF AN ITALIAN INN

The inn at present contains many more than it can possibly accommodate. We have secured the best rooms, or rather the *only* rooms – and besides ourselves and other foreigners, there are numbers of native travellers: some of whom arrived on horseback, and others with the Vetturini. A kind of gallery or corridor separates the sleeping rooms, and is divided by a curtain into two parts: the smaller is appropriated to us, as a saloon: the other half, as I contemplate it at this moment through a rent in the curtain, presents a singular and truly Italian spectacle – a huge black iron lamp, suspended by a chain from the rafters, throws a flaring and shifting light around. Some trusses of hay have been shaken down upon the floor, to supply the place of beds, chairs, and tables; and there, reclining in various attitudes, I see a number of dark-looking figures, some eating and drinking, some sleeping; some playing at cards, some telling stories with all the Italian variety of gesticulation and intonation; some silently looking on, or listening. Two or three common-looking fellows began to smoke their segars, but when it was suggested that this might incommode the ladies on the other side of the curtain, they with genuine politeness ceased directly. Through this motley and picturesque assemblage I have to make my way to my bed-room in a few minutes – I will take another look at them and then – *andiamo*!

Anna Jameson
Diary of an Ennuyée
1826

ROUGH COMFORT AND GOOD CHEER

Soon after dark, we halted for the night, at the *osteria* of La Scala: a perfectly lone house, where the family were sitting round a great fire in the kitchen, raised on a stone platform three or four feet high, and big enough for the roasting of an ox. On the upper, and only other floor of this hotel, there was a great wild rambling *sála*, with one very little window in a by-corner, and four black doors opening into four black bedrooms in various directions. To say nothing of another large black door, opening into another large black *sála*, with the staircase coming abruptly through a kind of trap-door in the floor, and the rafters of the roof looming above: a suspicious little press skulking in one obscure corner: and all the knives in the house lying about in various directions. The fireplace was of the purest Italian architecture, so that it was perfectly impossible to see it for the smoke. The waitress was like a dramatic brigand's wife, and wore the same style of dress upon her head. The dogs barked like mad; the echoes returned the compliments bestowed upon them; there was not another house within twelve miles; and things had a dreary, and rather a cut-throat, appearance.

They were not improved by rumours of robbers having come out, strong and boldly, within a few nights; and of their having stopped the mail very near that place. They were known to have waylaid some travellers not long before, on Mount Vesuvius itself, and were the talk at all the roadside inns. As they were no business of ours, however (for we had very little with us to lose), we made ourselves merry on the subject, and were very soon as comfortable as need be. We had the usual dinner in this solitary house; and a very good dinner it is, when you are used to it. There is something with a vegetable or some rice in it, which is a sort of short-hand or arbitrary character for soup, and which tastes very well, when you have flavoured it with plenty of grated cheese, lots of salt, and abundance of pepper. There is the half fowl of which this soup has been made. There is a stewed pigeon, with the gizzards and livers of himself and other birds stuck all round him. There is a bit of roast beef, the size of a small French roll. There are a scrap of Parmesan cheese, and five little withered apples, all huddled together on a small plate, and crowding one upon the other, as if each were trying to save itself from the chance of being eaten. Then there is coffee; and then there is bed.

Charles Dickens
Pictures from Italy
1846

THE RUSSIAN HOTEL AT THE END OF THE 19TH CENTURY

Now, as we went through Russia, staying here and staying there, sometimes sleeping in a cosy bed, sometimes on a board, we had a varied experience of Russian hotels. Like the little girls in the poem, –

> 'When they were good they were very good;
> When they were bad they were horrid.'

They all, however, had two abiding characteristics. The first was a power, amounting to absolute genius, of charging for things you never had – a faculty, maybe, not strictly limited to Russian hotels; and the second, abject horror at the idea you should need more than half a pint of water to wash in. Britishers, to put it plainly, must be a dirty set, else why should they desire to wash all over at least once a day? A Russian never needs more than a little can of water poured about his hands, and the brush of a damp towel across his features. One can understand, accordingly, why he has exercised his inventive abilities to make washing a disagreeable operation. Sometimes the water is in a brass, bottle-funnel-shaped arrangement fastened to the wall. You push up the long plug in the snout, and the water trickles up your sleeves and down your clothes in a spitefully human way.

When you go to a Russian hotel you are only supplied with a bare bed. For nights we lay shivering in the cold, attempting to acclimatize ourselves to the habit of sleeping without bedclothes. In time we learnt our error. Russian travellers carry their own bedding and pillows. Therefore, if you want covering, you must order and pay extra.

Further, it is the universal habit for folks to bring their own tea and sugar. An English landlord would rather resent his customers simply ordering hot water. In Russia it is different. Tea-drinking is the pastime for a couple of hours before dinner in the evening – not one or two glasses, but seven or eight, with slices of lemon to give it piquant flavour. Then you start on appetisers. These are generally placed on a side table, and consist of several glasses of vodka, some caviare, a morsel or two of salt herring, perhaps a bit of ham, some radishes, onions, and olives, and a slice of cheese. After that a start is made on an elaborate thirteen-course dinner.

J. F. Fraser
Round the World on a Wheel
1899

Not much could be expected from the inns in the busy lands of commerce – Germany, France, Italy; even less was available in the obscure refuges that dotted remote countryside or passed for accommodation in European borderlands. In these places it was pot-luck indeed. The traveller gave thanks to emerge in one piece:

'MAKE THE BEST OF THINGS'

Few human beings are encountered in these lonely regions: you meet now and then a Greek family migrating with furniture and household – a peasant or two, near some forlorn hut – or a travelling merchant, with laden mules and armed guards. The sun was setting as we arrived at a height overlooking the valley of the Kalamá, and caught sight of a little lake, immediately below my feet, surrounded by most beautiful scenery. I walked on alone by the side of that quiet, still water, enjoying the calm glades, and the pleasant wood of brown oak. There was a carcase of a horse, with a vulture soaring above it, and many falcons on the upper boughs of the trees, and there were numerous tombstones, and two or three dervish sepulchres in one of those quiet solitudes.

After sunset I reached the khan of Tzerovína – a solitary, walled, dilapidated building, not promising in appearance, with a distant background of the snowy Pindus range. Alas, for accommodation! All the little space of the khan was already fully crowded by a fat dervish in green and white, and some sixty or eighty Albanian guards, journeying to Berát, or Arghyró Kastro, so that no shelter remained but that of the lofty and wide stable; and even this, five minutes later had been denied me, for several parties came in, and those who could not find room in the stable slept outside. '*Bisogna adattarsi*,'* as the Romans say: the evening was bitterly cold, and a bad shelter is better than none.

A huge fire is lighted on a sort of hearth on one side of the windy, half-dismantled tenement, and Giorgio seizes upon all the khanjí offers by way of supper, so that there was no danger of starvation. The travelling groups of Albanians arranged themselves in different stalls of the building, forming, with mules and horses, many a wondrous fire-light scene. After their repast, they all sang furiously about Zulíki till late in the night, by which time I was fast asleep in a thick capote.

Edward Lear
Journals of a Landscape Painter in Greece and Albania
1851

A HOVEL IN SOUTHERN CALABRIA

Neither man nor horse could proceed farther under the broiling heat, and unrefreshed by food; so we found a most vile *taverna*, where, for want of better accommodation, we prepared to abide. Ciccio – the Phœnix of guides – stowed away the horse and baggage, and set the Turchi to get lots of eggs, which, with wine and snow, made our dinner. It was more difficult to find a place to eat it in, and we truly congratulated ourselves on not having come on to Condufóri last night. The wretched hut we were in was more than half choked up by the bed of a sick man, with barrels, many calf-skins filled with wine, and a projecting stone fire-place; moreover, it was as dark as Erebus; so in the palpable obscure I sat down on

* 'Make the best of things.'

59

a large live pig, who slid away, to my disgust, from under me, and made a portentous squeaking, to the disquiet of a horde of fowls, perched on every available spot above and below. The little light the place rejoiced in was disturbed by a crowd of thirty or forty Turchi, who glared at us with the utmost curiosity, and talked in the vernacular tongue without ceasing. We had also a glimpse now and then of our Hebe handmaid, the assistant or 'waitress' in the establishment, a woman with one eye, whose countenance struck both of us as a model of a Medusa: nor was her mistress (the hostess) much better. Spite of all this, we nevertheless greatly enjoyed our roasted eggs, and were soon ready to start again; for although the heat was great out of doors, yet it was nearly as much so within; besides, Bova was a weary way off, and Díghi Dóghi Dà made signs of impatience, so he paid for our lunch, and off we went once more into the blazing *fiumara*.

Edward Lear
Journals of a Landscape Painter in Southern Calabria
1852

THE WELCOME AT A HEDGE-INN OF THE FRENCH UPLANDS

The *auberge* of Bouchet St. Nicolas was among the least pretentious I have ever visited; but I saw many more of the like upon my journey. Indeed, it was typical of these French highlands. Imagine a cottage of two stories, with a bench before the door; the stable and kitchen in a suite, so that Modestine and I could hear each other dining; furniture of the plainest, earthen floors, a single bed-chamber for travellers, and that without any convenience but beds. In the kitchen cooking and eating go forward side by side, and the family sleep at night. Anyone who has a fancy to wash must do so in public at the common table. The food is sometimes spare; hard fish and omelette have been my portion more than once; the wine is of the smallest, the brandy abominable to man; and the visit of a fat sow, grouting under the table and rubbing against your legs, is no impossible accompaniment to dinner.

But the people of the inn, in nine cases out of ten, show themselves friendly and considerate. As soon as you cross the doors you cease to be a stranger; and although this peasantry are rude and forbidding on the highway, they show a tincture of kind breeding when you share their hearth. At Bouchet, for instance, I uncorked my bottle of Beaujolais, and asked the host to join me. He would take but little.

'I am an amateur of such wine, do you see?' he said, 'and I am capable of leaving you not enough.'

In these hedge-inns the traveller is expected to eat with his own knife; unless he ask, no other will be supplied: with a glass, a whang of bread, and an iron fork, the table is completely laid. My knife was cordially admired by the landlord of Bouchet, and the spring filled him with wonder.

'I should never have guessed that,' he said. 'I would bet,' he added, weighing it in his hand, 'that this cost you not less than five francs.'

When I told him it had cost me twenty, his jaw dropped.

He was a mild, handsome, sensible, friendly old man, astonishingly ignorant. His wife, who was not so pleasant in her manners, knew how to read, although I do not suppose she ever did so. She had a share of brains and spoke with a cutting emphasis, like one who ruled the roost.

'My man knows nothing,' she said, with an angry nod; 'he is like the beasts.'

And the old gentleman signified acquiescence with his head. There was no contempt on her part, and no shame on his; the facts were accepted loyally, and no more about the matter.

R. L. Stevenson
Travels with a Donkey
1879

RURAL ACCOMMODATION IN SPAIN: 1846

Many of these *ventas* have been built on a large scale by the noblemen or convent brethren to whom the village or adjoining territory belonged, and some have at a distance quite the air of a gentleman's mansion. Their walls, towers, and often elegant elevations glitter in the sun, gay and promising, while all within is dark, dirty, and dilapidated, and no better than a whitened sepulchre. The ground floor is a sort of common room for men and beasts; the portion appropriated to the stables is often arched over, and is very imperfectly lighted to keep it cool, so that even by day the eye has some difficulty at first in making out the details. The ranges of mangers are fixed round the walls, and the harness of the different animals suspended on the pillars which support the arches; a wide door, always open to the road, leads into this great stable; a small space in the interior is generally left unincumbered, into which the traveller enters on foot or on horseback; no one greets him; no obsequious landlord, bustling waiter, or simpering chambermaid takes any notice of his arrival: the *ventero* sits in the sun smoking, while his wife continues her uninterrupted *chasse* for 'small deer' in the thick covers of her daughters' hair; nor does the guest pay much attention to them; he proceeds to a gibbous water-jar, which is always set up in a visible place, dips in with the ladle, or takes from the shelf in the wall an *alcarraza* of cold water; refreshes his baked clay, refills it, and replaces it in its hole on the *taller*, which resembles the decanter stands in a butler's pantry: he then proceeds, unaided by ostler or boots, to select a stall for his beast – unsaddles and unloads, and in due time applies to the *ventero* for fodder; the difference of whose cool reception contrasts with the eager welcome which awaits the traveller at bedtime: his arrival is a godsend to the creeping tribe, who, like the *ventero*, have no regular larder; it is not upstairs that he eats, but where *he* is eaten like Polonius; the walls are frequently stained with the marks of nocturnal combats, of those internecine, truly Spanish *guerrillas*, which are waged without an Elliot treaty, against enemies who, if not exterminated, murder sleep. Were these fleas and French ladybirds unanimous, they would eat up a Goliath; but fortunately, like other Spaniards, they never act together, and are consequently conquered and slaughtered in detail; hence the proverbial expression for great mortality among men, *mueren como chinches*.

The vicinity of the kitchen fire being the warmest spot, and the nearest to the flesh-pot, is the *querencia*, the favourite 'resort' of the muleteers and travelling bagsmen, especially when cold, wet, and hungry. The first come are the best served, says the proverb, in the matters of soup and love. The earliest arrivals take the cosiest corner seats near the fire, and secure the promptest non-attendance; for the better class of guests there is sometimes a 'private apartment,' or the boudoir of the *ventera*, which is made over to those who bring courtesy in their mouths, and seem to have cash in their pockets; but these out-of-the-way curiosities of comfort do not always suit either author or artist, and the social kitchen is preferable to solitary state. When a stranger enters into it, if he salutes the company, 'My lords and knights, do not let your graces molest yourselves,' or courteously indicates his desire to treat them with respect, they will assuredly more than return the compliment, and as good breeding is instinctive in the Spaniard, will rise and insist on his taking the best and highest seat. Greater, indeed, is their reward and satisfaction, if they discover that the invited one can talk to them in their own lingo, and understands their feelings by circulating *his* cigars and wine *bota* among them.

Richard Ford
Gatherings from Spain
1846

RURAL ACCOMMODATION IN SPAIN: 1961

There is still the *fonda*, a brand of hotel which is found in the larger *pueblos* and which caters for people only, not horses. The bedrooms contain from one to four beds apiece which are tolerably comfortable, though the mattresses and pillows often appear to be filled with walnuts (actually lumpy flock). The eiderdown is unknown, so is the bedside mat. One pleasant respect in which these inns do differ from Ford's time lies in the complete absence of small bedfellows. In six weeks touring I did not meet with a single bug or flea and not because *'Quien duerme bien no le pican pulgas'* (He who sleeps well is not bitten by fleas.) Due to over-excitement and indigestion I often slept very badly.

The *posada* is an inn with stables attached, the animals being often better housed and better fed than the human beings. Both enter by the same front door, which in the smaller *posadas* leads directly into the living-room. Your horse is led through this into the great cavernous stables beyond, which are cool in summer and warm in winter. In the larger *posadas* there are big double doors, open during the day, which lead into a covered cobbled yard where the muleteers and the donkey boys sleep on straw palliasses. At the far end are the stables with rows of mangers, sometimes over a hundred, all along the walls with pegs above them (often the thigh bones of animals cemented in between the stones) to which you tie your halter rope. Borrow was fond of sleeping in mangers but if they were anything like the ones I saw, he must have curled up like a dog.

On either side of the cobbled yard are the kitchen and dining-room and stairs leading up to the bedroom. The furnishing is similar to that of the *fonda* but in the more remote districts there is no chest-of-drawers, so that you have to keep your clothes in the saddle-bags, hung on the end of the bed, your books on the window-sill and risk hanging your coat and hat and camera on the wall-pegs which may or may not remain *in situ*. At least one of the bedrooms is used as a store for barley, maize, onions, almonds, pumpkins and pomegranates. There is seldom any glass in the windows. Ill-fitting and dilapidated wooden shutters keep out some of the draughts and all of the light, a feeble artificial variety of which is provided by a 15-watt bulb usually hung over the foot of your bed.

The *posada* often has the advantage over the *fonda* in that it possesses only stable sanitation. When the water variety is attempted it is always a dismal failure, partly because there is never any water laid on. You simply ladle it into the pan from a large stone jar, and the stink from the drains is overpowering. The Spaniards possess a great variety of talents but plumbing is not one of them.

Penelope Chetwode
Two Middle-Aged Ladies in Andalusia
1963

Over the centuries, the battery of complaint directed against European lodgings was formidable. But things were not entirely black. Here and there, in palace, house or cottage, a welcome awaited which soothed the fretful spirit of the English traveller and sent him or her to a decent, peaceful sleep:

ICELANDIC TRANQUILLITY

Then turning a corner, we ride in through the lanes between the garth walls and into a little yard in front of a six-gabled house of the regular Icelandic type, turf walls ever so thick, and wooden gables facing the sunny side: these are Stockholm-tarred and have little white framed windows with small panes of glass in them: both walls and roof are just as green as the field they spring from; all doors are very low: I, who am but five foot six, used to bang my head about finely when I first came to Iceland: well, we went in and were welcomed by some woman-kind of Dean Asmundr, who told us the dean would be in presently; the Italian Dapples was here already, and had had his bedroom assigned to him; we sat in a funny little panelled parlour, where they brought us wine and biscuits pending the priest's arrival, who turned up presently, a little hard-bitten, apple-cheeked old man, of a type very common in Iceland: he was extremely hospitable and soon summoned us to dinner, or supper rather, for it was half-past nine by now; we had smoked mutton to eat, smoked salmon, Norway anchovies, Holstein cheese (like Gruyère) and ewe-milk cheese (*islandicé* mysu ostr), queer brown stuff and quite sweet, together with some plovers we had shot which they roasted for us: the dean was very gay, and kept on calling toasts which we drank in Danish brandy, though there was Bordeaux on the table too: altogether I have a keen remembrance of the joys of that dinner. Then the dean asked us into the parlour again and we sat there and wandered out into the home-mead. It was a beautiful evening still, and even the eastern sky we saw behind the great mountains of the Eyjafell range was quite red.

I walked round the home-field, which sloped gently down toward the marsh; the dew was falling like rain, as it always did after hot days here, and it was getting decidedly cold when I came in at last and went to a comfortable bed made up in the room where we had dined: for I needn't say that we five turned the house upside down with our requirements. That was the end of the day.

William Morris
Journal of Travel in Iceland
1871

Food and Drink
To the traveller, the question of food and drink was an important business. On the road, interest tends to revolve around mealtimes. In general, the English in Europe found eating habits a matter of curiosity rather than complaint. English conservatism was surprised by continental customs, but one sometimes gets the impression that there was, among the English, a certain wistful admiration for the variety, quantity and gusto of foreign meals:

EATING HABITS IN THE NETHERLANDS

They use to eate early in the morning, even before day, and the cloth is laid foure times in the day for very servants, but two of these times they set before them nothing but cheese and butter. They seeth all their meate in water falling of raine, and kept in Cesternes. They eate Mushromes and the hinder parts of frogges for great dainties, which frogges young men use to catch and present them to their Mistresses for dainties. I have seene a hundreth of Oysters in divers Cities sold sometimes for eight or twelve, yea for twenty or thirty stivers. They dresse fresh water fish with butter more then enough, and salted fishes savoury with butter & mustard: where they eate not at an Ordinary, but upon reckoning (as they doe in Villages and poorer Innes), there they weigh the cheese when it is set on Table, and taken away, being paid by the waight; and I have knowne some waggish Souldiers, who put a leaden bullet into the Cheese, making it thereby weigh little lesse then at first sitting downe, and so deceiving their Hosts: But in the chiefe Innes, a man shall eate at an Ordinary, and there Gentlemen and others of inferiour condition sit at the same Table, and at the same rate.

Fynes Moryson
Itinerary
1605–17

GOOD FELLOWSHIP ON THE LOWER RHINE

One of their customes I much disliked, that they sit exceeding long
at their meales, at the least an howre and halfe. And very seldome
do they go to supper before seven of the clocke. In most places
betwixt Colen and the farther end of the Netherlands even till I
came to Vlyshingen commonly called Flushing the farthest towne
of Zealand, I observed that they usually drinke beare & not Rhenish
wine, as in the higher parts of Germany. For they have no wine
in their country. This custome also I observed amongst those of
Cleveland, Gelderland, and Hollond, that whensoever one drinketh
to another, he shaketh his fellow by the hand, and whensoever the
men of the country come into an Inne to drinke, they use to take a
tinnen tankard full of beere in their hands, and sit by it an howre
together, yea sometimes two whole howres before they will let their
tankards go out of their hands.

Thomas Coryat
Crudities
1611

THE FASTIDIOUS TABLES OF ITALY

In generall the Italians, and more specially the Florentines, are
most neate at the Table, and in their Innes from morning to night
the Tables are spread with white cloathes, strewed with flowers
and figge leaves, with Ingestars or glasses of divers coloured wines
set upon them, and delicate fruits, which would invite a Man to eat
and drink, who otherwise hath no appetite, being all open to the
sight of passengers as they ride by the high way, through their
great unglased windowes. At the Table, they touch no meate with
the hand, but with a forke of silver or other mettall, each man
being served with his forke and spoone, and glasse to drinke. And
as they serve small peeces of flesh, (not whole joints as with us), so
these peeces are cut into small bits, to be taken up with the forke,
and they seeth the flesh till it be very tender. In Summer time,
they set a broad earthen vessel full of water upon the Table, wherein little glasses filled with wine doe swimme for coolenesse. They
use no spits to roast flesh, but commonly stew the same in earthen
pipkins, and they feed much upon little fishes and flesh cut and
fried with oyle. They have no skill in the Art of Cookery, and the
meate is served to the table in white glistering and painted dishes
of earth (whereof the finest are much esteemed with us). They are
not willingly invited to eate with other men, esteeming basely of
those, who live at other mens trenchers, calling them vulgarly

scroccatori d' i pasti, shifters for meales. And the reason hereof is, that they would not be tied to invite others againe, which in their pride they would doe, if they should be invited to them, and this is the chiefe cause that makes them nice to converse with strangers.

Fynes Moryson
Itinerary
1605–17

THIN FARE AT THE FRENCH 'TABLE D'HÔTE'

Rouen is dearer than Paris, and therefore it is necessary for the pockets of the people that their bellies should be wholesomely pinched. At the *table d'hôte*, at the hotel *Pomme de Pin*, we sat down, sixteen, to the following dinner: a soup, about 3lb of *bouilli*, one fowl, one duck, a small fricassee of chicken, *rôti* of veal, of about 2lb and two other small plates with a salad; the price 45 *sous* and 20 *sous* more for a pint of wine. At an ordinary of 20d a head in England, there would be a piece of meat which would, literally speaking, outweigh this whole dinner! The ducks were swept clean so quickly, that I moved from table without half a dinner. Such *table d'hôtes* are among the cheap things of France! of all *sombre* and *triste* meetings a French *table d'hôte* is foremost; for eight minutes a dead silence, and as to the politeness of addressing a conversation to a foreigner, he will look for it in vain. Not a single word has anywhere been said to me unless to answer some question; Rouen not singular in this.

Arthur Young
Travels in France
1788

ONE MEAL FOR THE GENTRY, ANOTHER FOR THE SERVANTS

Dinner is announced. There is very thin soup; there are very large loaves – one apiece; a fish; four dishes afterwards; some poultry afterwards; a dessert afterwards; and no lack of wine. There is not much in the dishes; but they are very good, and always ready instantly. When it is nearly dark, the brave Courier, having eaten the two cucumbers, sliced up in the contents of a pretty large decanter of oil, and another of vinegar, emerges from his retreat below, and proposes a visit to the Cathedral, whose massive tower frowns down upon the court-yard of the inn. Off we go; and very solemn and grand it is, in the dim light: so dim at last, that the polite, old, lanthorn-jawed Sacristan has a feeble little bit of candle in his hand, to grope among the tombs with – and looks among the grim columns, very like a lost ghost who is searching for his own.

Underneath the balcony, when we return, the inferior servants of the inn are supping in the open air, at a great table; the dish, a stew of meat and vegetables, smoking hot: and served in the iron cauldron it was boiled in. They have a pitcher of thin wine, and are very merry; merrier than the gentleman with the red beard, who is playing billiards in the light room on the left of the yard, where shadows, with cues in their hands, and cigars in their mouths, cross and recross the window, constantly. Still the thin Curé walks up and down alone, with his book and umbrella. And there he walks, and there the billiard-balls rattle, long after we are fast asleep.

Charles Dickens
Pictures from Italy
1846

AN HONOURABLE DEARTH ON THE SPANISH ROAD

At nine o'clock at night they will ask you what you want to eat.

'What have you got?'

'Whatever the señor wishes.'

And a Dutch auction begins. Meat, alas there isn't any; chicken, they regret; it comes down in the end to garlic soup and how many 'pairs of eggs' can you eat, with a chunk of garlic sausage thrown in? They have 'wonderful wine, the finest for miles' – but it turns out to be thin, vinegarish, and watered. The oil is rancid, but the stick fire blazes, the smoke fills the room, and there is war in your stomach that night unless you are used to the crude Spanish fry and to garlic as strong as acetylene. The food might turn out better than this, of course; there might be *bacalao*, if you can eat dry salted cod; there might be pork off the black pigs; and resinous wine, scraping the top off your tongue, with flavour of the pine cask. They might catch and kill that screeching chicken in the yard or give you goat cheese and the close white bread which has come in again after the years of war and starvation. But good or bad, full or meagre, the meal will not be squalid or sluttish. There will be a piety and honourableness about it, no scrambling round the trough. The woman's hard voice will command the room and one will break one's bread with the dignity of a lean person who speaks of other things. 'We give what we have' – not the 'you eat the official portion which you're given or go without' of our sour democracies. They still – even after the Civil War, in which so much of Spanish custom died – turn to their neighbour before they eat and say: 'Would you like this?' and even lift the plate.

'Please enjoy it yourself,' is the reply.

Being so noble, they could (they convey) do without food altogether.

V. S. Pritchett
The Spanish Temper
1954

RURAL MEALS IN SOUTHERN SPAIN

The staple diet of rural Andalusia consists of vegetable soups and stews (*cocidos* and *pucheros*). These are made with a basis of dried chickpeas and different sorts of beans, all very high in protein, stewed together with potatoes, onions, pimientos, garlic and any available green vegetables. Sometimes the beans are replaced by rice, and now and then there will be the added thrill of lumps of fat pork. When eating these *cocidos* and *pucheros* day after day, week after week, the lack of relish is compensated for by the knowledge of how wholesome they are.

Fish soup is popular – fresh sardines or little mussels in their shells in a saffron-coloured broth with many cloves of garlic and bits of bread floating in it. Prawns, squids, hake, bream and fresh anchovies are also brought from the coast to the inland *pueblos* in Vespa vans two or three times a week.

The Spanish soup which is deservedly famous outside Spain, *gazpacho*, is always eaten cold during the summer months, fresh cucumber being one of its essential ingredients.

The home-cured hams of Spain are also famous throughout Europe and the exquisite flavour varies with the district, those of Estramadura taking the top place. Thick slices are eaten raw, not smoked, and are not easily dealt with by delicate digestions. One can however always ask for it fried, a practice which horrifies the connoisseur. Apart from the products of the pig, meat is rarely met with outside the tourist areas. Cattle are bred for ploughing or fighting and not for milking or eating. Karakul sheep are bred for the skins of the new-born lambs. Kid, hare, rabbit, chicken and partridge are occasional luxuries. I had rabbit twice in six weeks, chicken once and partridge three times.

Fresh eggs are everywhere plentiful and can be had boiled according to the number of minutes you dictate, or poached in oil, when they are served in a soup-plate floating in half an inch of it. This brings us to bread, the great mopper-up. Spanish bread is superlative and is a pleasure to eat dry, which is very fortunate as neither butter nor jam are to be had in the *pueblos* (though one can buy slabs of quince jelly which has the consistency of damson cheese and is a good stomach binder.) It is all baked in flat, round, crusty loaves in stone ovens preheated with brushwood, like the old brick ones of our farmhouses and bake-houses and cottages, some of which still survive. In colour it is just off-white, being not over-refined yet not over coarse and dark. It is eaten in prodigious quantities by the Spaniards and I took to it myself in a big way and after the first week forgot that there was such a thing as butter.

Penelope Chetwode
Two Middle-Aged Ladies in Andalusia
1963

In ages when most supplies of water were anything but safe, some alcoholic drink accompanied most meals. This was normal, and consequently some degree of inebriation was regretted but not unexpected. Having no vineyards of their own, the English took a particular interest in wine. They also shared with the continentals a keen appreciation of good water – a copious source of pure water was worth a rare vintage:

A DRUNK AT THE VATICAN

As for the place where the Pilgrimes find one dinner, called the Popes table, it is thus: there is a certaine low roome at St. Peters Pallace, and without the gate, where every day at our nine of the clocke, there meete 21. pilgrimes; 14. from the Trinity, one having a bullet for all, and seven from St. Peters Penitentialls: where being received, the seven Jesuit Pilgrims get the upper place, and sit alone, yet all of them alike served, each of them having foure dishes of meat, besides bread & abundance of wine. The dinner done, their fragments are wrapt up in cleane paper, which they carry with them, and so departing, they, or like company come no more there. They are dayly served with a very venerable Prelat, and a few other serviceable Priests, but for the Popes presence with them, there is no such matter. The liberty being spoyld by a drunken Dutch-man about 60. yeeres agoe, who in presence of the Pope gave up againe his good cheare and strong wines, with a freer good will then perhaps they were allowed him, whereat the Pope grewe angry, notwithstanding the drunken fellowe cryed through his belching throate, Thankes Holy Father, Deere Holy Father, God blesse your Holinesse.

William Lithgow
Rare Adventures and Painful Peregrinations
1632

THE SPANISH THIRST

As the *bota* is always near every Spaniard's mouth who can get at one, all classes being ever ready, like Sancho, to give 'a thousand kisses', not only to his own legitimate *bota*, but to that of his neighbour, which is coveted more than wife: therefore no prudent traveller will ever journey an inch in Spain without getting one, and when he has, will never keep it empty, especially when he falls in with good wine. Every man's Spanish attendant will always find out, by instinct, where the best wine is to be had; good wine neither needs bush, herald, nor crier; in these matters, our experience of them tallies with their proverb, '*mas vale vino maldito, que no agua bendita*,' 'cursed bad wine is better than holy water'; at the same time, in their various scale of comparisons, there is good wine, better wine, and best wine, but no such thing as bad wine; of good wine, the Spaniards are almost as good judges as of good water; they rarely mix them, because they say that it is spoiling two good things. *Vino Moro*, or Moorish wine, is by no means indicative of uncleanness, or other heretical imperfections implied generally by that epithet; it simply means, that it is pure from never having been baptized with water, for which the Asturians, who keep small chandler's shops, are so infamous, that they are said, from inveterate habit, to adulterate even water; *aguan el agua*.

It is a great mistake to suppose, because Spaniards are seldom seen drunk, and because when on a journey they drink as much water as their beasts, that they have any Oriental dislike to wine; the rule is '*Agua como buey, y vino como Rey*', 'to drink water like an ox, and wine like a king'. The extent of the *given* quantity of wine which they will always swallow, rather suggests that their habitual temperance may in some degree be connected more with their poverty than with their will.

> Richard Ford
> *Gatherings from Spain*
> 1846

IN PRAISE OF WATER

Then, when the heavens and earth are on fire, and the sun drinks up rivers at one draught, when one burnt sienna tone pervades the tawny ground, and the green herb is shrivelled up into black gunpowder, and the rare pale ashy olive-trees are blanched into the livery of the desert; then, when the heat and harshness make even the salamander muleteers swear doubly as they toil along like demons indeed, will an Englishman discover that he is made of the same material, only drier, and learn to estimate water; but a good thirst is too serious an evil, too bordering on suffering, to be made, like an appetite, a matter of congratulation; for when all fluids evaporate, and the blood thickens into currant jelly, and the nerves tighten up into the catgut of an overstrung fiddle, getting attuned to the porcupinal irritability of the tension of the mind, how the parched soul sighs for the comfort of a Scotch mist, and fondly turns back to the uvula-relaxing damps of Devon! And oh! ye our fair readers, who chance to run such risks, and value complexion, take for heaven's sake a parasol and an *Alcarraza*.

This clay utensil – as its Arabic name *al Karaset* implies – is a porous refrigeratory vessel, in which water, when placed in, current of hot air, becomes chilled by evaporation; it is to be seen hung up on poles dangling from branches, suspended to waggons – in short, is part and parcel of a Spanish scene in hot weather and localities; every *posada* has rows of them at the entrance, and the first thing every one does on entering, before wishing even the hostess Good morning, or asking permission, is to take a full draught: all classes are learned on the subject, and although on the whole they cannot be accused of teetotalism, they are loud in their praises of the pure fluid. The common form of praise is *agua muy rica* – very rich water. According to their proverbs, good water should have neither taste, smell, nor colour, *ni sabor, olor, ni color*, which neither makes men sick nor in debt, nor women widows, *que no enferma, no adeuda, no enviuda*; and besides being cheaper than wine, beer, or brandy, it does not brutalize the consumer, nor deprive him of his common sense or good manners.

Richard Ford
Gatherings from Spain
1846

An abiding impression, both among the travellers and their hosts, was the eccentricity of eating habits. Strange meals were witnessed, and not just in remote provinces. Often, food and manners were as much a puzzle in France or Italy as in Albania or the mountains of southern Spain:

A PICNIC AVOIDS THE DANGERS OF FRENCH CUISINE

The people of this country dine at noon, and travellers always find an ordinary prepared at every *auberge*, or public-house, on the road. Here they sit down promiscuously, and dine at so much a-head.

The usual price is thirty sols for dinner, and forty for supper, including lodging; for this moderate expense they have two courses and a dessert. If you eat in your own apartment, you pay, instead of forty sols, three, and in some places four livres a-head. I and my family could not well dispense with our tea and toast in the morning, and had no stomach to eat at noon. For my own part, I hate the French cookery, and abominate garlick, with which all their ragouts in this part of the country are highly seasoned. We therefore formed a different plan of living upon the road. Before we left Paris, we laid in a stock of tea, chocolate, cured neats tongues, and *saucissons*, or Bologna sausages, both of which we found in great perfection in that capital, where indeed there are excellent provisions of all sorts. About ten in the morning we stopped to breakfast at some auberge, where we always found bread, butter, and milk. In the mean time, we ordered a *poulard* or two to be roasted, and these, wrapped in a napkin, were put into the boot of the coach, together with bread, wine, and water. About two or three in the afternoon, while the horses were changing, we laid a cloth upon our knees, and producing our store, with a few earthen plates, discussed our short meal without further ceremony. This was followed by a dessert of grapes and other fruit, which we had also provided. I must own I found these transient refreshments much more agreeable than any regular meal I ate upon the road. The wine commonly used in Burgundy is so weak and thin, that you would not drink it in England. The very best which they sell at Dijon, the capital of the province, for three livres a bottle, is, in strength, and even in flavour, greatly inferior to what I have drank in London. I believe all the first growth is either consumed in the houses of the noblesse, or sent abroad to foreign markets. I have drank excellent Burgundy at Brussels for a florin a bottle; that is little more than twenty pence sterling.

Tobias Smollett
Travels through France and Italy
1766

THE EFFICACY OF BOUILLON

A *bouillon* is an universal remedy among the good people of France; insomuch, that they have no idea of any persons dying, after having swallowed *un bon bouillon*. One of the English gentlemen, who were robbed and murdered about thirty years ago, between Calais and Boulogne, being brought to the post-house of Boulogne, with some signs of life, this remedy was immediately administered. 'What surprises me greatly,' said the postmaster, speaking of this melancholy story to a friend of mine, two years after it happened, 'I made an excellent *bouillon*, and poured it down his throat with my own hands, and yet he did not recover.' Now, in all probability, this *bouillon* it was that stopped his breath.

At Brignolles, where we dined, I was obliged to quarrel with the landlady, and threaten to leave her house, before she would indulge us with any sort of fleshmeat. It was meagre day, and she had made her provision accordingly. She even hinted some dissatisfaction at having heretics in her house. But, as I was not disposed to eat stinking fish, with ragouts of eggs and onions, I insisted upon a leg of mutton, and a brace of fine partridges, which I found in the larder.

Tobias Smollett
Travels through France and Italy
1766

WAITING FOR THE MILK IN CALABRIA

If you wish for milk at breakfast-time in these parts of the world, you ought to sit in the middle of the road with a jug at early dawn, for unless you seize the critical moment of the goats passing through the town, you may wish in vain. If you have any excursion to make, and require to start early, you may as well give up the idea, for the *Crapi* are 'not yet come'; and if you delay but a little while, you hear the tinkle of their bells, and perceive the last tails of the receding flock in vexatious perspective at the end of the street.

Edward Lear
Journal of a Landscape Painter in Southern Calabria
1852

THE GONDOLIER'S WEDDING

It was a heavy entertainment, copious in quantity, excellent in quality, plainly but well cooked. I remarked there was no fish. The widow replied that everybody present ate fish to satiety at home. They did not join a marriage feast at the San Gallo, and pay their nine francs, for that! It should be observed that each guest paid for his own entertainment. This appears to be the custom. Therefore attendance is complimentary, and the married couple are not at ruinous charges for the banquet. A curious feature in the whole proceeding had its origin in this custom. I noticed that before each cover lay an empty plate, and that my partner began with the first course to heap upon it what she had not eaten. She also took large helpings, and kept advising me to do the same. I said: 'No; I only take what I want to eat; if I fill that plate in front of me as you are doing, it will be great waste.' This remark elicited shrieks of laughter from all who heard it; and when the hubbub had subsided, I perceived an apparently official personage bearing down upon Eustace, who was in the same perplexity. It was then circumstantially explained to us that the empty plates were put there in order that we might lay aside what we could not conveniently eat, and take it home with us. At the end of the dinner the widow (whom I must now call my *comare*) had accumulated two whole chickens, half a turkey, and a large assortment of mixed eatables. I performed my duty and won her regard by placing delicacies at her disposition.

Meanwhile the room grew warm. The gentlemen threw off their coats – a pleasant liberty of which I availed myself, and was immediately more at ease. The ladies divested themselves of their shoes (strange to relate!) and sat in comfort with their stockinged feet upon the *scagliola* pavement. I observed that some cavaliers by special permission were allowed to remove their partners' slippers. This was not my lucky fate. My *comare* had not advanced to that point of intimacy. Healths began to be drunk. The conversation took a lively turn; and women went fluttering round the table, visiting their friends, to sip out of their glass, and ask each other how they were getting on. It was not long before the stiff veneer of *bourgeoisie* which bored me had worn off. The people emerged in their true selves: natural, gentle, sparkling with enjoyment, playful. Playful is, I think, the best word to describe them. They played with infinite grace and innocence, like kittens, from the old men of sixty to the little boys of thirteen. Very little wine was drunk. Each guest had a litre placed before him. Many did not finish theirs; and for very few was it replenished. When at last the dessert arrived, and the bride's comfits had been handed round, they began to sing. It was very pretty to see a party of three or four friends gathering round some popular beauty, and paying her compliments in verse – they grouped behind her chair, she sitting back in it and laughing up to them, and joining in the chorus. The words, '*Brunetta mia simpatica, ti amo sempre più*', sung after this fashion to Eustace's handsome partner, who puffed delicate whiffs from a Russian cigarette, and smiled her thanks, had a peculiar appropriateness. All the ladies, it may by observed in passing, had by this time lit their cigarettes. The men were smoking Toscani, Sellas, or Cavours, and the little boys were dancing round the table breathing smoke from their pert nostrils.

J. A. Symonds
Sketches and Studies in Italy and Greece
1898

THE REPRESENTATIVE DINER IN ITALY

Wonderful to observe, the representative diner. He always seems to know exactly what his appetite demands; he addresses the waiter in a preliminary discourse, sketching out his meal, and then proceeds to fill in the minutiæ. If he orders a common dish, he describes with exquisite detail how it is to be prepared; in demanding something out of the way he glows with culinary enthusiasm. An ordinary bill of fare never satisfies him; he plays variations upon the theme suggested, divides or combines, introduces novelties of the most unexpected kind. As a rule, he eats enormously (I speak only of dinner), a piled dish of macaroni is but the prelude to his meal, a whetting of his appetite. Throughout he grumbles, nothing is quite as it should be, and when the bill is presented he grumbles still more vigorously, seldom paying the sum as it stands. He rarely appears content with his entertainment, and often indulges in unbounded abuse of those who serve him. These characteristics, which I have noted more or less in every part of Italy, were strongly illustrated at the *Concordia*. In general, they consist with a fundamental good humour, but at Cotrone the tone of the dining-room was decidedly morose. One man – he seemed to be a sort of clerk – came only to quarrel. I am convinced that he ordered things which he knew the people could not cook just for the sake of reviling their handiwork when it was presented. Therewith he spent incredibly small sums; after growling and remonstrating and eating for more than an hour, his bill would amount to seventy or eighty *centesimi*, wine included. Every day he threatened to withdraw his custom; every day he sent for the landlady, pointed out to her how vilely he was treated, and asked how she could expect him to recommend the *Concordia* to his acquaintances. On one occasion I saw him push away a plate of something, plant his elbows on the table, and hide his face in his hands; thus he sat for ten minutes, an image of indignant misery, and when at length his countenance was again visible, it showed traces of tears.

George Gissing
By the Ionian Sea
1901

ALBANIAN HOSPITALITY

The plan of Khimáriot hospitality is this: the guest buys a fowl or two, and his hosts cook it, and help him to eat it. We all sat round the dish, and I, propping myself sideways on cushions, made shift to partake of it as well as I could; but a small candle being the only light allotted to the operation, I was not so adroit as my co-partners, who fished out the most interesting parts of the excellent fowl ragout with astonishing dexterity and success. The low round plate of tin was a perpetual shelter for eight or nine little cats, whom we pulled out from beneath by their tails at momentary intervals, when they wailed aloud, and rushed back again, pleased even by feeling the hot fowl through the table, as they could not otherwise enjoy it. After the ragout had nearly all been devoured, and its remains consigned to the afflicted cats, there came on a fearful species of cheese soup, with butter, perfectly fabulous as to filthiness; and after this, there was the usual washing of hands, *à la turque*, and the evening meal was done. Supper over, we all sat in a semicircle about the fire. Some six or eight of the townsmen came in – a sort of soirée – and drinking cups of coffee was the occupation for some hours. Albanian only is spoken, and very little Greek understood here. About ten or eleven, all but the family gradually withdrew; the old gentlemen, Achmét, and the rest of the Albanians, rolled themselves up in capotes, and slept, Anastásio placed himself across my feet, with his pistols by his side; and as for me, with my head on my knapsack, I managed to get an hour or two of early sleep, though the army of fleas, which assailed me as a newcomer, not to speak of the excursion cats, who played at bo-peep behind my head, made the rest of the night a time of real suffering, the more so that the great wood fire nearly roasted me, and was odious to the eyes, as a wood fire must needs be. Such are the penalties paid for the picturesque. But one does not come to Acroceraunia for food, sleep or cleanliness.

Edward Lear
Journals of a Landscape Painter in Greece and Albania
1851

TOWN AND COUNTRY EATING IN SPAIN

As the sun gets high, and man and beast hungry and weary, wherever a tempting shady spot with running water occurs, the party draws aside from the high road, like Don Quixote and Sancho Panza; a retired and concealed place is chosen, the luggage is removed from the animals, the hampers which lard the lean soil are unpacked, the table-cloth is spread on the grass, the *botas* are laid in the water to cool their contents; then out with the provision, cold partridge or turkey, sliced ham or *chorizo* – simple cates, but which are eaten with an appetite and relish for which aldermen would pay hundreds. They are followed, should grapes be wanting, with a soothing cigar, and a sweet slumber on earth's freshest softest lap. In such wild banquets Spain surpasses the Boulevards. Alas! that such hours should be bright and winged as sunbeams! Such is Peninsular country fare. The *olla*, on which the rider may restore exhausted nature, is only to be studied in larger towns; and dining, of which this is the foundation in Spain, is such a great resource to travellers, and Spanish cookery, again, is so Oriental, classical, and singular, let alone its vital importance, that the subject will properly demand a chapter to itself . . .

The veritable *olla* – the ancient time-honoured *olla podrida*, or pot pourri – the epithet is now obsolete – is difficult to be made: a tolerable one is never to be eaten out of Spain, since it requires many Spanish things to concoct it, and much care; the cook must throw his whole soul into the pan, or rather pot; it may be made in one, but two are better. They must be of earthenware; for, like the French *pot au feu*, the dish is good for nothing when made in an iron or copper vessel; take therefore two, and put them on their separate stoves with water. Place into No. 1, *Garbanzos*, which have been placed to soak over-night. Add a good piece of beef, a chicken, a large piece of bacon; let it boil once and quickly; then let it simmer: it requires four or five hours to be well done. Meanwhile place into No. 2, with water, whatever vegetables are to be had: lettuces, cabbage, a slice of gourd, of beef, carrots, beans, celery, endive, onions and garlic, long peppers. These must be previously well washed and cut, as if they were destined to make a salad; then add red sausages, or '*chorizos*'; half a salted pig's face, which should have been soaked over-night. When all is sufficiently boiled, strain off the water, and throw it away. Remember constantly to skim the scum off both saucepans. When all this is sufficiently dressed, take a large dish, lay in the bottom the vegetables, the beef in the centre, flanked by the bacon, chicken, and pig's face. The sausages should be arranged around, *en couronne*; pour over some of the soup of No. 1, and serve hot, as Horace did: *Uncta satis – ponuntur oluscula lardo.* No violets come up to the perfume which a coming *olla* casts before it; the mouth-watering bystanders sigh, as they see and smell the rich freight steaming away from them.

This is the *olla en grande*, such as Don Quixote says was eaten only by canons and presidents of colleges; like turtle soup, it is so rich and satisfactory that it is a dinner of itself. A worthy dignitary of Seville, in the good old times, before reform and appropriation had put out the churches' kitchen fire, and whose daily pot-luck was transcendental, told us, as a wrinkle, that he on feast-days used turkeys instead of chickens, and added two sharp Ronda apples, and three sweet potatoes of Malaga. His advice is worth attention: he was a good Roman Catholic canon, who believed everything, absolved everything, drank everything, ate everything, and digested everything.

Richard Ford
Gatherings from Spain
1846

PIG-KILLING IN A SPANISH MOUNTAIN VILLAGE

At roughly 9 p.m. we all downed tools and sat round two tables put together and ate a simple form of *paella* directly out of another huge frying-pan with dessert spoons. It was sloppier than the Valencian variety but very good all the same: saffron-coloured rice with sliced potatoes, garlic and pimientos with the seeds left in so that you had to cram masses of bread into your mouth to prevent the roof being removed. *'Picante! Picante!'* observed Hilario shovelling it in.

Back to work after supper, for we were making *Morcillas Negras* – black puddings. Three large saucepans of rice were put on to boil in quick succession and as one lot of onions finished cooking it was tipped into the largest black *olla* (cauldron) I have ever seen while another lot replaced it in the frying-pan. The cooked rice joined the cooked onions in the *olla* together with a mountain of bread crumbs, several pints of rendered lard, the chopped parsley, pounded peppercorns, nutmeg and cinnamon with the following ingredients put through a large meat mincer: the crisped pimientos, about fifty cloves of garlic and at least two pounds of blanched almonds. Then the blood of the pig was poured in, the mixture stirred well together and fed into sections of the intestinal tube each tied at one end, the other end being pulled over a metal tube fixed to the mincer. When a section was full, it was removed and tied at the other end and there was a long sausage-shaped black pudding. This process took most of the night. The children and I retired to bed at 11.30 p.m. but all the women of the household and their neighbours worked through until 5 a.m. the next morning.

When I came down at eight o'clock to feed the Marquesa I counted eighty-two loops of black pudding hanging from the beams. Breakfast was *sopa*, bread broken into a bowl with sugar and barley coffee poured over it. Got through as much as I could, leaving a few sops at the bottom. The poor women were yawning a lot but all up and about their business . . .

When we got back to the *posada* in the late afternoon everyone was busy in the kitchen making pork sausages and white puddings. Three enormous bowls of mince stood ready on the table, the one destined for the puddings containing, among other delicacies, the colossal lights of the pig, boiled and put through the mincing-machine and the tripe treated in the same way.

That night we had a royal feast to celebrate the *matanza* (pig killing): ten grown-ups sat round the two tables while the four children sat on low chairs by the fire. We had no plates or glasses or forks, just a spoon and a *navaja* apiece.

First course: Pig's broth with bits of bread floating in it.

Second course: Extra good *cocido* (chickpea and potato soup with cloves of garlic).

Third course: Two large earthenware bowls containing slices of fried black pudding and assorted chitterlings eaten off the points of our *navajas* with pickled pimientos.

Fourth course: A delicious pork and chicken stew served in the *olla* in which it was cooked, swimming in yellowish brown gravy and accompanied by a mountain of olives. This was great fun: you jabbed your *navaja* into a bit of meat and took pot-luck; you gnawed all the meat off the bone held in your fingers and tossed it over your shoulder onto the floor. At one point Felicidad fished out a hen's claw which she sucked clean with great relish.

Fifth course: Pomegranates.

White wine was passed round and round in a *porrón*, and after the excellent meal was over the women washed the spoons and the serving dishes, scrubbed the tables and swept up all the bones off the floor, leaving the kitchen cleaner than many a one I have visited in the British Isles, and what a way to solve the washing-up problem!

Penelope Chetwode
Two Middle-Aged Ladies in Andalusia
1963

Officials and Other Busybodies
The burdens imposed by officialdom upon British travellers in Europe were, in theory, quite heavy. Authority was fragmented. The writ of central government did not run very far. Regions, towns, even villages set imposts and taxes. Passports were demanded. On the other hand, most parts of Europe still retained something of the old pre-industrial tradition of hospitality to travellers. Even when England and France were at war, an Englishman might cross the French countryside with little disturbance. And since most of our travellers were well-off, and most local officials were poor, inefficient and corrupt, a judicious bribe smoothed many a foreigner's path. So

the official was more a nuisance than a barrier. He sniffed around, his palm itched and he made war (since foreign persons were largely beyond reach) on the seditious influence of foreign books:

DOOR-KEEPERS AND STREET LADIES: BOSWELL PAYS HIS WAY IN GERMANY

I must remark that at Dresden strangers pay monstrously dear for seeing the fine things, which is shameful when they are the property of a prince. My *valet de louage* told me that I must pay a ducat to the library-keeper and a florin to his man, which I was fool enough to do, as I would be genteel, forsooth. It seems, too, I must pay at the museum a louis to the principal keeper, two écus to another, and a guilder to the servant. Instead of this I made two guilders do the business. I know not how I divided it between the upper keeper and the servant. I forget, but no matter. The fellows looked strange and I saved six écus. The museum has indeed many great curiosities, but some of its richest pieces have been sold to repair the ruins of the war. I then walked to the garden, where I saw some fine antiques in bronze. I went to the French *comédie*, which is very pretty here. I saw the Elector, Prince Xavier, and several more of the Court. I was enlivened with new ideas. Yet again I went with those easy street girls, and between their thighs, merely for health. I would not embrace them. First, because it was dangerous. Next, because I could not think of being so united to miscreants. Both last night and this they picked my pocket of my handkerchief. I was angry at myself. I was obliged to own to my servant that I had been *avec des filles*. Man is sometimes low.

James Boswell
On the Grand Tour
1764.

THE CUSTOM-HOUSES AT VIENNA AND BERLIN

The approach to Vienna from the river, is not very unlike that of Venice, though there is much less water, for the Danube divides itself into three streams, about a mile and a half above the town; forty or fifty towers and spires may be seen from the water.

The custom-house did not disappoint my expectation of its being remarkably troublesome, particularly, in the article of *books*; all are stopped there, and read more scrupulously than at the inquisition of Bologna, in Italy; and mine, which, except music, were merely geographical and descriptive, were detained near a fortnight before

I could recover them; and his excellency Lord Viscount Stormont, his majesty's ambassador at this court, afterwards told me, that this was the only thing in which it was not in his power to assist me. On entering the town, I was informed that if a single book had been found in my *sac de nuit*, or travelling satchel, its whole contents would have been forfeited . . .

When I arrived at the gates of this city (Berlin), about nine o'clock in the morning, September 28th, I had hopes that I should have been suffered to pass peaceably to an inn, having received a passport at Treuenbrietzen, the first Prussian town I entered on the Saxony side, where I had submitted to a thorough rummage of my baggage, at the persuasion of the custom-house officers, who had assured me that I would prevent all future trouble upon entering Berlin. But this was merely to levy fees upon me, for, notwithstanding my passport, I was stopped three-quarters of an hour at the barrier, before I was taken into the custody of a sentinel; who mounting my post-wagon, with his musket on his shoulder, and bayonet fixed, conducted me, like a prisoner, through the principal streets of the city, to the custom-house. Here I was detained in the yard for more than two hours, shivering with cold, in all my wet garments, while everything was taken out of my trunk and writing box, and examined as curiously as if I had just arrived at Dover, from the capital of France.

Charles Burney
Continental Travels
1772

SUSPICIOUS BOOKS ARRIVE AT THE FRENCH-ITALIAN BORDER

We were summoned from our tea and patriotic effusions to attend the *Douane*. It was striking to have to pass and repass the piquets of soldiers stationed as a guard on bridges across narrow mountain-streams that a child might leap over. After some slight dalliance with our great-coat pockets, and significant gestures as if we might or might not have things of value about us that we should not, we proceeded to the Custom-house. I had two trunks. One contained books. When it was unlocked, it was as if the lid of Pandora's box flew open. There could not have been a more sudden start or expression of surprise, had it been filled with cartridge-paper or gun-powder. Books were the corrosive sublimate that eat out despotism and priestcraft – the artillery that battered down castle and dungeon-walls – the ferrets that ferreted out abuses – the lynx-

Examinations at the Custom-house

eyed guardians that tore off disguises – the scales that weighed right and wrong – the thumping make-weight thrown into the balance that made force and fraud, the sword and the cowl, kick the beam – the dread of knaves, the scoff of fools – the balm and the consolation of the human mind – the salt of the earth – the future rulers of the world! A box full of them was a contempt of the constituted Authorities; and the names of mine were taken down with great care and secrecy.

William Hazlitt
Notes of a Journey through France and Italy
1826

BRIBES ON THE SPANISH ROAD

The laws in Spain are indeed strict on paper, but those who administer them, whenever it suits their private interest, that is ninety-nine times out of a hundred, evade and defeat them; they obey the letter, but do not perform the spirit, *se obedece, pero no se cumple*; indeed, the lower classes of officials are compelled to eke out a livelihood by taking bribes and little presents, which, as *Backshish* in the East, may always be offered, and will always be accepted, as a matter of compliment. The *idea* of a bribe must be concealed; it shocks their dignity, their sense of honour, their *pundonor*: if, however, the money be given to the head person as something for his people to drink, the delicate attention is sacked by the chief, properly appreciated, and works its due effect.

Richard Ford
Gatherings from Spain
1846

THE 'ENGLISH MILORD' PASSES ON

Had it not been for the caprices of our guide, a wild gipsy Soorudgí, we should sooner have arrived at our destination than we did; that worthy having met with a fellow-gipsy on horseback, the twain indulged in convivial draughts of rakhee at two roadside khans to so great an extent that their merriment became boundless, and having loosened the baggage and led horses, they drove them facetiously in and out of fields of maize and corn – for we were now near the city – till their sport terminated in the lively new-comer subsiding into a quagmire, where his horse, anxious to make a good meal in the next field of gran-turco, left him to his fate. This catastrophe rather pleased me than not, till, on entering Monastír, our own Soorudgí suddenly gave way to pangs of conscience, and neither threats nor entreaties could prevent his returning for his lost friend, which meritorious act caused us an hour's delay ere we reached the barrier of the city.

Here we were interrogated by an official who, in the matter of passports, was soon satisfied by the αυτο´ς μιλο´ρδος Ιυγλις of Giorgio ('this English Milord', all English travellers being so termed in the East) and we passed onward. Close to the town, on the eastern side, stretches a wide common, used as a cemetery, and forming the unmolested abode of troops of dogs, who lie in groups of ten and twenty till the town scavengers bring them their morning and evening meal.

Edward Lear
Journals of a Landscape Painter in Greece and Albania
1851

FRONTIER TRANSACTIONS IN ROUMANIA

Full tilt we rode toward the Roumanian frontier. We whisked past a couple of cottages, over a brook, through a gate painted with the tricolour, and then suddenly realized we were in Roumanian territory. We had hardly turned our machines round and recrossed the brook before soldiers hastened from out the Hungarian cottages, armed from head to foot, guns across their shoulders, cartridges in their pouches, and imposing cocktail plumes nodding in their hats.

The Hungarian plains

We saluted them, showed our passports, produced our receipts, and suggested that they might be kind enough to hand over the bicycle tax of £2 10s. on each machine which we had paid on the German – Austrian frontier, and which was to be repaid on our reaching the Hungarian – Roumanian frontier.

Money! there wasn't so much on the frontier. And if there was, they were not going to part with it merely on the production of a receipt signed by some unknown officer on the other side of the empire. If we really wanted our £7 10s. we had better go to the village of Tolgyes, lying some way back off the main road.

We went to Tolgyes. We gave the officials our names, allowed them to calculate our heights, find out the colour of our eyes, and write down any peculiarities of feature or body. Then, to a parboiled, clear-eyed, and big-stomached gentleman, positively bursting with authority, we suggested the return of that money. Return! He laughed at the idea. Whoever heard of his Government paying any money to anybody? He became abusive. We threatened and scoffed.

The miserable village inn was discovered and then we telegraphed to Braunau, on the other side of Austria, to give authority for the money to be handed over. In a day and a half we got a reply that our telegram was not understood, and would we be more explicit? The official, noting our obstinacy, thought it well to wire Buda-Pest for instructions. He got no reply at all.

So we lounged about the filthy inn, cursed our fate, and vowed a cruel vengeance ultimately on all officials of whatever land. The

85

particular official against whom our vows were specially directed found wisdom on the second morning. He also found special instructions in his rules about the return of duty on bicycles. After keeping us dawdling about his office, and pretending he had been only following instructions, he slowly doled out the seventy-five florins. We picked up the money and gave him scowls as thanks.

Then upon our 'Rovers' we jumped and hied swiftly to the Roumanian frontier.

J. F. Fraser
Round the World on a Wheel
1899

RESCUED BY A MISSAL

Just as I was dropping happily off after midnight there was a clatter in the stone passage followed by a loud knock on the door. I sat up with a start and shouted '*Adelante!*' as I switched on the light. In marched two Civil Guards with carbines slung over their shoulders, followed by my landlord who was embarrassed and apologetic. I was thrilled. At last I should be able to produce the Marquesa's papers: for all Spanish horses and mules have identity papers with the names of their breeders and any change of ownership recorded on them to facilitate the police in case of theft. I dug out the plastic sponge-bag hidden in the depths of my *alforjas*, extracted my passport from it and the mare's papers, and handed them to the moustached leader of the two Guards. He looked far longer and asked far more questions about her papers than about mine, which I endeavoured to answer as best I could. Then he wanted to know what I was doing here, so I started off on my piece: 'I am English, I am on a tour in these Sierras; I have come from . . .' During my recitation both the Guards lit cigarettes. Then the leader started to examine a few books on the window-sill. 'Ah! I see you must be a Catholic as you have this Missal? *Muy bien, muy bien.*' And they all left the room.

Penelope Chetwode
Two Middle-Aged Ladies in Andalusia
1963

Tax-collectors, policemen and guards were not the only impediments to quiet progress. At various times the traveller was likely to have the assistance of servants, helpers, guides, interpreters and state functionaries. In general, these efforts were well-intentioned, but whether they saw the traveller efficiently on the way was more doubtful:

THE ANTIQUARY OF VERONA

Twilight drawing on, I left my haunt, and, stealing down stairs, enquired for a guide to conduct me to the amphitheatre; perhaps, the most entire monument of Roman days. The people of the house, instead of bringing me a quiet peasant, officiously delivered me up to an antiquary; one of those diligent, plausible young men, to whom, God help me! I have so capital an aversion. This sweet spark displayed all his little erudition, and flourished away upon cloacas and vomitoriums, with eternal fluency. He was very profound in the doctrine of conduits; and knew to admiration how the filthiness of all the amphitheatre was disposed of: but perceiving my inattention, and having just grace enough to remark, that I chose one side of the street, when he preferred the other; and sometimes trotted, through despair, in the kennel, he made me a pretty bow, I tipped him half a crown; and, seeing the ruins before me, traversed a gloomy arcade, and emerged alone into the arena.

William Beckford
Dreams, Waking Thoughts and Incidents
1783

THE POSTILION IS AMUSED ON THE ROAD TO FERRARA

There was a Postilion, in the course of this day's journey, as wild and savagely good-looking a vagabond as you would desire to see. He was a tall, stout-made, dark-complexioned fellow, with a profusion of shaggy black hair hanging all over his face, and great black whiskers stretching down his throat. His dress was a torn suit of rifle green, garnished here and there with red; a steeple-crowned hat, innocent of nap, with a broken and bedraggled feather stuck in the band; and a flaming red neck-kerchief hanging on his shoulders. He was not in the saddle, but reposed, quite at his ease, on a sort of low footboard in front of the postchaise, down among the horses' tails – convenient for having his brains kicked out, at any moment. To this Brigand, the Brave Courier, when we were at a reasonable trot, happened to suggest the practicability of going faster. He received the proposal with a perfect yell of derision; brandished his whip about his head (such a whip! it was more like a home-made bow); flung up his heels, much higher than the horses; and disappeared, in a paroxysm, somewhere in the neighbourhood of the axle-tree. I fully expected to see him lying in the road, a hundred yards behind, but up came the steeple-crowned hat again, next minute, and he was seen reposing, as on a sofa, entertaining himself with the idea, and crying, 'Ha ha! what next. Oh the devil!

87

Faster too! Shoo-hoo-o-o!' (This last ejaculation, an inexpressibly defiant hoot). Being anxious to reach our immediate destination that night, I ventured, by and by, to repeat the experiment on my own account. It produced exactly the same effect. Round flew the whip with the same scornful flourish, up came the heels, down went the steeple-crowned hat, and presently he reappeared, reposing as before and saying to himself, 'Ha ha! what next! Faster too! Oh the devil! Shoo-hoo-o-o!'

Charles Dickens
Pictures from Italy
1846

SPANISH COACHING OFFICIALS

The mail is organized on the plan of the French *malle-poste*, and offers, to those who can stand the bumping, shaking, and churning of continued and rapid travelling without halting, a means of locomotion which leaves nothing to be desired. The diligences also are imitations of the lumbering French model. It will be in vain to expect in them the neatness, the well-appointed turn-out, the quiet, time-keeping, and infinite facilities of the English original, but when one is once booked and handed over to the conductor, you arrive in due time at the journey's end. The 'guards' are realities, they consist of stout, armed, most picturesque, robber-like men and no mistake, since many, before they were pardoned and pensioned, have frequently taken a purse on the Queen's highway; for the foreground of your first sketch, they are splendid fellows, and worth a score of marshals. They are provided with a complete arsenal of swords and blunderbusses, so that the cumbrous machine rolling over the sea of plains looks like a man-of-war, and has been compared to a marching citadel. Again in suspicious localities a mounted escort of equally suspicious look gallops alongside, nor is the primitive practice of black mail altogether neglected: the consequences of these admirable precautions is, that the diligences are seldom or never robbed; the thing, however, is possible.

The whole of this garrisoned Noah's ark is placed under the command of the *Mayoral* or conductor, who like all Spanish men in authority is a despot, and yet, like them, is open to the conciliatory influences of a bribe. He regulates the hours of toil and sleep, which latter – blessings, says Sancho, on the man who invented it! – is uncertain, and depends on the early or late arrival of the diligence and the state of the roads, for all that is lost of the fixed time on the road is made up for by curtailing the time allowed for repose. One of the many good effects of setting up diligences is the bettering the inns on the road; and it is a safe and general rule to travellers in Spain, whatever be their vehicle, always to inquire in every town which is the *posada* that the diligence stops at.

Richard Ford
Gatherings from Spain
1846

AN AUDIENCE WITH ALI BEY

In the arabesqued and carved corridor, to which a broad staircase conducted me, were hosts of Albanian domestics; and on my letter of introduction being sent into the Bey, I was almost instantly asked into his room of reception – a three-windowed, square chamber (excellent, according to the standard of Turkish ornament, taste, and proportion) – where, in a corner of the raised divan, sat Alí, Bey of Króia – a lad of eighteen or nineteen, dressed in the usual blue frock-coat now adopted by Turkish nobles or officers. A file of kilted and armed retainers were soon ordered to marshal me into a room where I was to sleep, and the little Bey seemed greatly pleased with the fun of doing hospitality to so novel a creature as a Frank. My dormitory was a real Turkish chamber; and the raised cushions on three sides of it – the high, square, carved wooden ceiling – the partition screen of lofty woodwork, with long striped Brusa napkins thrown over it – the guns, horse-gear, etc., which covered the walls – the fire-place – closets – innumerable pigeon-holes – green, orange, and blue stained-glass windows – all appeared so much the more in the light of luxuries and splendours when found in so remote a place as Króia. It was not easy to shake off the attentions of ten full-dressed Albanian servants, who stood in much expectation, till, finding I was about to take off my shoes, they made a rush at me as the Jews did at Saloníki, and showed such marks of disappointment at not being allowed to make themselves useful, that I was obliged to tell Giorgio to explain that we Franks were not used to assistance every moment of our lives, and that I should think it obliging of them if they would leave me in peace. After changing my dress, the Bey sent to say that supper should be served in an hour, he having eaten at sunset, and in the meantime he would be glad of my society; so I took my place on the sofa by the little gentleman's side, and Giorgio, sitting on the ground, acted as interpreter. At first Alí Bey said little, but soon became immensely loquacious, asking numerous questions about Stamboul, and a few about Franks in general – the different species of whom he was not very well informed. At length, when the conversation was flagging, he was moved to discourse about ships that went without sails, and coaches that were impelled without horses; and to please him I drew a steamboat and a railway carriage; on which he asked if they made any noise; and I replied by imitating both the inventions in question in the best manner I could think of – 'Tik-tok, tik-tok, tik-tok, tokka, tokka, tokka, tokka, tokka - tok' (crescendo), and 'Squish-squash, squish-squash, squish-squash, thump-bump' – for the land and sea engines respectively – a noisy novelty, which so intently delighted Alí Bey, that he fairly threw himself back on the divan, and laughed as I never saw Turk laugh before.

Edward Lear
Journals of a Landscape Painter in Greece and Albania
1851

THE CALABRIAN MULETEER AND GUIDE

We had engaged a muleteer for an indefinite time: the expense for both guide and quadruped being six carlini daily; and if we sent him back from any point of our journey it was agreed that his charges should be defrayed until he reached Reggio. Our man, a grave tall fellow of more than fifty years of age, and with a good expression of countenance, was called Ciccio, and we explained to him that our plan was to do always just as we pleased – going straight a-head or stopping to sketch, without reference to any law but our own pleasure; to all which he replied by a short sentence ending with – '*Dógo; díghi, dóghi, dághi, dà*' – a collection of sounds of frequent recurrence in Calabrese lingo, and the only definite portion of that speech we could ever perfectly master. What the '*Dógo*' was we never knew, though it was an object of our keenest search throughout the tour to ascertain if it were animal, mineral, or vegetable. Afterwards, by constant habit, we arranged a sort of conversational communication with friend Ciccio, but we never got on well unless we said '*Dógo si*,' or '*Dógo no*' several times as an *ad libitum* apoggiatura, winding up with '*Díghi, dóghi, dághi, dà*,' which seemed to set all right. Ciccio carried a gun, but alas! wore no pointed hat; nothing but a Cicilian long blue cap.

Edward Lear
Journals of a Landscape Painter in Southern Calabria
1852

And just occasionally, neither rank nor influence nor bribe sufficed. The figure of authority loomed alarmingly large. The traveller seemed to be on the edge of an incident:

A BRUSH WITH THE FRENCH LAW

A polite gendarme threw his shadow on the path.

'*Monsieur est voyageur?*' he asked.

And the *Arethusa*, strong in his innocence, forgetful of his vile attire, replied – I had almost said with gaiety: 'So it would appear.'

'His papers are in order?' said the gendarme. And when the *Arethusa* with a slight change of voice, admitted he had none, he was informed (politely enough) that he must appear before the Commissary.

The Commissary sat at a table in his bedroom, stripped to the shirt and trousers, but still copiously perspiring; and when he turned upon the prisoner a large meaningless countenance, that was (like Bardolph's) 'all whelks and bubukles ', the dullest might have been prepared for grief. Here was a very stupid man, sleepy with the heat and fretful at the interruption, whom neither appeal nor argument could reach.

THE COMMISSARY. You have no papers?

THE ARETHUSA. Not here.

THE COMMISSARY. Why?

THE ARETHUSA. I have left them behind in my valise.

THE COMMISSARY. You know, however, that it is forbidden to circulate without papers?

THE ARETHUSA. Pardon me: I am convinced of the contrary. I am here on my rights as an English subject by the international treaty.

THE COMMISSARY (*with scorn*). You call yourself an Englishman?

THE ARETHUSA. I do.

THE COMMISSARY. Humph. What is your trade?

THE ARETHUSA. I am a Scottish advocate.

THE COMMISSARY. (*with singular annoyance*). A Scottish advocate! Do you then pretend to support yourself by that in this Department?

The *Arethusa* modestly disclaimed the pretension. The Commissary had scored a point.

THE COMMISSARY. Why, then, do you travel?

THE ARETHUSA. I travel for pleasure.

THE COMMISSARY (*pointing to the knapsack, and with sublime incredulity*). Avec ça? Voyez-vous, je suis un homme intelligent! (With that? Look here, I am a person of intelligence!)

The culprit remained silent under this home thrust, the Commissary relished his triumph for awhile, and then demanded (like the postman, but with what different expectations!) to see the contents of the knapsack. And here the *Arethusa*, not yet sufficiently awake to his position, fell into a grave mistake. There was little or no furniture in the room except the Commissary's chair and table; and to facilitate matters, the *Arethusa* (with all the innocence on earth) leant the knapsack on a corner of the bed. The Commissary fairly bounded from his seat; his face and neck flushed past purple, almost into blue; and he screamed to lay the desecrating object on the floor.

The inquisitor resumed his seat.

THE COMMISSARY (*after a pause*). *Eh bien, je vais vous dire ce que vous êtes. Vous êtes allemand et vous venez chanter à la foire.* (Well, then, I will tell you what you are. You are a German and have come to sing at the fair.)

THE ARETHUSA. Would you like to hear me sing? I believe I could convince you of the contrary.

THE COMMISSARY. *Pas de plaisanterie, monsieur!*

THE ARETHUSA. Well, sir, oblige me at least by looking at this book. Here, I open it with my eyes shut. Read one of these songs – read this one – and tell me, you who are a man of intelligence, if it would be possible to sing it at a fair?

THE COMMISSARY (*critically*). *Mais oui. Très bien.*

THE ARETHUSA. *Comment, monsieur!* What! But you do not observe it is antique. It is difficult to understand even for you and me; but for the audience at a fair, it would be meaningless.

THE COMMISSARY (*taking a pen*). *Enfin, il faut en finir.* What is your name?

THE ARETHUSA (*speaking with the swallowing vivacity of the English*). Robert-Louis Stev'ns'n.

THE COMMISSARY. (*aghast*). *Hé! Quoi?*

THE ARETHUSA (*perceiving and improving his advantage*). Rob'rt-Lou's-Stev'ns'n.

THE COMMISSARY. (*after several conflicts with his pen*). *Eh bien, il faut se passer du nom. Ça ne s'écrit pas.* (Well, we must do without the name: it is unspellable.)

The above is a rough summary of this momentous conversation, in which I have been chiefly careful to preserve the plums of the Commissary; but the remainder of the scene, perhaps because of his rising anger, has left but little definite in the memory of the *Arethusa*. The Commissary was not, I think, a practised literary man; no sooner, at least, had he taken pen in hand and embarked on the composition of the *procès-verbal*, than he became distinctly more uncivil and began to show a predilection for that simplest of all forms of repartee: 'You lie!' Several times the *Arethusa* let it pass, and then suddenly flared up, refused to accept more insults or to answer further questions, defied the Commissary to do his worst, and promised him, if he did, that he should bitterly repent it. Perhaps if he had worn his proud front from the first, instead of beginning with a sense of entertainment and then going on to argue, the thing might have turned otherwise; for even at this eleventh hour the Commissary was visibly staggered. But it was too late; he had been challenged; the *procès-verbal* was begun; and he again squared his elbows over his writing, and the *Arethusa* was led forth a prisoner.

R. L. Stevenson
An Inland Voyage
1873

THE ALBANIANS RECEIVE THE FOREIGN ARTIST
WITH SUSPICION

Sunrise: and I am drawing the plain and hills from the *Piazza de' Cani*; lines of convicts are passing from the Barracks, carrying offal in tubs to the ghouly burying-grounds and followed by some hundreds of dogs, who every now and then give way to their feelings and indulge in a general battle among themselves. It is no easy matter to pursue the fine arts in Monastír, and I cannot but think – will matters grow worse as I advance into Albania? for all the passers-by having inspected my sketching, frown, or look ugly, and many say, '*Shaitán*', which means, Devil; at length one quietly wrenches my book away and shutting it up returns it to me, saying, '*Yok, Yok!*'* so as numbers are against me, I bow and retire. Next, I essay to draw on one of the bridges, but a gloomy sentinel comes and bullies me off directly, indicating by signs that my profane occupation is by no manner of means to be tolerated; and farther on, when I thought I had escaped all observation behind a friendly buttress, out rush legions of odious hounds (all bare-hided and very like jackals) and raise such a din, that, although by means of a pocket full of stones I keep them at bay, yet they fairly beat me at last, and give me chase open-mouthed, augmenting their detestable pack by fresh recruits at each street-corner. So I gave up this pursuit of knowledge under difficulties, and returned to the khan.

Giorgio was waiting to take me to the Pashá; so dressing in my 'best', thither I went, to pay my first visit to an Oriental dignitary. All one's gathered and hoarded memories, from books or personal relations, came so clearly to my mind as I was shown into the great palace or *serai* of the Governor, that I seemed somehow to have seen it all before; the ante-room full of attendants, the second state-room with secretaries and officers, and, finally, the large square

---

* 'No, no!'

hall, where – in a corner, and smoking the longest nargilleh, the serpentine foldings of which formed all the furniture of the chamber save the carpets and sofas – sat the Seraskíer Pashá himself – one of the highest grandees of the Ottoman empire. Emím Seraskíer Pashá was educated at Cambridge, and speaks English fluently. He conversed for some time agreeably and intelligently, and after having promised me a Kawás, the interview was over, and I returned to the khan, impatient to attack the street-scenery of Monastír forthwith under the auspices of my guard. These availed me much, and I sketched in the dry part of the river-bed with impunity – ay, and even in the Jews' quarter, though immense crowds collected to witness the strange Frank and his doings; and the word, '*Scroo, Scroo,*' resounded from hundreds of voices above and around. But a clear space was kept around me by the formidable baton of the Kawás, and I contrived thus to carry off some of the best views of the town ere it grew dark.

Edward Lear
Journals of a Landscape Painter in Greece and Albania
1851

MONEY CHANGING IN DEEPEST RUSSIA

After several days of plodding over sandy wastes and sleeping in our clothes in the hovels of muzjiks, we made a halt for a couple of nights at the town of Ekaterindar, a big, busy, electric-lighted city, with a main street nearly two miles long, and a population of over a hundred and twenty thousand.

Now to be 'stumped' and have not the wherewithal to pay your way, while at the same time your pocket-book bulges with bank notes, is an anomaly. And it was our condition at Ekaterindar. Never before did we realize the uselessness of Bank of England five-pound notes. Ekaterindar is on the road to nowhere, and English notes may be interesting as works of art, but they won't settle a hotel bill. When we presented two for this laudable purpose, the landlord fingered them curiously, turned them over, held them up to the light, sniffed at them, and then shook his head. He didn't understand. We waved him aside, and marched to the local bank. The full force of manager, clerks, office boy, and sweeper alternately examined our money. 'Could the notes be changed?' we asked. No; they had never seen anything like them before, and, casting a suspicious side glance, they insinuated they had never seen anything like us before; they were sorry they could not help us, perhaps some tradesman might oblige, Russia wasn't England, and so on.

We tried another bank. No doubt was expressed about our being honourable, upright gentlemen, but really there was so much counterfeit foreign paper money about, that, without making any suggestions, they were regretfully obliged, etc. Next we attempted to beguile an apothecary, then a manufacturer, then somebody else; in fact, we waited upon all the butchers, bakers, and candlestick-makers in Ekaterindar. When we got weary and footsore we sat down and looked at one another dismally. We were in a hole. Our total funds in Russian money amounted to something under half a sovereign. Would we be cast into prison as vagabonds, or hastened off to Siberia, or would it be advisable to put our bicycles in pawn till the one thing needful was forthcoming? We went back to the hotel, ordered a good lunch, though we knew not how or when it was to be paid for, and discussed futile schemes. In the middle of it all a gentleman came and spoke to us in German. He had seen us in Odessa, and was interested in our journey. We told him our trouble.

'What blithering silly fools these people in Ekaterindar must be!' or something to that effect, he said in German. Open flew his pocket-book, and in fifteen seconds our minds were easy. But faith in Bank of England notes was shaken.

J. F. Fraser
Round the World on a Wheel
1899

Danger, Discomforts and Minor Troubles

In four hundred years of war, social unrest and turmoil, before the modern nation-state imposed an authoritarian grip on all aspects of national life, Europe was often a dangerous place. Robbers, brigands and bandits operated in remote areas more or less with impunity. Lonely roads were preyed on by highwaymen. Even in populous lands, outlaws prowled up to the very gates of large cities. Poor, repressed countrymen were not beyond brutal reprisals against anyone whose luck was better than theirs. And unregulated sea-lanes, infested with pirates, were particularly hazardous. The travel-ler, an easy mark, was likely to suffer, and paid not infrequently, with his life:

THE DANGERS OF 16TH CENTURY RUSSIA

For as themselves are verie hardlie and cruellie dealte withall by their chiefe magistrates and other superiours, so are they as cruell one against an other, specially over their inferiours and such as are under them. So that the basest and wretchedest *Christianoe* (as

95

they call him) that stoupeth and croucheth like a dogge to the gentleman, and licketh up the dust that lieth at his feete, is an intollerable tyrant where he hath the advantage. By this meanes the whole countrie is filled with rapine and murder. They make no account of the life of a man. You shall have a man robbed sometime in the very streats of their townes, if hee goe late in the evening, and yet no man to come forth out of his doores to rescue him, though hee heare him crie out. I will not speake of the straungenesse of the murders and other cruelties committed among them, that would scarsly bee beleeved to bee done among men, specially such as professe themselves Christians.

The number of their vagrant and begging poore is almost infinite, that are so pinched with famine and extreame neede, as that they begge after a violent and desperate manner, with 'give mee and cut mee, give mee and kill mee,' and such like phrases. Whereby it may bee gheassed what they are towardes straungers, that are so unnaturall and cruell towardes their owne. And yet it may bee doubted whither is the greter, the crueltie or intemperancie that is used in that countrie. I will not speake of it, because it is so foule and not to bee named. The whole countrie overfloweth with all sinne of that kinde. And no marveile, as having no lawe to restraine whoredomes, adulteries, and like uncleannesse of life.

As for the truth of his word, the Russe for the most part maketh small regard of it, so he may gaine by a lie and breache of his promise. And it may be saide truely (as they know best that have traded most with them) that from the great to the small (except some fewe that will scarcely be founde) the Russe neither beleeveth any thing that an other man speaketh, nor speaketh any thing himselfe worthie to be beleeved.

Giles Fletcher
Of the Russe Common Wealth
1591

THE '*BRAVI*' OF VENICE AND AN ENGLISHMAN
ENSLAVED IN THE GALLEYS

There are certaine desperate and resolute villaines in Venice, called Braves, who at some unlawfull times do commit great villainy. They wander abroad very late in the night to and fro for their prey, like hungry Lyons, being armed with a privy coate of maile, a gauntlet upon their right hand, and a little sharpe dagger called a stiletto. They lurke commonly by the water side, and if at their time of the night, which is betwixt eleven of the clocke and two, they happen to meete any man that is worth the rifling, they will presently stabbe him, take away all about him that is of any worth, and when they have thoroughly pulled his plumes, they will throw him into one of the channels: but they buy this booty very deare if they are after apprehended. For they are presently executed.

I observed one thing in Venice that I utterly condemned, that if two men should fight togetheer at sharpe openly in the streets, whereas a great company will suddenly flocke together about them, all of them will give them leave to fight till their hearts ake, or till they welter in their owne blood, but not one of them hath the honesty to part them, and keepe them asunder from spilling each others blood: also if one of the two should be slaine they will not offer to apprehend him that slew the other (except the person slaine be a Gentleman of the citie) but suffer him to go at randome whither he list, without inflicting any punishment upon him. A very barbarous and unchristian thing to winke at such effusion of Christian blood, in which they differ (in my opinion) from all Christians. The like I understand is to be observed in Milan and other cities of Italy.

There happened a thing when I was in Venice, that moved great commiseration and sympathie in me: I saw a certain English-man one Thomas Taylour, born in Leicester-shire, endure great slavery in one of the Venetian galleys: for whose inlargement I did my utmost endeavour, but all would not serve. I would to God he had not committed that fault which deserved that condemnation to the galleys. For indeed he tooke pay before hand of the Venetians for service in their warres, and afterward fled away. But being againe apprehended, they have made him with many trickling teares repent his flying from them.

Thomas Coryat
Crudities
1611

THE FREEBOOTERS OF THE LOWER RHINE

I observed in a great many places, on both sides of the Rhene, more gallowes and wheeles betwixt Mentz and Colen, then ever I saw in so short a space in all my life, especially within few miles of Colen, by reason that the rusticall Corydons of the country, which are commonly called the Boores and the Free-booters, do commit many notorious robberies neere the Rhene, who are such cruell and bloody horseleaches (the very Hyenæ & Lycanthropi of Germany) that they seldome robbe any man but forthwith they cut his throat. And some of them doe afterward escape, by reason of the woodes neere at hand in which they shelter themselves free from danger. Yet others are sometimes taken, and most cruelly excarnificated and tortured upon these wheeles, in that manner that I have before mentioned in some of my observations of France. For I sawe the bones of many of them lie uppon the wheele, a doleful spectacle for any relenting Christian to beholde. And upon those gallowes in divers places I sawe murderers hang, partly in chaines, and partly without chaines. A punishment too good for these Cyclopicall Anthropophagi, these Caniball man-eaters.

Thomas Coryat
Crudities
1611

PIRATES OF THE AEGEAN

Believe me, Greeks are Greeks still; for falsenesse and treachery they still deserve *Iphigenia's* character of them in Euripides, *Trust them and hang them*, or rather hang them first for sureness.

Dr John Covel
Diaries
1670–79

A FRENCH MOB, 1789

Night – I have been witness to a scene curious to a foreigner; but dreadful to Frenchmen that are considerate. Passing through the square of the Hôtel de Ville, the mob were breaking the windows with stones, notwithstanding an officer and a detachment of horse was in the square. Perceiving that their numbers not only increased, but that they grew bolder and bolder every moment, I thought it worth staying to see what it would end in, and clambered on to the roof of a row of low stalls opposite the building against which their malice was directed. Here I beheld the whole commodiously. Perceiving that the troops would not attack them, except in words and menaces, they grew more violent, and furiously attempted to beat the doors in pieces with iron crows; placing ladders to the windows. In about a quarter of an hour, which gave time for the assembled magistrates to escape by a back door, they burst all open, and entered like a torrent with a universal shout of the spectators. From that minute a shower of casements, sashes, shutters, chairs, tables, sofas, books, papers, pictures, etc., rained incessantly from all the windows of the house, which is 70 or 80 feet long, and which was then succeeded by tiles, skirting boards, bannisters, framework, and every part of the building that force could detach. The troops, both horse and foot, were quiet spectators. They were at first too few to interpose, and, when they became more numerous, the mischief was too far advanced to admit of any other conduct than guarding every avenue around, permitting none to go to the scene of action, but letting everyone that pleased retire with his plunder; guards being at the same time placed at the doors of the churches, and all public buildings. I was for two hours a spectator at different places of the scene, secure myself from the falling furniture, but near enough to see a fine lad of about fourteen crushed to death by something as he was handing plunder to a woman, I suppose his mother, from the horror that was pictured in her countenance. I remarked several common soldiers, with their white cockades, among the plunderers, and instigating the mob even in sight of the officers of the detachment. There were amongst them people so decently dressed, that I regarded them with no small surprise; they destroyed all the public archives; the streets for some way around strewed with papers. This has been a wanton mischief, for it will be the ruin of many families unconnected with the magistrates.

Arthur Young
Travels in France
1789

THE ENGLISH TRAVELLER IN THE MIDST OF THE FRENCH REVOLUTION

JAN. 14th. Plots! plots! The Marquis La Fayette, last night, took two hundred prisoners in the Champs-Elysées; out of eleven hundred that were collected. They had powder and ball, but no muskets. Who and what are they is the question; but an answer is not so easily to be had. *Brigands*, according to some accounts, that have collected in Paris for no good purpose; people from Versailles by others; Germans by a third; but everyone would make you believe, they are an appendix to a plot laid for a counter-revolution. Reports are so various and contradictory, that no dependence is to be placed on them; nor credit given to one-tenth of what is asserted. It is singular, and has been much commented on, that La Fayette would not trust his standing troops, as they may be called, that is the eight thousand regularly paid, and of whom the French guards form a considerable portion, but he took, for the expedition, the *bourgeoise* only; which has elated the latter as much as it has disgusted the former. The moment seems big with events; there is an anxiety, an expectation, an uncertainty, and suspense that is visible in every eye one meets; and even the best informed people, and the least liable to be led away by popular reports, are not a little alarmed at the apprehension of some unknown attempt that may be made to rescue the King, and overturn the National Assembly. Many persons are of opinion, that it would not be difficult to take the King, Queen, and Dauphin away, without endangering them, for which attempt the Tuileries is particularly well situated, provided a body of troops, of sufficient force, were in readiness to receive them. In such a case, there would be a civil war, which, perhaps, would end in despotism, whatever party came off victorious; consequently such an attempt, or plan, could not originate in any bosom from true patriotism.

Arthur Young
Travels in France
1790

THE ONLY REMAINING ROMANTIC SITUATION

As to the real amount of the danger of travelling this road, as far as I can learn, it is this – there is at present a possibility but no probability of your being robbed or kidnapped, if you go in the daytime and by the common method of a *Vetturino*, stopping two nights on the road. If you go alone, and with a determination to set time, place, and circumstances at defiance, like a personified representation of John Bull, maintaining the character of your countrymen for sturdiness and independence of spirit, you stand a very good chance of being shot through the head: the same thing might happen to you, if you refused your money to an English footpad; but if you give it freely, like a gentleman, and do not stand too nicely upon a punctilio, they let you pass like one. If you have no money about you, you must up into the mountain, and wait till you can get it. For myself, my remittances have not been very regular even in walled towns; how I should fare in this respect upon the forked mountain, I cannot tell, and certainly I have no wish to try. A friend of mine said that he thought it *the only romantic thing going*, this of being carried off by the banditti; that life was become too tame and insipid without such accidents, and that it would not be amiss to put one's-self in the way of such an adventure, like putting in for the grand prize in the lottery.

William Hazlitt
Notes of a Journey through France and Italy
1826

CORSICAN BRIGANDAGE

The Corsican system of brigandage is so very different from that of
the Italians, Sicilians, and Greeks, that a word may be said about
its peculiar character. In the first place, it has nothing at all to do
with robbery and thieving. The Corsican bandit took to a free life
among the *macchi*, not for the sake of supporting himself by lawless
depredation, but because he had put himself under a legal and
social ban by murdering some one in obedience to the strict code of
honour of his country. His victim may have been the hereditary foe
of his house for generations, or else the newly made enemy of
yesterday. But in either case, if he had killed him fairly, after a
due notification of his intention to do so, he was held to have fulfilled
a duty rather than to have committed a crime. He then betook
himself to the dense tangles of evergreens which I have described,
where he lived upon the charity of countryfolk and shepherds. In
the eyes of those simple people it was a sacred duty to relieve the
necessities of the outlaws, and to guard them from the bloodhounds
of justice. There was scarcely a respectable family in Corsica who
had not one or more of its members thus *alla campagna*, as it was
euphemistically styled. The Corsicans themselves have attributed
this miserable state of things to two principal causes. The first of
these was the ancient bad government of the island: under its
Genoese rulers no justice was administered, and private vengeance
for homicide or insult became a necessary consequence among the
haughty and warlike families of the mountain villages. Secondly,
the Corsicans have been from time immemorial accustomed to wear
arms in everyday life. They used to sit at their house doors and
pace the streets with musket, pistol, dagger, and cartouch-box on
their persons; and on the most trivial occasion of merriment or
enthusiasm they would discharge their firearms. This habit gave a
bloody termination to many quarrels, which might have ended more
peaceably had the parties been unarmed; and so the seeds of *ven-
detta* were constantly being sown. Statistics published by the
French Government present a hideous picture of the state of bloodshed in Corsica even during this century. In one period of thirty
years (between 1821 and 1850) there were 4319 murders in the
island. Almost every man was watching for his neighbour's life, or
seeking how to save his own; and agriculture and commerce were
neglected for this grisly game of hide-and-seek.

J. A. Symonds
Sketches and Studies in Italy and Greece
1898

CALABRIAN BRIGANDAGE

The men who gave the French so much trouble were political brigands, allies of Bourbonism. They were commanded by creatures like
Mammone, an anthropophagous monster whose boast it was that
he had personally killed 455 persons with the greatest refinements
of cruelty, and who wore at his belt the skull of one of them, out of
which he used to drink human blood at mealtime; he drank his own
blood as well; indeed, he 'never dined without having a bleeding
human heart on the table'. This was the man whom King Ferdinand
and his spouse loaded with gifts and decorations, and addressed as
'Our good Friend and General – the faithful Support of the Throne.'
The numbers of these savages were increased by shiploads of profes-
sional cut-throats sent over from Sicily by the English to help their
Bourbon friends. Some of these actually wore the British uniform;
one of the most ferocious was known as 'L'Inglese' – the
Englishman.

It is good to bear these facts in mind when judging of the present
state of this province, for the traces of such a reign of terror are
not easily expunged. Good, also, to remember that this was the
period of the highest spiritual eminence to which South Italy has
ever attained. Its population of four million inhabitants were then
consoled by the presence of no less than 120,000 holy persons – to
wit, 22 archbishops, 116 bishops, 65,500 ordained priests, 31,800
monks, and 23,600 nuns. Some of these ecclesiastics, like the Bishop
of Capaccio, were notable brigand-chiefs.

It must be confessed that the French were sufficiently cold-
blooded in their reprisals. Colletta himself saw, at Lagonegro, a
man impaled by order of a French colonel; and some account of
their excesses may be gleaned from Duret de Tavel, from Rivarol
(rather a disappointing author), and from the flamboyant epistles
of P. L. Courier, a soldier-scribe of rare charm, who lost everything
in this campaign. 'J'ai perdu huit chevaux, mes habits, mon linge,
mon manteau, mes pistolets, mon argent (12,247 francs). . . . Je ne
regrette que mon Homère (a gift from the Abbé Barthélemy), et
pour le ravoir, je donnerais la seule chemise qui me reste.'

But even that did not destroy the plague. The situation called for
a genial and ruthless annihilator, a man like Sixtus V, who asked
for brigands' heads and got them so plentifully that they lay 'thick
as melons in the market' under the walls of Rome, while the Castel
Sant' Angelo was tricked out like a Christmas tree with quartered
corpses – a man who told the authorities, when they complained of
the insufferable stench of the dead, that the smell of living iniquity
was far worse. Such a man was wanted. Therefore, in 1810, Murat

gave *carte blanche* to General Manhes, the greatest brigand-catcher
of modern times, to extirpate the ruffians, root and branch. He had
just distinguished himself during a similar errand in the Abruzzi
and, on arriving in Calabria, issued proclamations of such inhuman
severity that the inhabitants looked upon them as a joke. They
were quickly undeceived. The general seems to have considered
that the end justified the means, and that the peace and happiness
of a province was not to be disturbed year after year by the malig-
nity of a few thousand rascals; his threats were carried out to the
letter, and, whatever may be said against his methods, he certainly
succeeded. At the end of a few months' campaign, every single
brigand, and all their friends and relations, were wiped off the face
of the earth – together with a very considerable number of innocent
persons. The high roads were lined with decapitated bandits, the
town walls decked with their heads; some villages had to be abandoned, on account of the stench; the Crati river was swollen with
corpses, and its banks whitened with bones. God alone knows the
cruelties which were enacted; Colletta confesses that he 'lacks courage to relate them.'

Norman Douglas
Old Calabria
1915

*And the traveller who avoided the bandit was still subject to the
normal perils of the journey – storms at sea, villainous roads, broken
equipment, drunken coachmen, runaway animals, avalanche and
flood. The traveller who arrived with pocket unpicked, health unim-
paired, and dignity unruffled was lucky indeed:*

A STORM IN THE MEDITERRANEAN

Here, on the 15th, forsaking our galley, we encountered a little foul
weather, which made us creep *terra, terra*, as they call it, and so a
vessel that encountered us advised us to do; but our patron, striving
to double the point of Savona, making out into the wind put us into
great hazard; for blowing very hard from land betwixt those horrid
gaps of the mountains, it set so violently, as raised on the sudden
so great a sea, that we could not recover the weather-shore for
many hours, insomuch that, what with the water already entered,
and the confusion of fearful passengers (of which one who was an
Irish bishop, and his brother, a priest, were confessing some as at
the article of death), we were almost abandoned to despair, our pilot

Boats of the Mediterranean

himself giving us up for lost. And now, as we were weary with pumping and laving out the water, almost sinking, it pleased God on the sudden to appease the wind, and with much ado and great peril we recovered the shore, which we now kept in view within half a league in sight of those pleasant villas, and within scent of those fragrant orchards which are on this coast, full of princely retirements for the sumptuousness of their buildings, and nobleness of the plantations, especially those at St. Pietro d'Arena; from whence, the wind blowing as it did, might perfectly be smelt the peculiar joys of Italy in the perfumes of orange, citron, and jasmine flowers, for divers leagues seaward.

John Evelyn
Diary
1644

ALARMS AND EXCURSIONS IN THE MUD OF TUSCANY

Here, however, another difficulty occurred. There was but one chaise, and a dragoon officer in the imperial troops insisted upon his having bespoke it for himself and his servant. A long dispute ensued, which had like to have produced a quarrel. But at length, I accommodated matters, by telling the officer that he should have a place in it gratis, and his servant might ride a-horseback. He accepted the offer without hesitation; but, in the mean time, we set out in the coach before them, and having proceeded about a couple of miles, the road was so deep from a heavy rain, and the beasts were so fatigued, that they could not proceed. The postilions scourging the poor animals with great barbarity, they made an effort, and pulled the coach to the brink of a precipice, or rather a kind of hollow way, which might be about seven or eight feet lower than the road. Here my wife and I leaped out, and stood under the rain, up to the ancles in mud; while the postilions still exercising their whips, one of the fore horses fairly tumbled down the descent, and hung by the neck, so that he was almost strangled before he could be disengaged from the traces, by the assistance of some foot travellers that happened to pass. While we remained in this dilemma, the chaise, with the officer and my servant, coming up, we exchanged places; my wife and I proceeded in the chaise, and left them with Miss C– and Mr R–, to follow in the coach. The road from hence to Florence is nothing but a succession of steep mountains, paved and conducted in such a manner, that one would imagine the design had been to render it impracticable by any sort of wheel-carriage. Notwithstanding all our endeavours, I found it would be impossible to enter Florence before the gates were shut. I flattered and threatened the driver by turns. But the fellow, who had been remarkably civil at first, grew sullen and impertinent. He told me I must not think of reaching Florence. That the boat would not take the carriage on board; and that from the other side, I must walk five miles before I should reach the gate that was open. But he would carry me to an excellent osteria, where I should be entertained and lodged like a prince. I was now convinced that he had lingered on purpose to serve this in keeper; and I took it for granted that what he told me of the distance between the ferry and the gate was a lie. It was eight o'clock when we arrived at his inn. I alighted with my wife to view the chambers, desiring he would not put up his horses. Finding it was a villainous house, we came forth, and by this time, the horses were put up. I asked the fellow how he durst presume to contradict my orders, and commanded him to put them to the chaise. He asked in his turn if I was mad? If I thought I and the lady had strength and courage enough to walk five miles in the dark, through a road which we did not know, and which was broke up by a continued rain of two days? I told him he was an impertinent rascal, and, as he still hesitated, I collared him with one hand, and shook my cane over his head with the other. It was the only weapon I had, either offensive or defensive; for I had left my sword and musquetoon in the coach. At length the fellow obeyed, though with great reluctance, cracking many severe jokes upon us in the mean time, and being joined in his raillery by the innkeeper, who had all the external marks of a ruffian. The house stood in a solitary situation, and not a soul appeared but these two miscreants, so that they might have murdered us without fear of detection. 'You do not like the apartments?' said one; 'to be sure they were not fitted up for persons of your rank and quality!' 'You will be glad of a worse chamber,' continued the other, 'before you get to bed.' 'If you walk to Florence tonight, you will sleep so sound, that the fleas will not disturb you.' 'Take care you do not take up your night's lodging in the middle of the road, or in the ditch of the city-wall.' I fired inwardly at these sarcasms, to which, however, I made no reply; and my wife was almost dead with fear. In the road from hence to the boat, we met with an ill-looking fellow, who offered his service to conduct us into the city; and such was our situation, that I was fain to accept his proposal, especially as we had two small boxes in the chaise by accident, containing some caps and laces belonging to my wife. I still hoped the postilion had exaggerated in the distance between the boat and the city-gate, and was confirmed in this opinion by the ferryman, who said we had not above half a league to walk. Behold us then in this expedition; myself wrapped up in a very heavy great coat, and my cane in my hand. I did not imagine I could have walked a couple of miles in this equipage, had my life been depending; my wife, a delicate creature, who had scarce ever walked a mile in her life, and the ragamuffin before us, with our boxes under his arm. The night was dark and wet; the road slippery and dirty; not a soul was seen, nor a sound was heard; all was silent, dreary and horrible. I laid my account with a violent fit of illness from the cold I should infallibly catch, if I escaped assassination, the fears of which were the more troublesome, as I had no weapon to defend our lives. While I laboured under the weight of my great coat, which made the streams of sweat flow down my face and shoulders, I was plunging in the mud, up to the mid-leg, at every step; and at the same time obliged to support my wife, who wept in silence, half dead with terror and fatigue.

Tobias Smollett
Travels through France and Italy
1766

GREEK SAILORS IN HEAVY WEATHER

We were nearing the isle of Cyprus, when there arose half a gale of wind, with a heavy chopping sea.

We were at length in such a position, that by holding on our course for about half an hour, we should get under the lee of the island, and find ourselves in smooth water, but the wind had been gradually freshening; it now blew hard, and there was a heavy sea running.

As the grounds for alarm arose, the crew gathered together in one close group; they stood pale and grim under their hooded capotes like monks awaiting a massacre, anxiously looking by turns along the pathway of the storm, and then upon each other, and then upon the eye of the Captain, who stood by the helmsman. Presently the Hydriot came aft, more moody than ever, the bearer of fierce remonstrance against the continuing of the struggle; he received a resolute answer, and still we held our course. Soon there came a heavy sea that caught the bow of the brigantine as she lay jammed in betwixt the waves; she bowed her head low under the waters, and shuddered through all her timbers, then gallantly stood up again over the striving sea with bowsprit entire. But where were the crew? – It was a crew no longer, but rather a gathering of Greek citizens; – the shout of the seamen was changed for the murmuring of the people – the spirit of the old Demos was alive. The men came aft in a body, and loudly asked that the vessel should be put about, and that the storm be no longer tempted. Now, then, for speeches: – the Captain, his eyes flashing fire, his frame all quivering with emotion – wielding his every limb, like another and a louder voice – pours forth the eloquent torrent of his threats, and his reasons, his commands, and his prayers; he promises – he vows – he swears that there is safety in holding on – safety, *if Greeks will be brave!* The men hear and are moved, but the gale rouses itself once more, and again the raging sea comes trampling over the timbers that are the life of all. The fierce Hydriot advances one step nearer to the Captain, and the angry growl of the people goes floating down the wind; but they listen, they waver once more, and once more resolve, then waver again, thus doubtfully hanging between the terrors of the storm and the persuasion of glorious speech, as though it were the Athenian that talked, and Philip of Macedon that thundered on the weather-bow.

Brave thoughts winged on Grecian words gained their natural mastery over Terror; the Brigantine held on her course, and reached smooth water at last.

Alexander Kinglake
Eothen
1844

DECEPTIVE IMPRESSIONS ON SPANISH ROADS

It must be also admitted that the respectability and character of many a Spaniard is liable to be misunderstood, when he sets forth on any of his travels, except in a public wheel conveyance; as we said in our ninth chapter, he assumes the national costume of the road, and leaves his wife and long-tailed coat behind him. Now as most Spaniards are muffled up and clad after the approved melodrame fashion of robbers, they may be mistaken for them in reality; indeed they are generally sallow, have fierce black eyes, uncombed hair, and on these occasions neglect the daily use of towels and razors; a long beard gives, and not in Spain alone, a ferocious ruffian-like look, which is not diminished when gun and knife are added to match faces *à la* Brutus. Again, these worthies thus equipped, have sometimes a trick of staring rather fixedly from under their slouched hat at the passing stranger, whose, to them, outlandish costume excites curiosity and suspicion; naturally therefore some difficulty does exist in distinguishing the merino from the wolf, when both are disguised in the same clothing – a *zamarra* sheepskin to wit. A private Spanish gentleman, who, in his native town, would be the model of a peaceable and inoffensive burgess, or a respectable haberdasher, has, when on his commercial tour, altogether the appearance of the Bravo of Venice, and such-like heroes, by whom children are frightened at a minor theatre. In consequence of the difficulty of outliving what has been learnt in the nursery, many of our countrymen have, with the best intentions, set down the bulk of the population of the Peninsula as one gang of robbers – they have exaggerated their numbers like Falstaff's men of buckram.

Richard Ford
Gatherings from Spain
1846

A BRUTAL DRIVER IN CORSICA, AND THE CONSEQUENCES

At *kilomètre* eleven and a half is a neat little forest-house and a mill. The guardiano and his family, sitting outside their dwelling, make a picture, combined with groups of trees and the beautiful river, here close below the highway, and dashing foamily over its worn stones. Beyond this point the road makes a sharp turn, and for the moment Peter is lost sight of. Latterly his swearing has been so horrible, and his cruelty so odious, that I have thought at times that he is not quite sane; consequently, I have walked nearer the carriage, and it was only by the accident of my having stopped a little while at the forest-house, to make some inquiries about the distance, that he had got considerably ahead, for here the ascent is not steep.

But on turning the corner of the road just mentioned there was a shocking sight, and one that became more so at each moment. Taking this opportunity of being alone Peter had given way to a burst of rage and violent blows with his whip handle on the poor beasts' heads. In vain did both I and Giorgio shout, running forward. Even then the carriage stood at right angles to the side of the road, and not far from the edge of it, above the river, while at every blow the poor horses backed nearer to the ravine.

One more blow – carriage and horses are quite at the side of the precipice! –

Yet one more blow, struck with an infernal scream from bad Peter, and the horses back for the last time! And then–

Down, down, go all into the ravine!

Nothing was left on the road but the abominable old fellow, kneeling, and wailing to the Madonna and all the saints, whom a minute before he had been blaspheming.

Edward Lear
Journal of a Landscape Painter in Corsica
1868

When the great dangers from man and nature were overcome, minor pinpricks from the same sources continued to annoy. Officious soldiers or men of foolish honour might block the traveller's path; a variety of animals, from fleas to wolves, lay in wait. And there was a special anxiety reserved for those travellers who lay sick in some rotten hostelry many miles from home and comfort:

A FRISKY NIGHT IN MALAGA

We staid one night with mine Host on shoar, and we had a proud fellow which entertain'd us a while with a song or two to a *Guitarra*. He first lay'd by his old threadbare cloak with great deliberation and wonderfull gravity; then, with his dagger behind and his hat cock't, his eyes staring, his browes bent, and his *Mostachos* new brush't, he yell'd and acted with that strange state and fiercenesse, as if he had been swaggering at some desperate criminals and threatening to hang them; but, with a *Real* or two we came off well enough. After supper and a little chat we thought of our lodgings. All that lay on twills and bedsteads were sorely bitten with little bugs, which left hard knobs and pimples wherever they seised. I, with one or two more, had the fortune to putt our twills for coolnesse into the middle of the floor, which (as all above stairs as well as those below are) was laid with brick, and we escaped all these pestilent companions. These insects, so well known in all hot countryes (but to us never seen before), are here called *chismes* and *chinches*, and in Italian *cimici*, from the Latin *cimex*, in French *punaises*; they are shaped much like a spider, but far lesse, with six legges and a bottled breech, the back being often reddish. They are truly cal'd by Pliny most nasty animals, for besides their venomous bite they have (especially if they are bruised) a most intolerable filthy smel. One of our comrades, catching one in the night as it was preying upon him, and thinking it had been a flea (after a slovingly custome which he had got), *bit it with his teeth, thinking so to kill it*; but the abominable stink set him on vomiting in such a manner as he verily thought he had been poyson'd; which make me amazed how they came to be prescribed inwardly by the antients as a medicine against feavers, unlesse it was that (after the Italian proverbe, *Un Diavolo scaccia il altro*) 'one devil drives out another'; but, perhaps, being drunk in wine, they may go down whole, and not prove so nauseous.

Dr John Covel
Diaries
1670–79

THE DIFFICULTIES OF A CODE OF HONOUR

A certain noble lord of our country, when he was yet a commoner, on his travels, involved himself in a dilemma of this sort at the court of Lorrain. He had been riding out, and strolling along a public walk, in a brown study, with his horsewhip in his hand, perceived a caterpillar crawling on the back of a marquis, who chanced to be before him. He never thought of the *petit-maître*; but lifting up his whip, in order to kill the insect, laid it across his shoulders with a crack, that alarmed all the company in the walk. The marquis's sword was produced in a moment, and the aggressor in great hazard of his life, as he had no weapon of defence. He was no sooner waked from his reverie than he begged pardon, and offered to make all proper concessions for what he had done through mere inadvertency. The marquis would have admitted his excuses, had there been any precedent of such an affront washed away without blood. A conclave of honour was immediately assembled; and after long disputes, they agreed, that an involuntary offence, especially from *such a kind of man, d'un tel homme*, might

be atoned by concessions. That you may have some idea of the
small beginning from which many gigantic quarrels arise, I shall
recount one that lately happened at Lyons, as I had it from the
mouth of a person who was an ear and eye witness of the transaction. Two Frenchmen, at a public ordinary, stunned the rest of
the company with their loquacity. At length one of them, with a
supercilious air, asked the other's name. 'I never tell my name,'
said he, 'but in a whisper.' 'You may have very good reasons for
keeping it a secret,' replied the first. 'I will tell you,' resumed the
other. With these words, he rose; and going round to him, pro-
nounced, loud enough to be heard by the whole company, '*Je
m'appelle Pierre Paysan; et vous êtes un impertinent.*' So saying, he
walked out. The interrogator followed him into the street, where
they justled, drew their swords, and engaged. He who asked the
question was run through the body; but his relations were so powerful, that the victor was obliged to fly his country. He was tried and
condemned in his absence; his goods were confiscated; his wife broke
her heart; his children were reduced to beggary; and he himself is
now starving in exile.

Tobias Smollett
Travels through France and Italy
1766

SICKNESS IN SOUTHERN ITALY

Whilst my fever was high, little groups of people often came into
the room, to stand and stare at me, exchanging, in a low voice,
remarks which they supposed I did not hear, or, hearing, could not
understand; as a matter of fact, their dialect was now intelligible
enough to me, and I knew that they discussed my chances of surviving. Their natures were not sanguine. A result, doubtless, of the
unhealthy climate, every one at Cotrone seemed in a more or less
gloomy state of mind. The hostess went about uttering ceaseless
moans and groans; when she was in my room I heard her constantly
sighing: 'Ah, Signore! Ah, Cristo!' – exclamations which, perhaps,
had some reference to my illness, but which did not cease when I
recovered. Whether she had any private reason for depression I
could not learn; I fancy not; it was only the whimpering and queru-
lous habit due to low health. A female servant, who occasionally
brought me food (I found that she also cooked it), bore herself in
much the same way. This domestic was the most primitive figure
of the household. Picture a woman of middle age, wrapped at all
times in dirty rags (not to be called clothing), obese, grimy, with
dishevelled black hair, and hands so scarred, so deformed by labour

and neglect, as to be scarcely human. She had the darkest and fiercest eyes I ever saw. Between her and her mistress went on an unceasing quarrel: they quarrelled in my room, in the corridor, and, as I knew by their shrill voices, in places remote; yet I am sure they did not dislike each other, and probably neither of them ever thought of parting. Unexpectedly, one evening, this woman entered, stood by the bedside, and began to talk with such fierce energy, with such flashing of her black eyes, and such distortion of her features, that I could only suppose that she was attacking me for the trouble I caused her. A minute or two passed before I could even hit the drift of her furious speech; she was always the most difficult of the natives to understand, and in rage she became quite unintelligible. Little by little, by dint of questioning, I got at what she meant. There had been *guai*, worse than usual; the mistress had reviled her unendurably for some fault or other, and was it not hard that she should be used like this after having *tanto, tanto lavorato!* In fact, she was appealing for my sympathy, not abusing me at all. When she went on to say that she was alone in the world, that all her kith and kin were *freddi morti* (stone dead), a pathos in her aspect and her words took hold upon me; it was much as if some heavy-laden beast of burden had suddenly found tongue, and protested in the rude beginnings of articulate utterance against its hard lot. If only one could have learnt, in intimate detail, the life of this domestic serf! How interesting, and how sordidly picturesque against the background of romantic landscape, of scenic history! I looked long into her sallow, wrinkled face, trying to imagine the thoughts that ruled its expression. In some measure my efforts at kindly speech succeeded, and her 'Ah, Cristo!' as she turned to go away, was not without a touch of solace.

George Gissing
By the Ionian Sea
1901

CHAPTER 3

People and Places

Foreigners

Foreigners are odd and not to be trusted: that is the oldest rule of national life and is generally applied by nations the world over. And experience suggests that insular lands, snug behind the moat of their seas, are more suspicious than others. England is no exception. The quantity of insult and contempt heaped by the English on less fortunate European countries is quite remarkable. Bad feeling usually increased with the distance from the blessed homeland and older travellers, who did not mince their words, set the tone for our national discourse on foreigners by treating the far-flung Europeans as barely human:

THE CONDITION OF THE RUSSIANS

As touching the naturall habite of their bodies, they are for the most parte of a large sise and of very fleshly bodies, accounting it a grace to bee somewhat grosse and burley, and therefore they nourish and spread their beardes to have them long and broad. But, for the most part, they are very unweldy and unactive withall. Which may bee thought to come partly of the climate, and the numbnes which they get by the cold in winter, and partly of their diet, that standeth most of rootes, onions, garlike, cabbage, and such like things that breed grosse humors, which they use to eate alone and with their other meates.

Their diet is rather much then curious. At their meales they beginne commonly with a *chark*, or small cuppe, of *aqua vitæ* (which they call Russe wine) and then drinke not till towardes the ende of their meales, taking it in largely and all together, with kissing one another at every pledge. And therefore after dinner there is no talking with them, but every man goeth to his bench to take his afternoones sleepe, which is as ordinary with them as their nightes reste. When they exceede and have varietie of dishes, the first are their baked meates (for roste meates they use little) and then their broathes or pottage. To drinke drunke, is an ordinary matter with them every day in the weeke. Their common drinke is mead; the poorer sort use water, and thinne drink called quasse, which is

Russian peasant houses

nothing els (as wee say) but water turned out of his wittes, with a little branne meashed with it.

This diet would breede in them many diseases, but that they use bathstoves or hote houses in steede of all phisicke, commonly twise or thrise every weeke. All the winter time, and almost the whole sommer, they heat their *peaches*, which are made lyke the Germane bathstoaves, and their *potlads*, like ovens, that so warme the house, that a straunger at the first shall hardly like of it. These two extremities, specially in the winter, of heat within their houses and of extreame colde without, together with their diet, maketh them of a darke and sallow complexion, their skinnes beyng tanned and parched both with colde and with heate, specialy the women, that for the greater parte are of farre worse complexions then the men. Whereof the cause I take to bee, their keeping within the hote houses, and busying themselves about the heating and using of their bathstoves and peaches.

The Russe, because that hee is used to both these extremities of heat and of cold, can beare them both a great deale more patiently than straungers can doo. You shal see them sometimes (to season their bodies) come out of their bathstoves all on a froth, and fuming as hote almost as a pigge at a spitte, and presently to leape into the river starke naked, or to poure colde water all over their bodies, and that in the coldest of all the winter time. The women, to mende the bad hue of their skinnes, use to paint their faces with white and redde colours, so visibly that every man may perceyve it. Which is made no matter, because it is common and liked well by their husbandes, who make their wives and daughters an ordinarie allowance to buy them colours to paint their faces withall, and delight themselves much to see them of fowle women to become such faire images. This parcheth the skinne, and helpeth to deforme them when their painting is of.

Giles Fletcher
Of the Russe Common Wealth
1591

GERMANS AT THEIR DRINK

And to say truth, the Germans are in high excesse subject to this vice of drinking, scarce noted with any other nationall vice, so that as their Doctors and Artisans, affecting the knowledge onely of one science, or manuall art, doe become excellent therein, so this nation in generall, and every part or member thereof, practising night and day the faculty of drinking, become strong & invincible professors therein. In Saxony, when the gates of the Cities are to be shut, while they that dwell in the suburbs, passing out, doe reele from one side of the streete to the other, as if it were too narrow for them to walke in, while they stumble and fall in the durt, while they by stradling with their legges as if a Cart should passe betweene them, doe for the most part beare up themselves from falling, yet jostle every post, pillar, and passenger by the way, while the gates of the City seeme not wide enough for them to passe, except the wals also were pulled downe.

For howsoever the richer sort hide this intemperance for the most part, by keeping at home, surely the vulgar yeeld this daily spectacle. Yet in truth it is no shame, especialy in Saxony, even to spew at the Table in their next fellowes bosome, or to pisse under the Table, and afterwards in their beds. And I know not how the fellowship of drunkards is so pleasing to them, as a man shall with no other quality make so many friends as with this, so as he that wil be welcome in their company, or desires to learne their language, must needs practice this excesse in some measure. When they drinke, if any man chance to come in and sit in the roome, though he be a stranger of another Nation, they doe not onely conjure him to pledge them by the bond of friendship, of his Fathers Nobility, and his Mothers chastity, but (if need be) compell him by force therunto, vulgarly crying, *Kanstunight sauffen und fressen, so kanstu keinem hern wol dienen*; If thou canst not swill and devoure, thou canst serve no Master well. In the meane time, they like not to drinke great draughts, wherein our Countrey-men put them downe, but they will spend an Age in swoping and sipping. Their Coachmen are in this kind so tender hearted to their Horses, that out of a fellow feeling of thirst, they will suffer them to drinke in standing water, scarce covering their shooes, when they sweat by the high way. Once I observed that my selfe and seven consorts after dinner upon a full gorge, had sixteene great pots to drinke at parting, at which time one of our consorts being a Horseman, and not fit to ride, was taken into our Coach, and sitting by me, now laughing, then weeping, and often knocking his head against mine, at last defiled me by casting his stomacke in my bosome.

Fynes Moryson
Itinerary
1605–17

ARMED GREEKS AND LECHEROUS WOMEN

In all my travels through this Realme, I never could see a Greeke come forth of his house unarmed: and after such a martiall manner, that on his head he weareth a bare steele cap, a bow in his hand, a long sword by his side, a broad Ponard overthwart his belly, and a round Target hanging at his girdle. They are not costly in apparell, for they weare but linnen cloathes, and use no shooes but bootes of white leather, to keepe their legges in the fields from the prickes of a kind of Thistle, wherewith the Countrey is overcharged like unto little bushes or short shrubs which are marvelous sharpe, and offensive unto the inhabitants, whereof, often a day to my great harme, I found their bloody smart: The women generally weare linnen breaches as men do, and bootes after the same manner, and their linnen coates no longer then the middle of their thighes, and are insatiably inclined to Venery, such is the nature of the soyle and climate. The Cretans are excellent good Archers, surpassing all the Orientall people therein, couragious and valiant upon the Sea, as in former time they were; and they are naturally inclined to singing: so that commonly after meat, Man, Wife, and Child of

each family, will for the space of an houre, sing with such a harmony, as is wonderfull melodious to the hearer; yea, and they
cannot forgoe the custome of it.

William Lithgow
Rare Adventures and Painful Peregrinations
1632

MEAN-SPIRITED DANES

The Common People are mean spirited, not Warlike in their
Tempers, as formerly; inclined to gross Cheating, and to suspect
that others have a design to cheat them; therefore unwilling to go
out of a road they have been accustomed to: insomuch that if you
offer them great profit for a thing which they have not been used
formerly to sell, they will refuse to part with it, as suspecting that
you see an advantage in such a Purchase, which as yet is unknown
to them, but which they hope to find out. I remember one instance:
Seeing great Flocks of Green Geese in the Fields near the Town, I
sent to buy some, but they being never used to sell, or eat Geese,
in that Countrey, till they are big and old; it was not possible to
perswade any body to part with one of them, though double the
price of a big one were offered for each. They asked what we desired
to buy them for? What we would do with them? &c. for they could
not be perswaded, any one would be so foolish as to eat them whilst
young, or little; after a Week, an old Woman, to whom Money had
been offered for a dozen, came and brought four to sell, saying, *That
neither she, nor her Geese, had thriven since she had refused to sell
them at a good price; for the Kite had the night before kill'd eight
of her stock, and that now the remaining four were at my service.*
Thus the Superstition of this old woman procured us the first Green
Geese that I believe were ever eaten in *Denmark*; but after that
they had taken notice that we fatted, and killed them for eating,
they furnisht us with them as often as desired. I would not omit
this silly Story, because it gives a more lively Idea of the Temper
of the Common People, than any Description I could make. In their
Markets they will ask the same price for stinking Meat, as for fresh;
for lean, as for fat, if it be of a kind. And the sure way not to
obtain, is to seem to value, and to ask importunately, a thing which
otherwise they themselves would desire should be done. This last
Remark is not peculiar to the Common People only.

Robert Molesworth
An Account of Denmark
1694

About our closer neighbours, in particular the Latin peoples, travel-
lers were hardly more polite. The point was that these races, despite
some mitigating virtues, had something wrong with them. *It is*
surprising how nearly universal this English opinion was; there was
almost no dissenting opinion until the sane voice of William Hazlitt
was heard. After Hazlitt, though criticism still predominated, a cer-
tain respect and even affection became more common:

FRENCH AND SPANIARDS COMPARED

The Sicilians have a Proverb, as having experience of both, that
the French are wiser than they seeme, and the Spaniards seeme
wiser than they are: And even as the Spaniard is extremely proud
in the lowest ebbe of Fortune: So is the French man exceeding
impatient, cowardly desperate, and quite discouraged in the pinch
of sterne calamity. The Spaniard and the French man have an
absolute opposition, and conditionall disagreement in all fashions;
and in their riding both different, and defective: For the Spaniard
rideth like a Monkey mounted on a Camell, with his knees and
heeles alike aside, sitting on the sadle, like to a halfe ballast ship,
tottering on top-tempestuous waves: And the French man, hangeth
in the stirrop, at the full reach of his great toe, with such a long-
legged ostentation, pricking his horse with neck-stropiat spurres,
and beating the wind with his long waving limbes, even as the
Turkes usually do, when they are tossed at their Bairam, hanging
betweene two high trees, reciprocally waving in the ayre, from the
force of two long bending ropes.

William Lithgow
Rare Adventures and Painful Peregrinations
1632

UNBALANCED BEHAVIOUR IN GENOA

The first palace we went to visit was that of Hieronymo del Negros,
to which we passed by boat across the harbour. Here I could not
but observe the sudden and devilish passion of a seaman, who
plying us was intercepted by another fellow, that interposed his
boat before him and took us in; for the tears gushing out of his
eyes, he put his finger in his mouth and almost bit it off by the
joint, showing it to his antagonist as an assurance to him of some
bloody revenge, if ever he came near that part of the harbour again.
Indeed this beautiful city is more stained with such horrid acts of
revenge and murders, than any one place in Europe, or haply in

the world, where there is a political government, which makes it unsafe to strangers. It is made a galley matter to carry a knife whose point is not broken off.

John Evelyn
Diary
1644

RANK AND HONOUR IN AUSTRIA: 1716

It is not from Austria that one can write with vivacity, and I am already infected with the phlegm of the country. Even their amours and their quarrels are carried on with a surprising temper, and they are never lively but upon points of ceremony. There, I own, they shew all their passions; and 'tis not long since two coaches, meeting in a narrow street at night, the ladies in them not being able to adjust the ceremonial of which should go back, sat there with equal gallantry till two in the morning, and were both so fully determined to die upon the spot, rather than yield in a point of that importance, that the street would never have been cleared till their deaths, if the emperor had not sent his guards to part them; and even then they refused to stir, till the expedient could be found out of taking them both out in chairs, exactly in the same moment. After the ladies were agreed, it was with some difficulty that the *pas* was decided between the two coachmen, no less tenacious of their rank than the ladies.

This passion is so omnipotent in the breasts of the women, that even their husbands never die but they are ready to break their hearts, because that fatal hour puts an end to their rank, no widows having any place at Vienna. The men are not much less touched with this point of honour, and they do not only scorn to marry, but even to make love to any woman of a family not as illustrious as their own; and the pedigree is much more considered by them, than either the complexion or features of their mistresses.

Lady Mary Wortley Montagu
Travel Letters
1763

FRENCH MANNERS AND FRENCH RELIGION

What strikes me the most upon the whole is, the total difference of manners between them and us, from the greatest object to the least. There is not the smallest similitude in the twenty-four hours. It is obvious in every trifle. Servants carry their lady's train, and put her into her coach with their hat on. They walk about the streets in the rain with umbrellas to avoid putting on their hats; driving themselves in open chaises in the country without hats, in the rain, too, and yet often wear them in a chariot in Paris when it does not rain. The very footmen are powdered from the break of day, and yet wait behind their master, as I saw the Duc of Praslin's do, with a red pocket-handkerchief about their necks. Versailles, like everything else, is a mixture of parade and poverty, and in every instance exhibits something most dissonant from our manners. In the colonnades, upon the staircases, nay, in the antechambers of the royal family, there are people selling all sorts of wares. While we were waiting in the Dauphin's sumptuous bedchamber, till his dressing-room door should be opened, two fellows were sweeping it, and dancing about in sabots to rub the floor.

One does not learn a whole nation in four or five months; but, for the time, few, I believe, have seen, studied, or got so much acquainted with the French as I have.

By what I said of their religious or rather irreligious opinions, you must not conclude their people of quality, atheists – at least not the men – Happily for them, poor souls! they are not capable of going so far into thinking. They assent to a great deal, because it is the fashion, and because they don't know how to contradict. They are ashamed to defend the Roman Catholic religion, because it is quite exploded; but I am convinced they believe it in their hearts. They hate the parliaments and the philosophers, and are rejoiced that they may still idolize royalty.

The generality of the men, and more than the generality, are dull and empty. They have taken up gravity, thinking it was philosophy and English, and so have acquired nothing in the room of their natural levity and cheerfulness. However, as their high opinion of their own country remains, for which they can no longer assign any reason, they are contemptuous and reserved, instead of being ridiculously, consequently pardonably, impertinent. I have wondered, knowing my own countrymen, that we had attained such a superiority. – I wonder no longer, and have a little more respect for English *heads* than I had.

Horace Walpole
Letters
1765–66

ROMAN PRIDE

I witnessed a scene last night, which was a good illustration of that extraordinary indolence for which the Romans are remarkable. Our *laquais* Camillo suffered himself to be turned off, rather than put wood on the fire three times a day; he would rather, he said, 'starve in the streets than break his back by carrying burthens like an ass; and though he was miserable to displease the *Onoratissimo Padrone*, his first *duty* was to take care of his own health, which, with the blessing of the saints, he was determined to do.' R– threw him his wages, repeating with great contempt the only word of his long speech he understood. '*Asino!*' '*Sono Romano, io,*' replied the fellow, drawing himself up with dignity. He took his wages, however, and marched out of the house.

The impertinence of this Camillo was sometimes amusing, but oftener provoking. He piqued himself on being a profound anti-quarian, would confute Nibby, and carried Nardini in his pocket, to whom he referred on all occasions: yet the other day he had the impudence to assure us that Caius Cestus was an English Prot-estant, who was excommunicated by Pope Julius Cæsar; and took his Nardini out of his pocket to prove his assertion.

Anna Jameson
Diary of an Ennuyée
1826

A FEW GOOD WORDS FOR THE FRENCH

They are not handsome, but good-natured, expressive, placid. They retain the look of peasants more than the town's-people with us, whether from living more in the open air, or from greater health and temperance, I cannot say. What I like in their expression (so far) is not the vivacity, but the goodness, the simplicity, the thoughtful resignation. The French are full of gesticulation when they speak; they have at other times an equal appearance of repose and content. You see the figure of a girl sitting in the sun, so still that her dress seems like streaks of red and black chalk against the wall; a soldier reading; a group of old women (with skins as tough, yellow, and wrinkled as those of a tortoise) chatting in a corner and laughing till their sides are ready to split; or a string of children tugging a fishing-boat out of the harbour as evening goes down, and making the air ring with their songs and shouts of merriment (a sight to make Mr Malthus shudder!). Life here glows, or spins carelessly round on its soft axle. The same animal spirits that supply a fund of cheerful thoughts, break out into all the extravagance of mirth and social glee. The air is a cordial to them, and they drink drams of sunshine. My particular liking to the French is, however, confined to their natural and unsophisticated character. The good spirits 'with which they are clothed and fed', and which eke out the deficiencies of fortune or good government, are perhaps too much for them, when joined with external advantages, or artificial pretensions. Their vivacity becomes insolence in office; their success, presumption; their gentility, affectation and grimace. But the national physiognomy (taken at large) is the reflection of good temper and humanity. One thing is evident, and decisive in their favour – they do not insult or point at strangers, but smile on them good-humouredly, and answer them civilly. . . .

The French physiognomy is like a telegraphic machine, ready to shift and form new combinations every moment. It is commonly too light and variable for repose; it is careless, indifferent, but not sunk in indolence, nor wedded to ease: as on the other hand, it is restless, rapid, extravagant, without depth or force. Is it not the same with their feelings, which are alike incapable of a habit of quiescence, or of persevering action or passion? It seems so to me. Their freedom from any tendency to drunkenness, to indulge in its dreamy stupor, or give way to its incorrigible excesses, confirms by analogy the general view of their character. I do not bring this as an accusation against them, I ask if it is not the fact; and if it will not account for many things observable in them, good, bad, and indifferent? In a word, mobility without *momentum* solves the whole riddle of the French character.

William Hazlitt
Notes of a Journey through France and Italy
1826

SPANISH IMPRACTICALITY

If you called on a Spanish gentleman, and, finding him out, wished afterwards to write him a note, and inquired of his man or maid servant the number of the house; – 'I do not know, my lord,' was the invariable answer, 'I never was asked it before, I have never looked for it: let us go out and see. Ah! it is number 36.' Wishing once to send a parcel by the wagon from Merida to Madrid, 'On what day, my lord,' said I to the pot-bellied, black-whiskered *ventero*, 'does your *galera* start for the Court?' 'Every Wednesday,' answered he; 'and let not your grace be anxious' – '*Disparate* – nonsense,' exclaimed his copper-skinned, bright-eyed wife, 'why do you tell the English knight such lies? the wagon, my lord, sets out on Fridays.' During the logomachy, or the few words which ensued between the well-matched pair, our good luck willed, that the *mayoral* or driver of the vehicle should come in, who forthwith informed us that the days of departure were Thursdays; and he was right. This occurred

122

in the provinces; take, therefore, a parallel passage in the capital, the heart and brain of the Castiles. '*Señor, tenga Usted la bondad* – My lord,' said I to a portly, pompous bureaucrat, who booked places in the dilly to Toledo, – 'have the goodness, your grace, to secure me one for Monday, the 7th.' – 'I fear,' replied he, politely, for the *negocio* had been prudently opened by my offering him a real Havannah, 'that your lordship has made a mistake in the date. Monday is the 8th of the current month.' – which it was not. Thinking to settle the matter, we handed to him, with a bow, the almanack of the year, which chanced to be in our pocket-book. '*Señor*,' said he gravely, when he had duly examined it, 'I knew that I was right; this one was printed at Seville,' – which it was – 'and we are here at Madrid, which is *otra cosa*, that is, altogether another affair.'

Richard Ford
Gathering from Spain
1846

PUZZLED OPINIONS IN SOUTHERN ITALY

There is always in these provincial towns a knot of neighbours who meet in the house of the great man of each little place, to discuss the occurrences of the day for an hour or two before supper; already a long perspective of such hours oppressed me, loaded with questions about Inghilterra and our own plans and circumstances. 'Cosa c'e da vedere in Bagaládi?'* said our host's coterie with one voice, when they heard we wanted to go there – and one elder was fiercely incredulous, proposing that, if, as we said, we were in search of the beautiful or remarkable, we should set out directly for Montebello or Mélito, or any place but Bagaládi. He also explained the position and attributes of England to the rest of the society, assuring them that we had no fruit of any sort, and that all our bread came from Egypt and India: and as for our race, with a broad contempt for minute distinctions, he waid we were 'tutti Francesi,' an assertion we faintly objected to, but were overruled by – 'in somma – siete sempre una razza di Francesi: è lo stesso.'**

Edward Lear
Journals of a Landscape Painter in Southern Calabria
1852

* 'What should there be to see in Bagaládi?'
** 'In a word, you are a sort of Frenchmen; it's all the same.'

SPANISH INDIFFERENCE

At Guadix the cave-dwellers have been visited by so many motorists now that they are vain of themselves as a curiosity, but they do not molest as much as Italian peasants and children; dignity and self-containment, the restful and smiling indifference of the Spaniards, are their protection. Like the rest of their nation they regard the foreigner as fantastic, abnormal, absurd, a person of the wrong religion and intolerable ideas. Envy and covetousness do not exist. They are shocked by the sight of wealth and the kind of work we have to do in order to get it. The general attitude of the Spaniard, from the cave-dweller to the grandee, to those who point out the beauties of social reform, better health and housing, is possibly polite agreement, but it is generally angry resentment; fundamentally, the attitude is that it is we who live in a spiritual slum which the Spaniards could rescue us from, if they felt the effort worth while – but they do not. In a few years we shall have blown ourselves to pieces or killed ourselves off by a germ warfare, and the survivors will then see the irresistible but unattainable advantage of the Spanish way of life.

V. S. Pritchett
The Spanish Temper
1954

For thoroughgoing prejudice and wholesale vituperation of foreigners, no Englishman outdid Tobias Smollett M. D. His travel book on France and Italy, published in 1766, was a catalogue of withering observation and malicious comment. Smollett was a sick man on his travels, and some allowance may be made for that; but his book was not greatly different in kind from the accounts of other travellers. Smollett only surpassed them in the energy, passion and comprehensiveness of his condemnations. He has a flavour of his own:

CHARACTER AND MANNERS OF THE FRENCH

If a Frenchman is capable of real friendship, it must certainly be the most disagreeable present he can possibly make to a man of a true English character. You know, madam, we are naturally taciturn, soon tired of impertinence, and much subject to fits of disgust. Your French friend intrudes upon you at all hours; he stuns you with his loquacity; he teases you with impertinent questions about your domestic and private affairs; he attempts to meddle in all your concerns, and forces his advice upon you with the most unwearied importunity; he asks the price of everything you wear, and, so sure as you tell him, undervalues it without hesitation; he affirms it is in a bad taste, ill contrived, ill made; that you have been imposed upon both with respect to the fashion and the price; that the marquis of this, or the countess of that, has one that is perfectly elegant, quite in the *bon ton*, and yet it cost her little more than you gave for a thing that nobody would wear.

If a Frenchman is admitted into your family, and distinguished by repeated marks of your friendship and regard, the first return he makes for your civilities is to make love to your wife, if she is handsome; if not, to your sister, or daughter, or niece. If he suffers a repulse from your wife, or attempts in vain to debauch your sister, or your daughter, or your niece, he will, rather than not play the traitor with his gallantry, make his addresses to your grandmother; and ten to one but in one shape or another he will find means to ruin the peace of a family in which he has been so kindly entertained. What he cannot accomplish by dint of compliment and personal attendance, he will endeavour to effect by reinforcing these with billets-doux, songs, and verses, of which he always makes a provision for such purposes. If he is detected in these efforts of treachery, and reproached with his ingratitude, he impudently declares that what he has done was no more than simple gallantry, considered in France as an indispensable duty on every man who pretended to good breeding. Nay, he will even affirm that his endeavours to corrupt your wife, or deflower your daughter, were the most genuine proofs he could give of his particular regard for your family.

They have not even the implements of cleanliness in this country. Every chamber is furnished with an *armoire*, or clothes-press, and a chest of drawers, of very clumsy workmanship. Every thing shows a deficiency in the mechanic arts. There is not a door, nor a window, that shuts close. The hinges, locks, and latches, are of iron, coarsely made, and ill-contrived. The very chimnies are built so open, that they admit both rain and sun, and all of them smoke intolerably. If there is no cleanliness among these people, much less shall we find delicacy, which is the cleanliness of the mind. Indeed they are utter strangers to what we call common decency; and I could give you some high-flavoured instances, at which even a native of Edinburgh would stop his nose. There are certain mortifying views of human nature, which undoubtedly ought to be concealed as much as possible, in order to prevent giving offence; and nothing can be more absurd than to plead the difference of custom in defence of those usages, which cannot fail giving disgust to the organs and senses of all mankind. Will custom exempt from the imputation of gross indecency a French lady, who shifts her frowsy smock in presence of a male visitant, and talks to him of her *lavement*, her *medicine*, and her *bidet*?

I shall not even deny, that the French are by no means deficient in natural capacity; but they are, at the same time, remarkable for a natural levity, which hinders their youth from cultivating that capacity. This is reinforced by the most preposterous education, and the example of a giddy people, engaged in the most frivolous pursuits. A Frenchman is by some Jesuit, or other monk, taught to read his mother tongue, and to say his prayers in a language he does not understand. He learns to dance and to fence by the masters of those noble sciences. He becomes a complete connoisseur in dressing hair, and in adorning his own person, under the hands and instructions of his barber and valet-de-chambre. If he learns to play upon the flute or the fiddle, he is altogether irresistible. But he piques himself upon being polished above the natives of any other country by his conversation with the fair sex. In the course of this communication, with which he is indulged from his tender years, he learns like a parrot, by rote, the whole circle of French compliments, which you know are a set of phrases, ridiculous even to a proverb; and these he throws out indiscriminately to all women without distinction, in the exercize of that kind of address which is here distinguished by the name of gallantry; it is no more than his making love to every woman who will give him the hearing. It is an exercize, by the repetition of which he becomes very pert, very familiar, and very impertinent. Modesty, or diffidence, I have already said, is utterly unknown among them, and therefore I wonder there should be a term to express it in their language. . . .

A Frenchman will sooner part with his religion than with his hair, which, indeed, no consideration will induce him to forego. I know a gentleman afflicted with a continual headach, and a defluxion on his eyes, who was told by his physician, that the best chance he had for being cured, would be to have his head close shaved, and bathed every day in cold water. 'How!' cried he; 'cut my hair? Mr doctor, your most humble servant!' He dismissed his physician, lost his eyesight, and almost his senses, and is now led about with his hair in a bag, and a piece of green silk hanging like a screen before his face. Count Saxe and other military writers, have demonstrated the absurdity of a soldier's wearing a long head of hair; nevertheless every soldier in this country wears a long queue, which makes a delicate mark on his white clothing; and this ridiculous foppery has descended even to the lowest class of people. The *décrotteur*, who cleans your shoes at the corner of the Pont

Neuf, has a tail of this kind hanging down to his rump, and even the peasant who drives an ass loaded with dung, wears his hair *en queue*, though, perhaps, he has neither shirt nor breeches. This is the ornament upon which he bestows much time and pains, and in the exhibition of which he finds full gratification for his vanity. Considering the harsh features of the common people in this country, their diminutive stature, their grimaces, and that long appendage, they have no small resemblance to large baboons walking upright; and perhaps this similitude has helped to entail upon them the ridicule of their neighbours.

Tobias Smollett
Travels through France and Italy
1766

Given their willingness to think the worst, English travellers were often brought up short by the realities of living abroad. Matters were ripe for misunderstanding. There was likely to be some element of puzzlement or comedy in the simplest transaction:

'HUMAN BEINGS WHO DON'T UNDERSTAND ENGLISH'

I did my exercises nobly. I was in superb spirits. Mademoiselle Stensen and other young ladies drank tea at our house. I was very gay. They begged me to repeat to them something in English. I repeated Erskine's beautiful stanza, 'I fly, yet I love you, my fair.' They thought it Russian. I also repeated Mr Johnson's verses, 'On Thames's banks' &c., and they thought them no less rude. How curious is this! Here are human beings who don't understand English; and to whom Mr Samuel Johnson does not exist, and Erskine seems a savage. Mademoiselle Stensen taught me a sweet song, 'Je reconnais les atteintes, qui m'ont autrefois charmé' &c. It touched me sensibly and made me own, 'That brings back to my mind a married woman with whom I used to be deeply in love.' I must be on my guard.

James Boswell
On the Grand Tour
1764

THE ROMANS IN CHURCH

The scene in all the churches is the strangest possible. The same monotonous, heartless, drowsy chaunting, always going on; the same dark building, darker from the brightness of the street without; the same lamps dimly burning; the self-same people kneeling here and there; turned towards you, from one altar or other, the same priest's back, with the same large cross embroidered on it; however different in size, in shape, in wealth, in architecture, this church is from that, it is the same thing still. There are the same dirty beggars stopping in their muttered prayers to beg; the same miserable cripples exhibiting their deformity at the doors; the same blind men, rattling little pots like kitchen pepper-castors; their depositories for alms; the same preposterous crowns of silver stuck upon the painted heads of single saints and Virgins in crowded pictures, so that a little figure on a mountain has a head-dress bigger than the temple in the foreground, or adjacent miles of landscape; the same favourite shrine or figure, smothered with little silver hearts and crosses, and the like: the staple trade and show of all the jewellers; the same odd mixture of respect and indecorum, faith and phlegm: kneeling on the stones, and spitting on them, loudly; getting up from prayers to beg a little, or to pursue some other worldly matter: and then kneeling down again, to resume the contrite supplication at the point where it was interrupted. In one church, a kneeling lady got up from her prayers, for a moment, to offer us her card, as a teacher of Music; and in another, a sedate gentleman with a very thick walking-staff, arose from his devotions to belabour his dog, who was growling at another dog: and whose yelps and howls resounded through the church, as his master quietly relapsed into his former trains of meditation – keeping his eye upon the dog, at the same time, nevertheless.

Charles Dickens
Pictures from Italy
1846

THE FOREIGNER CREATES A STIR IN ALBANIA

In this, the first town I had seen in Northern Albania, the novelty of the costumes is striking; for, rich as is the clothing of all these people, the tribes of Ghegheria surpass all their neighbours in gorgeousness of raiment, by adding to their ordinary vestments a long surtout of purple, crimson, or scarlet, trimmed with fur, or bordered with gold thread, or braiding. Their jackets and waistcoats are usually black, and their whole outer man contrasts strongly with that of their white neighbours of Berát, or many-hued brethren of Epirus. Other proofs were not wanting of my being in a new land; for, as we advanced slowly through the geese-frequented kennels (a running stream with *trottoirs* on each side, and crossed by stepping-stones, is a characteristic of this place), my head was continually saluted by small stones and bits of dirt, the infidel air of my white hat courting the notice and condemnation of the orthodox Akhri-dhani; 'And,' quoth Giorgio, 'unless you take to a Fez, Vossignoria will have no peace, and possibly lose an eye in a day or two.' . . .

We halted at the khan of Episkopí, close to a little stream full of capital water cresses which I began to gather and eat with some bread and cheese, an act which provoked the Epirote bystanders of the village to ecstatic laughter and curiosity. Every portion I put into my mouth, delighted them as a most charming exhibition of foreign whim; and the more juvenile spectators instantly com-menced bringing me all sorts of funny objects, with an earnest request that the Frank would amuse them by feeding thereupon forthwith. One brought a thistle, a second a collection of sticks and wood, a third some grass; a fourth presented me with a fat grasshopper – the whole scene was acted amid shouts of laughter, in which I joined as loudly as any. We parted amazingly good friends, and the wits of Episkopí will long remember the Frank who fed on weeds out of the water.

Edward Lear
Journals of a Landscape Painter in Greece and Albania
1851

A STRANGER IN A FRENCH MOUNTAIN TOWN

I soon became a popular figure, and was known for miles in the country. *Où'st-ce que vous allez?* was changed for me into *Quoi, vous rentrez au Monastier ce soir?* and in the town itself every urchin seemed to know my name, although no living creature could pro-nounce it. There was one particular group of lace-makers who brought out a chair for me whenever I went by, and detained me from my walk to gossip. They were filled with curiosity about England, its language, its religion, the dress of the women, and were never weary of seeing the Queen's head on English postage-stamps or seeking for French words in English journals. The langu-age, in particular, filled them with surprise.

'Do they speak *patois* in England?' I was once asked; and when I told them not, 'Ah, then, French?' said they.

'No, no,' I said, 'not French.'

'Then,' they concluded, 'they speak *patois*.'

You must obviously either speak French or *patois*. Talk of the force of logic – here it was in all its weakness. I gave up the point, but proceeding to give illustrations of my native jargon, I was met with a new mortification. Of all *patois* they declared that mine was the most preposterous and the most jocose in sound. At each new word there was a new explosion of laughter, and some of the younger ones were glad to rise from their chairs and stamp about the street in ecstasy; and I looked on upon their mirth in a faint and slightly disagreeable bewilderment. 'Bread,' which sounds a commonplace, plain-sailing monosyllable in England, was the word that most delighted these good ladies of Monastier; it seemed to them frolicsome and racy, like a page of *Pickwick*; and they all got it carefully by heart, as a stand-by, I presume, for winter evenings. I have tried it since then with every sort of accent and inflection, but I seem to lack the sense of humour.

R. L. Stevenson
Travels with a Donkey
1879

ARRIVAL IN SOUTHERN ITALY

The surf was high; it cost much yelling, leaping, and splashing to gain the dry beach. Meanwhile, not without apprehension, I had eyed the group awaiting our arrival; that they had their eyes on me was obvious, and I knew enough of southern Italians to foresee my reception. I sprang into the midst of a clamorous conflict; half a dozen men were quarrelling for possession of me. No sooner was my luggage on shore than they flung themselves upon it. By what force or authority I know not, one of the fellows triumphed; he turned to me with a satisfied smile, and – presented his wife.

'*Mia sposa, signore!*'

Wondering, and trying to look pleased, I saw the woman seize the portmanteau (a frightful weight), fling it on to her head, and march away at a good speed. The crowd and I followed to the *dogana*, close by, where as rigorous a search was made as I have ever had to undergo. I puzzled the people; my arrival was an unwonted thing, and they felt sure I was a trader of some sort. Dismissed under suspicion, I allowed the lady to whom I had been introduced to guide me townwards. Again she bore the portmanteau on her head, and evidently thought it a trifle, but as the climbing road lengthened, and as I myself began to perspire in the warm sunshine, I looked at my attendant with uncomfortable feelings. It

Southern Italy

was a long and winding way, but the woman continued to talk and laugh so cheerfully that I tried to forget her toil. At length we reached a cabin where the *dazio* (town dues) officer presented himself, and this conscientious person insisted on making a fresh examination of my baggage; again I explained myself, again I was eyed suspiciously; but he released me, and on we went. I had bidden my guide take me to the best inn; it was the *Leone*, a little place which looked from the outside like an ill-kept stable, but was decent enough within. The room into which they showed me had a delightful prospect. Deep beneath the window lay a wild, leafy garden, and lower on the hillside a lemon orchard shining with yellow fruit; beyond, the broad pebbly beach, far seen to north and south, with its white foam edging the blue expanse of sea.

George Gissing
By the Ionian Sea
1901

Although there was more than enough ill-feeling to go round, not all meetings between the English and the continentals were characterized by prejudice and blindness. When they came across the poor or the oppressed, English travellers generally showed a sympathy and a tender-heartedness which compensated somewhat for their muddled heads:

FREE PEASANTS OF SWEDEN

As in the course of this route I constantly took my repast during the day, and passed every night in the cottages, I had frequent opportunities of observing the customs, manners, and food of the peasants. Upon entering a cottage, I usually found all the family employed in carding flax, spinning thread, and in weaving coarse linen, and sometimes cloth. The peasants are excellent contrivers, and apply the coarsest materials to some useful purpose. They twist ropes from swines' bristles, horses' manes, and bark of trees, and use eel-skins for bridles. Their food principally consists of salted flesh and fish, eggs, milk, and hard bread. At Michaelmas they usually kill their cattle, and salt them for the ensuing Winter and Spring. Twice in the year they bake their bread in large round cakes, which are strung upon files of sticks, and suspended close to the ceilings of the cottages. They are so hard as to be occasionally broken with a hatchet, but are not unpleasant. The peasants use beer for their common drink, and are much addicted to malt spirits. In the districts towards the western coasts, and at no great distance inland, tea and coffee are not unusually found in the Swedish cottages, which are procured in great plenty, and at a cheap rate, from Gotheborg.

The peasants are well clad in strong cloth of their own weaving. Their cottages, though built with wood, and only of one story, are comfortable and commodious. The room in which the family sleep is provided with ranges of beds in tiers (if I may so express myself), one above the other: upon the wooden testers of the beds in which the women lie are placed others for the reception of the men, to which they ascend by means of ladders.

To a person who has just quitted Germany, and been accustomed to tolerable inns, the Swedish cottages may perhaps appear miserable hovels; to me, who had been long used to places of far inferior accommodation, they seemed almost palaces. The traveller is able to procure many conveniences, and particularly a separate room from that inhabited by the family, which could seldom be obtained in the Polish and Russian villages. During my course through those two countries, a bed was a phænomenon which seldom occurred, excepting in the large towns, and even then not always completely equipped; but the poorest huts of Sweden were never deficient in this article of comfort: an evident proof that the Swedish peasants are more civilized than those of Poland and Russia.

After having witnessed the slavery of the peasants in those two countries, it was a pleasing satisfaction to find myself again among freemen, in a kingdom where there is a more equal division of property; where there is no vassalage, where the lowest order enjoy a security of their persons and property; and where the advantages resulting from this right are visible to the commonest observer.

William Coxe
Travels into Poland, Russia, Sweden, and Denmark
1784

THE CEMETERY KEEPER OF BOLOGNA

In the pleasant Cemetery at Bologna I found myself walking next Sunday morning, among the stately marble tombs and colonnades, in company with a crowd of Peasants, and escorted by a little Cicerone of that town, who was excessively anxious for the honour of the place, and most solicitous to divert my attention from the bad monuments: whereas he was never tired of extolling the good ones. Seeing this little man (a good-humoured little man he was, who seemed to have nothing in his face, but shining teeth and eyes) looking, wistfully, at a certain plot of grass, I asked him who was buried there. 'The poor people, Signore,' he said with a shrug and a smile, and stopping to look back at me – for he always went on a little before, and took off his hat to introduce every new monument. 'Only the poor, Signore! It's very cheerful. It's very lively. How green it is, how cool! It's like a meadow! There are five,' - holding up all the fingers of his right hand to express the number, which an Italian Peasant will always do, if it be within the compass of his ten fingers, – 'there are five of my little children buried there, Signore; just there; a little to the right. Well! Thanks to God! It's very cheerful. How green it is, how cool it is! It's quite a meadow!'

He looked me very hard in the face, and seeing I was sorry for him, took a pinch of snuff (every Cicerone takes snuff), and made a little bow; partly in deprecation of his having alluded to such a subject, and partly in memory of the children and of his favourite Saint. It was as unaffected and as perfectly natural a little bow, as ever man made. Immediately afterwards, he took his hat off altogether, and begged to introduce me to the next monument; and his eyes and his teeth shone brighter than before.

Charles Dickens
Pictures from Italy
1846

THE SPANISH MULETEER

The Spanish muleteer is a fine fellow; he is intelligent, active, and enduring; he braves hunger and thirst, heat and cold, mud and dust; he works as hard as his cattle, never robs or is robbed; and while his betters in this land put off everything till to-morrow except bankruptcy, he is punctual and honest, his frame is wiry and sinewy, his costume peculiar; many are the leagues and long, which we have ridden in his caravan, and longer his robber yarns, to which we paid no attention; and it must be admitted that these cavalcades are truly national and picturesque.

Richard Ford
Gatherings from Spain
1846

MUSLIM HOSPITALITY AND GREEK ACCOMPLISHMENTS

While taking a parting cup of coffee with the postmaster, I unluckily set my foot on a handsome pipe-bowl (pipe-bowls are always snares to near-sighted people moving over Turkish floors, as they are scattered in places quite remote from the smokers, who live at the farther end of prodigiously long pipe-sticks) – crash; but nobody moved; only on apologizing through Giorgio, the polite Mohammedan said: 'The breaking of such a pipe-bowl would indeed, under ordinary circumstances, be disagreeable; but in a friend every action has its charm!' – a speech which recalled the injunction of the Italian to his son on leaving home, 'Whenever anybody treads upon your foot in company, and says, "Scusatemi," only reply: "Anzi – mi ha fatto un piacere!" '*

The morning seemed lowering, and a drizzling rain soon fell. This perpetual haze must end in some one or two days' hard rain before the weather clears, and I speculate where the durance is to be borne the while. Avoiding the grass-grown raised pavement, which is the post-road in Turkey, wherever mud or water prevent your using the broad track parallel to which it leads, we advanced by well-worn paths over a plain somewhat similar to that of yesterday, but which became more marshy, and in parts more cultivated, as we approached the hills of Vodhená, backed by the dark cloudy mountains beyond. From time to time we pass herds of buffaloes; falcons are numerous on all sides, and, added to yesterday's ornithology, there are hooded crows, rooks, coots, quails, and plovers. At eleven,

---

* 'Excuse me.' 'On the contrary, you have done me a pleasure.'

we arrive at Arnaoutlík, a village of Greek and Bulgarian Christian peasants.

Of Giorgio, dragoman, cook, valet, interpreter, and guide, I have had as yet nothing to complain; he is at home in all kinds of tongues, speaking ten fluently, an accomplishment common to many of the travelling Oriental Greeks, for he is a Smyrniote by birth. In countenance my attendant is somewhat like one of those strange faces, lion or griffin, which we see on door-knockers or urn-handles, and a grim twist of his under-jaw gives an idea that it would not be safe to try his temper too much. In the morning he is diffuse, and dilates on past journeys; after noon his remarks become short, and sententious – not to say surly. Any appearance of indecision evidently moves him to anger speedily. It is necessary to watch the disposition of a servant on whom so much of one's personal comfort depends, and it is equally necessary to give as little trouble as possible, for a good dragoman has always enough to do without extra whims or worryings from his employer.

Edward Lear
Journals of a Landscape Painter in Greece and Albania
1851

THE DIGNITY OF LABOUR IN SOUTHERN ITALY

Later in the day I came upon a figure scarcely less impressive. Beyond the new quarter of the town, on the ragged edge of its wide, half-peopled streets, lies a tract of olive orchards and of seedland; there, alone amid great bare fields, a countryman was ploughing. The wooden plough, as regards its form, might have been thousands of years old; it was drawn by a little donkey, and traced in the soil – the generous southern soil – the merest scratch of a furrow. I could not but approach the man and exchange words with him; his rude but gentle face, his gnarled hands, his rough and scanty vesture, moved me to a deep respect, and when his speech fell upon my ear, it was as though I listened to one of the ancestors of our kind. Stopping in his work, he answered my inquiries with careful civility; certain phrases escaped me, but on the whole he made himself quite intelligible, and was glad, I could see, when my words proved that I understood him. I drew apart, and watched him again. Never have I seen man so utterly patient, so primævally deliberate. The donkey's method of ploughing was to pull for one minute, and then rest for two; it excited in the ploughman not the least surprise or resentment. Though he held a long stick in his hand, he never made use of it; at each stoppage he contemplated the ass, and then gave utterance to a long 'Ah-h-h!' in a note of the most affectionate remonstrance. They were not driver and beast, but comrades in labour. It reposed the mind to look upon them.

George Gissing
By the Ionian Sea
1901

THE KRAVARITES OF NORTHERN GREECE

The Kravara covers, I think, about fifty square miles, but the figure has no meaning in such a terrain. A score of villages lurk there; not one was visible and there was no hint of the presence of man or beast, not a leaf or a grass blade. Under a sharp sky where late winter was turning into early spring, the sphinx-like region was replete with enigmas. . . .

It was vital to get out of Greece as early as possible. The Bulgarians, although they were fellow-Orthodox, were stingy and xenophobe and hated the Greeks. The Serbs were not bad. Things began to look up the moment the Danube was crossed: Rumanians were more prosperous and more open-handed; the place teemed with cattle and fowl and livestock of every kind, even buffaloes, that the Rumanians used for ploughing. The Hungarians were good but of course they were Catholic; lots of livestock, specially horses. It was the same in Poland. Someone interrupted here and asked, with that curly backhanded scoop that always accompanies the mention of theft, whether the old ones ever lifted things. Not often, no, Uncle Elias said. The point was to use one's wits. But a few of them used to 'vanish' things. . . . One pinched the laundry off the line at one end of a village and sold it back at the other. Poultry was hard to resist. Experts would peer into hen-coops with a two-legged fox's glance then spit and roast their takings in the woods. Hens, ducks, geese, guinea fowl and turkeys flew into their embrace. Sheep and lambs sometimes met the same fate. One gifted Kravarite had the mysterious knack of silencing pigs, nobody knew how: once he removed a farrow of six without a note being heard from either the sow or the piglets; he got away with four in his bag and one under each arm. There were several specialists in this line. Property dwindled at their passage, movables moved, barnyards depleted, orchards lightened, eggs melted away by the clutch the moment they were laid from under the sitting fowl; whole landscapes yielded a sporadic toll. Some professionals were irresistibly seductive in their patter; if the coast were clear, alms and a square meal were sometimes followed by the flattening (as the rather short-sighted phrase goes in vulgar Greek) of the hostess. Used as they were to the fierce morality of Greek village life, the ease and fre-

quency of these favours filled young beggars with surprise. Their
itineraries were starred with brisk hurly-burlies in barns and ricks
and sometimes by snug nights indoors. Eastern Europe, Uncle Elias
thought, must have been full of small Kravarites; Russia,
especially. . . .

For Russia was the place! Uncle Elias's eyes blazed at the
memory. The Russia of the Tsars beckoned them like the promised
land. The inhabitants were moody, drunk, rough, a bit mad; but
they were Orthodox like the Greeks and very pious; also super-
stitious, kind-hearted, reckless, gullible and generous. It was no
good since the Revolution; you couldn't get into it. In their early
heyday, the Kravarites irrupted into the empire from Poland, after
doing the rounds of the Balkans and Eastern Europe; or, striking
across the Danube at Rustchuk, they followed the dotted line of
Bucharest and Yassy to Czernovits, the easternmost wing-tip of the
Hapsburg monarchy (before it was Rumanian and then Russian),
at the end of the Carpathians: (that peculiar multi-lingual town
that has enriched so many theatres and circuses with comic turns,
and, they say, with lifelong child-performers carefully stunted from
the cradle with spirits). From here they advanced into Podolia, a
Babel world full of great estates and of the huddling beards and
elflocks of the Hasidim. Many took a shorter cut, heading straight
for Bessarabia and crossing the Prut and the Dniestr into the
Ukraine; no passports then! Here the Black Sea coastline beckoned.
They haunted Krim Tartary and the Sea of Azov, and thrust on to
the Caucasus, pausing on the way among the Greek communities of
the ports: Odessa, Taganrog, Mariupol, Rostov-on-the-Don. Farther
south, scattered across the Caucasus between the shores of the
Black Sea and the Caspian, were whole villages of Lazi; others
proliferated near Trebizond in Asia Minor, all speaking Greek. 'You
couldn't understand much,' Uncle Elias said, 'but it was Greek all
right. They'd been there since the time of *Megaléxandros* – what
do I know? Perhaps even earlier than Alexander. . . .' Sometimes
they would swerve north to Kiev, Smolensk, Moscow, St Petersburg
and the shores of the Baltic. Great cities loomed and churches,
castles, palaces, avenues and bridges with many spans. . . . Carriages with six horses . . . ! Cavalry all in white with breastplates
and helmets . . . ! Many struck east to Kazan, Perm and Omsk. . . .
What rivers! the Dniepr, the Don, the Volga! Uncle Elias conjured
up oceans of wheat, forests, mountains, horses – hundreds galloping
together – huge herds of sheep and cattle, wide extents of snow;
Cossacks, barges, nomads, turbans, caravans of gypsies and slant-
eyed men in giant fur hats dressed all in sheepskin: 'you could
smell them a mile off.' Some wanderers stayed away for years. A

few left their interim-hoards with Greek traders in Taganrog or Rostov while they plunged farther east, recovered them on their way home and worked their passages to Constantinople and Piraeus on steamers and sailing ships. Back at last in the Aetolian thorpes that hovered round us in the dark, their deceptive tatters, and perhaps their hollow staves, yielded their lucre: a chinking shower of northern and transpontine gold from a dozen vanished mints: dinars, levas, sovereigns, piastres, lei, pengös, thalers, zlotys and roubles stamped with the heads of Hapsburgs, Obrenovitches, Karageorgevitches, Saxe-Coburg-Gothas, Hohenzollerns and Romanoffs: the crown of St Stephen, St George's charger, rampant lions, and a whole metallic flight of single- and double-headed eagles emblematic of a world as remote as the Heptarchy.

Patrick Leigh Fermor
Roumeli: Travels in Northern Greece
1966

Men and Women
In male-dominated societies, few things interest the citizens of one country more than the role and position of women in another. Relations between the sexes were subtly different on the continent, and English travellers, both men and women, viewed the difference with a mixture of censoriousness and slightly illicit admiration:

THE WIVES OF HOLLAND

The wives of Holland buy and sell all things at home, and use to saile to Hamburg and into England for exercise of traffique. I heard from credible men, that the Citizens of Enchusen, within thirty yeeres then past, used to marry a wife, and put her away at the yeeres end, if they liked her not; which barbarous custome, Civility and Religion hath since abolished: and at Delph I did see two examples, of men who having buried their wives, did after marry their wives Sisters. It is no rare thing for blowes to happen betweene man and wife, and I credibly heard that they have slight punishments for that fault, and my selfe did heare the Crier summon a man to answer the beating of his wife before a Magistrate.

The multitude of women is farre greater then of men, which I not only formerly heard from others, but my selfe observed to be true, by the daily meetings of both sexes, where a man may see sixty or more women sliding upon the yce, and otherwise recreating themselves, with five or six or much fewer men. But the reason

thereof is not easily yeelded, since wee cannot say that the men
are much consumed by the Civill warres, their Army consisting
altogether of strangers, and few or no Hollanders, except some
willingly served, for otherwise they cannot be pressed by authority,
but onely for the defence of the City or Towne wherein they dwell:
except these reasons thereof may bee approved, that the watery
Provinces breed flegmaticke humors, which together with the mens
excessive drinking, may disable them to beget Males; or that the
Women (as I have heard some Hollanders confese) not easily finding
a Husband, in respect of this disparity of the Sexes in number,
commonly live unmarried till they be thirty yeeres old, and as
commonly take Husbands of twenty yeeres age, which must needs
make the Women more powerfull in generation. And the Women
not onely take young Men to their Husbands, but those also which
are most simple and tractable: so as by the foresaid priviledge of
Wives to dispose goods by their last will, and by the contracts in
respect of their Dowry (which to the same end use to be warily
drawne) they keepe their Husbands in a kind of awe, and almost
alone, without their Husbands intermedling, not onely keepe their
shops at home, but exercise trafficke abroad.

Fynes Moryson
Itinerary
1605–17

THE SCANDALOUS FASHIONS OF VENICE

Almost all the wives, widowes and mayds do walke abroad with
their breastes all naked, and many of them have their backes also
naked even almost to the middle, which some do cover with a slight
linnen, as cobwebbe lawne, or such other thinne stuffe: a fashion
me thinkes very uncivill and unseemely, expecially if the beholder
might plainly see them. For I beleeve unto many that have *prurien-
tem libidinem*, they would minister a great incentive & fomentation
of luxurious desires. There is one thing used of the Venetian women,
and some others dwelling in the cities and towns subject to the
Signiory of Venice, that is not to be observed (I thinke) amongst
any other women in Christendome: a thing made of wood, and
covered with leather of sundry colors, some with white, some redde,
some yellow. It is called a Chapiney, which they weare under their
shoes. Many of them are curiously painted; some also I have seene
fairely gilt: so uncomely a thing (in my opinion) that it is pitty this
foolish custom is not cleane banished and exterminated out of the
citie. There are many of these Chapineys of great height, even half
a yard high, which maketh many of their women that are very

short, seeme much taller then the tallest women we have in
England. Also I have heard that this is observed amongst them,
that by how much the nobler a woman is, by so much the higher
are her Chapineys. All their Gentlewomen, and most of their wives
and widowes that are of any wealth are assisted and supported
eyther by men or women when they walke abroad, to the end they
may not fall. They are borne up most commonly by the left arme,
otherwise they might quickly take a fall. For I saw a woman fall a
very dangerous fall, as she was going down the staires of one of the
little stony bridges with her high Chapineys alone by her selfe: but
I did nothing pitty her, because shee wore such frivolous and (as I
may truely terme them) ridiculous instruments, which were the
occasion of her fall. For both I my selfe, and many other strangers
(as I have observed in Venice) have often laughed at them for their
vaine Chapineys.

Thomas Coryat
Crudities
1611

THE MANAGEMENT OF THE HEART IN VIENNA
IN THE EARLY 18TH CENTURY

A woman, till five-and-thirty, is only looked upon as a raw girl, and
can possibly make no noise in the world till about forty. I don't know
what your ladyship may think of this matter; but 'tis a considerable
comfort to me, to know there is upon earth such a paradise for old
women; and I am content to be insignificant at present, in the
design of returning when I am fit to appear no where else. I cannot
help lamenting on this occasion, the pitiful case of too many good
English ladies, long since retired to prudery and ratafia, whom if
their stars had luckily conducted hither, would shine in the first
rank of beauties. Besides, that perplexing word *reputation* has quite
another meaning here than what you give it at London; and getting
a lover is so far from losing, than 'tis properly getting reputation;
ladies being much more respected in regard to the rank of their
lovers, than that of their husbands.

But what you'll think very odd, the two sects that divide our
whole nation of petticoats, are utterly unknown in this place. Here
are neither coquettes nor prudes. No woman dares appear coquette
enough to encourage two lovers at a time. And I have not seen any
such prudes as to pretend fidelity to their husbands, who are certainly the best natured set of people in the world, and look upon
their wives' gallants as favourably as men do upon their deputies,
that take the troublesome part of their business off their hands.

140

They have not however the less to do on that account; for they are generally deputies in another place themselves; in one word, 'tis the established custom for every lady to have two husbands, one that bears the name, and another that performs the duties. And these engagements are so well known, that it would be a downright affront, and publicly resented, if you invited a woman of quality to dinner, without, at the same time, inviting her two attendants of lover and husband, between whom she sits in state with great gravity. The sub-marriages generally last twenty years together, and the lady often commands the poor lover's estate, even to the utter ruin of his family.

These connections, indeed, are as seldom begun by any real passion as other matches; for a man makes but an ill figure that is not in some commerce of this nature; and a woman looks out for a lover as soon as she's married, as part of her equipage, without which she could not be genteel; and the first article of the treaty is establishing the pension, which remains to the lady, in case the gallant should prove inconstant. This chargeable point of honour I look upon as the real foundation of so many wonderful instances of constancy. I really know some women of the first quality, whose pensions are as well known as their annual rents, and yet nobody esteems them the less; on the contrary, their discretion would be called in question, if they should be suspected to be mistresses for nothing.

Lady Mary Wortley Montagu
Travel Letters
1763

FEMALE MUSICIANS OF VENICE

The sight of the orchestra still makes me smile. You know, I suppose, it is entirely of the female gender; and that nothing is more common, than to see a delicate white hand journeying across an enormous double bass; or a pair of roseate cheeks puffing with all their efforts at a french-horn. Some of them are grown old and Amazonian, who have abandoned their fiddles and their lovers, take vigorously to the kettledrum; and one poor limping lady, who had been crossed in love, now makes an admirable figure on the bassoon. Good night! I am quite exhausted with composing a chorus for these same Amazons.

William Beckford
Dreams, Waking Thoughts and Incidents
1783

THE BURDENS OF THE ALBANIAN WOMEN

It was half past one when we arrived, and before I go out to sketch, Anastásio cooks a lunch of eggs roasted and fried in butter, of which he partakes with Pietone. This last accomplished person does not indulge in shoes, and I observe that when his hands are occupied, he holds his pipe in his toes, and does any other little office with those, to us, useless members. Throughout the whole of the day's journey I have seen numbers of women carrying burthens of incredible size and weight – from one hundred and fifty to one hundred and eighty pounds, I am assured, is no unusual loading. These poor creatures are indeed little like women in appearance, for their faces are worn into lines and furrows of masculine hardness by excessive and early toil; and as they labour pitifully up the rocky paths, steadying their steps with a staff, or cross the stony torrent beds, bent nearly double beneath their loads, they seem less like human beings than quadrupeds. A man's blood boils to see them accompanied by a beast of a husband or brother, generally on horseback, carrying – what? – nothing but a pipe! And when he is tired of smoking, or finds himself over-clad, he gives the woman his pipe to hold, or throws his capote over her load! The ponderous packages of wool, grain, sticks, etc., born by these hard-worked creatures are hung to their neck by two strong straps; their dress is dark blue, with a blue handkerchief on the head – dark full trowsers – no petticoat, an apron – and red worked woollen gaiters. They are short and strongly made in person, with very light hair; their eyes are almost universally soft gray, and very pretty, but the rest of the face, apart from the worn and ground-down expression, is too broad and square in form to be prepossessing.

Edward Lear
Journals of the Landscape Painter in Greece and Albania
1851

FORTHRIGHT LANGUAGE IN RURAL FRANCE

One thing was notable about these women, from the youngest to the oldest, and with hardly an exception. In spite of their piety, they could twang off an oath with Sir Toby Belch in person. There was nothing so high or so low, in heaven or earth or in the human body, but a woman of this neighbourhood would whip out the name of it, fair and square, by way of conversational adornment. My landlady, who was pretty and young, dressed like a lady and avoided *patois* like a weakness, commonly addressed her child in the language of a drunken bully. And of all the swearers that I have ever heard, commend me to an old lady in Goudet, a village of the Loire. I was making a sketch, and her curse was not yet ended when I had finished it and took my departure. It is true she had a right to be angry; for here was her son, a hulking fellow, visibly the worse for a drink before the day was well begun. But it was strange to hear her unwearying flow of oaths and obscenities, endless like a river, and now and then rising to a passionate shrillness, in the clear and silent air of the morning. In city slums, the thing might have passed unnoticed; but in a country valley, and from a plain and honest countrywoman, this beastliness of speech surprised the ear.

R. L. Stevenson
Travels with a Donkey
1879

But the great curiosity, which teased the imagination more than any other, concerned love and sexual gratification. The morals of the continent were, in the English view, dubious. Wantonness, sexual corruption and easy compliance derided sober virtue. It was a highly-coloured world of cynicism and danger. 'The worthy Corsicans,' wrote the sex-hungry Boswell, 'thought it proper to give a moral lesson to a young traveller just come from Italy. They told me that in their country I should be treated with the greatest hospitallity; but if I attempted to debauch any of their women, I might expect instant death.' Young men found this world hard to resist:

MIXED BATHING IN SWITZERLAND

Also I have noted another strange thing amongst them that I have not a littled wondred at. Men and women bathing themselves to-gether naked from the middle upward in one bathe: whereof some of the women were wives (as I was told) and men partly bachelers, and partly married men, but not the husbands of the same women. Yet their husbands have bene at that time at Hinderhove, and some of them in the very place standing hard by the bathe in their cloathes, and beholding their wives not onely talking and familiarly discoursing with other men, but also sporting after a very pleasant and merry manner. Yea sometimes they sing merily together but especially that sweet & most amorous song of *solus cum solâ*; I meane another mans wife, & another man naked upward (as I have aforesaid) in one bath. Yet all this while the husband may not be jelous though he be at the bathes, and seeth too much occasion of jealousie ministred unto him. For the verie name of jealousie is odious in this place. But let these Germanes and Helvetians do as they list, and observe these kind of wanton customes as long as they will; for mine owne part were I a married man, and meant to spend some little time here with my wife for solace and recreation sake, truly I should hardly be perswaded to suffer her to bath her selfe naked in one and the selfe same bath with one onely bachelar or married man with her, because if she was faire, and had an attractive countenance, she might perhaps cornifie me. Here also I saw many passing faire yong Ladies and Gentlewomen naked in the bathes with their wooers and favorites in the same. For at this time of the yeare many woers come thither to solace themselves with their beautifull mistresses. Many of these yong Ladies had the haire of their head very curiously plaited in locks, & they wore certaine pretty garlands upon their heads made of fragrant and odoriferous flowers. A spectacle exceeding amorous.

Thomas Coryat
Crudities
1611

ITALIAN PILGRIMS AND CONCUBINES

Before I came neare to Loreto by tenne miles, I overtooke a Caroch, wherein were two Gentlemen of Rome, and their two Concubines; who when they espied me, saluted me kindly, enquiring of what Nation I was? whither I was bound? and what pleasure I had to travell alone? After I had to these demands given satisfaction, they intreated me to come up in the Caroch, but I thankfully refused, and would not, replying the way was faire, the weather seasonable, and my body unwearied. At last they perceiving my absolute refusall, presently dismounted on the ground, to recreate themselves in my company: and incontinently, the two young unmarried Dames came forth also, and would by no perswasion of me, nor their familiars mount againe; saying, they were all Pilgrimes, and bound to Loreto (for devotion sake) in pilgrimage, and for the pennance enjoyned to them by their Father Confessour. Truely so farre as I could judge, their pennance was small, being carried with horses, and the appearance of their devotion much lesse: for lodging at Recanati, after supper, each youth led captive his dearest Darling to an unsanctified bed, and left me to my accustomed repose.

William Lithgow
Rare Adventures and Painful Peregrinations
1632

WOMEN BOUGHT AND SOLD

I have seene men and women as usually sold here in Markets, as Horses and other beasts are with us: A Ship of Marseilles, called the great Dolphin, lying here forty dayes at the Galata, the Maister Gunner, named Monsieur Nerack, and I falling in familiar acquaintance, upon a time he told me secretly that he would gladly for Conscience and Merits sake, redeeme some poore Christian slave from Turkish Captivity. To the which, I applauded his advice, and told him the next Friday following I would assist him to so worthy an action: Friday comes, and he and I went for Constantinople, where the Market of the slaves being ready, we spent two houres in viewing, and reviewing five hundreth Males and Females. At last I pointed him to have bought an old man or woman, but his minde was contrary set, shewing me that he would buy some virgin, or young widdow, to save their bodies undefloured with Infidels. The price of a virgin was too deare for him, being a hundred Duckets, and widdows were farre under, and at an easier rate: When we did visite and search them that we were mindfull to buy, they were strip'd starke naked before our eyes, where the sweetest face, the youngest age, and whitest skin was in greatest value and request: The Jewes sold them, for they had bought them from the Turkes: At last we fell upon a Dalmation widdow, whose pittifull lookes, and sprinkling teares, stroke my soule almost to the death for compassion: whereupon I grew earnest for her relief, and he yeelding to my advice, she is bought and delivered unto him, the man being 60. yeares of age, and her price 36. Duckets.

William Lithgow
Rare Adventures and Painful Peregrinations
1632

LOVE IN A SPANISH NUNNERY

My Lord Baltimore had then a daughter in one of these Nunneryes which we saw (I think it was at *San Bernado*); she was but a girl, and placed there only for education, and undoubtedly (setting religion aside) it is a way of breeding infinitely beyond all our English Schools. A very lovely sister there beg'd a silver pick-tooth and case of me, and return'd me for it a pretty little picture of the VM, curiously wrought, all with coloured straw. Platonic love is here very much esteem'd and practised, and really I have that charity and Justice to believe it may be done with perfect innocence. In one place we found a jolly Friar talking at the grate with the Sisters, who, with great civility, retired as soon as we came in.

Once, as we were sitting by them, in came a surly, stately Don, very richly attired; and after a profound reverence towards the Ladys, and a kind of scornfull nod to us, he lean'd his head to the wall by the side of the grate, and with his armes and leggs acrosse, and his eyes fixt upon one of them (which was very ingenious, but not handsome), he stood thare in such a fixed posture as, had it not been sometimes for a sneaking silly sigh (true or feign'd, I know not), you would have thought he rather saw Medusa's head then his dear Dulcinea's face. He spoil'd all our mirth; all was hush'd, and after a decent pause we left him to his *Devotions.* He askt our Interpreter whether we were Catholics; he answered Yes, and all past very well.

One of our English Merchants there (of good repute, though I shall not vouch the truth of his story), hearing me recount this adventure, told us that about 7 or 8 years before, soon after his first coming to Malaga, he had got acquainted with a young Sister, and often waited upon her, as well to divert himself as to perfect his Spanish Tounge; for there at the grate you have all the newes that is stirring, and the best and most refined language. He by degrees was wheedled into such fondnesse, as the presents which he had at several times made her came in a short time to about 40lb. He found (being but a young beginner) that his visits were more seldome, and his presents very few and meane, and at last he came no more at her at all, nor answer'd one line, though he received many most passionate ones from her, and there had past many such (as the manner is) betwixt them before. Not long after, he was one evening set upon by a Rogue (which she had hired), and was desperately wounded, and narrowly escaped with his life. The *Rufian* soon after confest it, being himself mortally wounded and taken in such another enterprise.

Dr. John Covel
Diaries
1670–79

PESTERED BY WHORES IN NAPLES

We went by coach to take the air, and see the diversions, or rather madness, of the Carnival; the courtesans (who swarm in this city to the number, as we are told, of 30,000 registered and paying a tax to the State) flinging eggs of sweet water into our coach, as we passed by the houses and windows. Indeed, the town is so pestered with these cattle, that there needs no small mortification to preserve from their enchantment, whilst they display all their natural and artificial beauty, play, sing, feign compliment, and by a thousand studied devices seek to inveigle foolish young men.

John Evelyn
Diary
1645

A GALLANT PROPOSITION IN VIENNA

But one of the pleasantest adventures I ever met with in my life was last night, and it will give you a just idea in what a delicate manner the *belles passions* are managed in this country. I was at the assembly of the Countess of – , and the young Count of – leading me down stairs, asked me how long I was to stay at Vienna? I made answer, that my stay depended on the emperor, and it was not in my power to determine it. Well, madam, (said he) whether your time here is to be long or short, I think you ought to pass it agreeably, and to that end you must engage in a *little affair of the heart.* – My heart (answered I gravely enough) does not engage very easily, and I have no design of parting with it. I see, madam, (said he sighing) but the ill nature of that answer, I am not to hope for it, which is a great mortification to me that am charmed with you. But, however, I am still devoted to your service; and since I am not worthy of entertaining you myself, do me the honour of letting me know whom you like best among us, and I'll engage to manage the affair entirely to your satisfaction. – You may judge in what manner I should have received this compliment in my own country; but I was well enough acquainted with the way of this, to know that he really intended me an obligation, and I thanked him with a very grave courtesy for his zeal to serve me, and only assured him I had no occasion to make use of it.

Lady Mary Wortley Montagu
Travel Letters
1763

BOSWELL GOES ADRIFT IN AMSTERDAM AND BERLIN

At nine I went into the Amsterdam boat. The *roef* was hired, so I was all night amongst ragamuffins. Yet were my thoughts sweet and lively till the last two hours when I sunk to gloom.

SATURDAY 26 MAY, 1764: I came to Grub's, an English house. I was restless. I was fretful. I despised myself.

At five I went to a bawdy-house. I was shown upstairs, and had a bottle of claret and a *juffrouw*. But the girl was much fitter for being wrapped in the blankets of salivation than kissed between the sheets of love. I had no armour, so did not fight. It was truly ludicrous to talk in Dutch to a whore. This scene was to me a rarity as great as peas in February. Yet I was hurt to find myself in the sinks of gross debauchery. This was a proper way to consider the thing. But so sickly was my brain that I had the low scruples of an Edinburgh divine.

I went to Blinshall's at eight. He talked of religious melancholy like a good sound fellow. He pleased me by saying it was bodily. I was so fretted as to be glad of any relief. I supped with Blinshall's landlord, Connal, an Irish peruke-maker who it seems was once a young fellow of fortune in London, and acquainted with Pope and many more men of genius. It was a queer evening. At six I had been so tired as to go to Farquhar's and drink amongst the blackguards a bottle of wine. I shall never forget that lowness; for low it was indeed. At eleven we parted. I resolved to go to a *speelhuis* but had no guide. I therefore very madly sought for one myself and strolled up and down the Amsterdam streets, which are by all accounts very dangerous at night. I began to be frightened and to think of Belgic *knives*. At last I came to a *speelhuis*, where I entered boldly. I danced with a fine lady in laced riding-clothes, a true blackguard minuet. I had my pipe in my mouth and performed like any common sailor. I had near quarrelled with one of the musicians. But I was told to take care, which I wisely did. I spoke plenty of Dutch but could find no girl that elicited my inclinations. I was disgusted with this low confusion, came home and slept sound . . .

TUESDAY 11 SEPTEMBER 1764: To punish my extravagant rodomontading, and to bring up my affairs and compose my spirit, I had sitten up all night. Grievous was it to the flesh till seven in the morning, when my blood took a fine flow. I was quite drunk with brisk spirits, and about eight, in came a woman with a basket of chocolate to sell. I toyed with her and found she was with child. Oho! a safe piece. Into my closet. 'Habs er ein Man?' 'Jar, in den Gards bei Potsdam.'* To bed directly. In a minute – over. I rose cool and astonished, half angry, half laughing. I sent her off. Bless me, have I now commited adultery? Stay, a soldier's wife is no wife. Should I now torment myself with speculations on sin, and on losing in one morning the merit of a year's chastity? No: this is womanish. Nay, your elegant mystics would not do so. Madame Guyon was of opinion that sin should be forgotten as soon as possible, as being an idea too gross for the mind of a saint, and disturbing the exercise of sweet devotion. Her notion is ingenious. I am sorry that this accident has happened, I know not how. Let it go. I'll think no more

* 'Have you a husband?' 'Yes, in the Guards at Potsdam.'

of it. Divine Being! Pardon the errors of a weak mortal. Give me
more steadiness. Let me grow more perfect. What a curious thing
is it to find a strict philosopher speculating on a recent fault! Well,
I shall not be proud. I shall be a mild and humble Christian.

James Boswell
Boswell in Holland; & On the Grand Tour
1764

A CASE OF DELICACY

I forthwith took possession of my bed-chamber – got a good fire –
order'd supper; and was thanking Heaven it was no worse – when
a voiture arrived with a lady in it and her servant maid.

As there was no other bed-chamber in the house, the hostess
without much nicety, led them into mine, telling them, as she
usher'd them in, that there was nobody in it but an English gentleman – that there were two good beds in it, and a closet within the
room which held another. – The accent in which she spoke of this
third bed did not say much for it – however, she said there were
three beds, and but three people – and she durst say, the gentleman
would do anything to accommodate matters. – I left not the lady a
moment to make a conjecture about it – so instantly made a declar-
ation that I would do anything in my power.

The lady was Piedmontese of about thirty, with a glow of health
in her cheeks. – The maid was a Lyonoise of twenty, and as brisk
and lively a French girl as ever moved. – There were difficulties
every way – and the obstacle of the stone in the road, which brought
us into the distress, great as it appeared whilst the peasants were
removing it, was but a pebble to what lay in our ways now – I have
only to add, that it did not lessen the weight which hung upon our
spirits, that we were both too delicate to communicate what we felt
to each other upon the occasion.

We sat down to supper; and had we not had more generous wine
to it than a little inn in Savoy could have furnish'd, our tongues
had been tied, till necessity herself had set them at liberty – but
the lady having a few bottles of Burgundy in her voiture, sent down
her Fille de Chambre for a couple of them; so that by the time
supper was over, and we were left alone, we felt ourselves inspired
with a strength of mind sufficient to talk, at least, without reserve
upon our situation. We turn'd it every way, and debated and considered it in all kind of lights in the course of a two hours nego-
tiation; at the end of which the articles were settled finally betwixt
us, and stipulated for in form and manner of a treaty of peace –
and I believe with as much religion and good faith on both sides,

as in any treaty which has yet had the honour of being handed
down to posterity.

They were as follows:

First, As the right of the bed-chamber is in Monsieur – and he
thinking the bed next to the fire to be the warmest, he insists upon
the concession on the lady's side of taking up with it.

Granted, on the part of Madame; with a proviso, That as the
curtains of that bed are of a flimsey transparent cotton, and appear
likewise too scanty to draw close, that the Fille de Chambre shall
fasten up the opening, either by corking pins, or needle and thread,
in such a manner as shall be deem'd a sufficient barrier on the side
of Monsieur.

2dly. It is required on the part of Madame, that Monsieur shall
lie the whole night through in his robe de chambre.

Rejected: inasmuch as Monsieur is not worth a robe de chambre;
he having in his portmanteau but six shirts and a black silk pair
of breeches.

The mentioning of the silk pair of breeches made an entire change
of the article – for the breeches were accepted as an equivalent for
the robe de chambre; and so it was stipulated and agreed upon,
that I should lie in my black silk breeches all night.

3dly. It was insisted upon, and stipulated for by the lady, that
after Monsieur was got to bed, and the candle and fire extinguished,
that Monsieur should not speak one single word the whole night.

Granted; provided Monsieur's saying his prayers might not be
deem'd an infraction of the treaty.

There was but one point forgot in this treaty, and that was the
manner in which the lady and myself should be obliged to undress
and get to bed – there was one way of doing it, and that I leave to
the reader to devise; protesting as I do, that if it is not the most
delicate in nature, 'tis the fault of his own imagination – against
which this is not my first complaint.

Now when we were got to bed, whether it was the novelty of the
situation, or what it was, I know not; but so it was, I could not shut
my eyes; I tried this side and that and turn'd and turn'd again, till
a full hour after midnight; when Nature and patience both were
wearing out – O my God! said I.

You have broke the treaty, Monsieur, said the lady, who had no
more sleep than myself. – I begg'd a thousand pardons – but insisted
it was no more than an ejaculation – she maintained 'twas an entire
infraction of the treaty – I maintain'd it was provided for in the
clause of the third article.

The lady would by no means give up the point, though she
weaken'd her barrier by it; for in the warmth of the dispute, I

could hear two or three corking pins fall out of the curtain to the ground.

Upon my word and honour, Madame, said I – stretching my arms out of bed by way of asseveration –

(– I was going to have added, that I would not have trespass'd against the remotest idea of decorum for the world) –

– But the Fille de Chambre hearing there were words between us, and fearing that hostilities would ensue in course, had crept silently out of her closet, and it being totally dark, had stolen so close to our beds, that she had got herself into the narrow passage which separated them, and had advanced so far up as to be in a line betwixt her mistress and me –

So that when I stretch'd out my hand, I caught hold of the Fille de Chambre's –

Laurence Sterne
A Sentimental Journey
1768

LOVE AND MARRIAGE IN RURAL GREECE

A few Khimáriotes were idling below the shady trees, and Anastásio were soon surrounded and welcomed back to his native haunts, though I perceived that some bad news was communicated to him, as he changed colour during the recital of the intelligence, and clasping his hands exclaimed aloud with every appearance of real sorrow. The cause of this grief was, he presently informed me, the tidings of the death of one of his cousins, at Vunó, his native place, a girl of eighteen, whose extreme beauty and good qualities had made her a sort of queen of the village, which, said Anastásio, I shall find a changed place, owing to her decease. 'I loved her,' said he, 'with all my heart, and had we been married, as we ought to have been, our lives might have been most thoroughly happy.' Having said thus much, and begging me to excuse his grief, he sat down with his head on his hand, in a mood of woe befitting such a bereavement. Meanwhile I reposed till the moment came for a fresh move onwards when lo! with the quickness of light the afflicted Anastásio arose, and ran to a group of women advancing towards the olive-trees, among whom one seemed to interest him not a little, and as she drew nearer I perceived that she was equally affected by the chance meeting – finally, they sate down together, and conversed with an earnestness which convinced me that the new-comer was a friend, at least, if not a sister, to the departed and lamented cousin of Vunó. It was now time to start, and as the mules were loading, the Khimáriote girl lingered, and I never saw a more exquisitely handsome face than hers. She was a perfect model of beauty, as she stood knitting, hardly bending beneath the burden she was carrying – her fine face half in shade from a snowy handkerchief thrown negligently over her head. She vanished when we were leaving Palása, but reappeared below the village, and accompanied Anastásio for a mile or more through the surrounding olive grounds, and leaving him at least with a bitter expression of melancholy which it was impossible not to sympathise with. 'Ah, Signore,' said Anastásio, 'she was to have been my wife, but now she is married to a horrid old man of Avlóna, who hates her, and she hates him, and so they will be wretched all their lives.' '*Corpo di Bacco!* Anastásio, why you told me just now you were to be married to the girl who has just died at Vunó!' 'So I was, Signore; but her parents would not let me marry her, so I have not thought about her any more – only now that she is dead I cannot help being very sorry; but Fortína, the girl who has just gone back, was the woman I loved better than anybody.' 'Then why didn't you marry her?' '*Perchè*, perchè,' said the afflicted Anastásio, '*perchè*, I have a wife already, Signore, in Vunó, and a little girl six years old. *Sì signor, sì.*'

Edward Lear
Journals of a Landscape Painter in Greece and Albania
1851

CANDOUR IN SPANISH SEXUAL LIFE

The great poverty of the masses in Spain has enormously increased prostitution, but Spaniards are not indignant about that. Passive, fatalistic, they accept the brothel and the prostitute as an ineluctable part of life, accept them with charity, pleasure, and indulgence.

The unabashed candour of the Spaniards, men and women, in their conversations about sexual love and the bodily passions is neither sensual nor obsessive. They talk without timidity or reserve. The common oaths or exclamations heard in any café or at any street corner are sexual. Everywhere, people swearing by their private parts with a Rabelaisian freedom and laughter. In their speech nothing is hidden. And under the puritanism of behaviour is something primitive and animal. It does not occur to them to conceal their admiration or their desire as they turn in the street to gaze at the woman who catches their eye; and the women, who make absolutely no response, nevertheless are very gratified by this admiration. They pity those women of other countries where public admiration is restrained; they condemn the women of those countries where such an admiration has an open response. Formal,

formal! How often, how many scores of times during the day, does one hear that almost military virtue in behaviour exalted! Preserve the formal, and after that – the whole mystery of private life, which no one can generalize about.

V. S. Pritchett
The Spanish Temper
1954

Wonders
It shines through all written accounts – the variety and strangeness of human behaviour. All travellers returned from the continent touched by wonders; the order and simplicity of a small national world was never quite the same again:

THE GALLEY-SLAVES OF MARSEILLES

We went then to visit the galleys, being about twenty-five in number; the Capitaine of the Galley Royal gave us most courteous entertainment in his cabin, the slaves in the interim playing both loud and soft music very rarely. Then he showed us how he commanded their motions with a nod, and his whistle making them row out. The spectacle was to me new and strange, to see so many hundreds of miserably naked persons, their heads being shaven close, and having only high red bonnets, a pair of coarse canvas drawers, their whole backs and legs naked, doubly chained about their middle and legs, in couples, and made fast to their seats, and all commanded in a trice by an imperious and cruel seaman. One Turk amongst the rest he much favoured, who waited on him in his cabin, but with no other dress than the rest, and a chain locked about his leg, but not coupled. This galley was richly carved and gilded, and most of the rest were very beautiful. After bestowing something on the slaves, the capitaine sent a band of them to give us music at dinner where we lodged. I was amazed to contemplate how these miserable caitiffs lie in their galley crowded together; yet there was hardly one but had some occupation, by which, as leisure and calms permitted, they got some little money, insomuch as some of them have, after many years of cruel servitude, been able to purchase their liberty. The rising-forward and falling-back at their oar, is a miserable spectacle, and the noise of their chains, with the roaring of the beaten waters, has something of strange and fearful in it to one unaccustomed to it. They are ruled and

153

chastized by strokes on their backs and soles of their feet, on the least disorder, and without the least humanity, yet are they cheerful and full of knavery.

John Evelyn
Diary
1644

TESTING THE GROTTO OF THE DOG AT LAGO D'AGNANO

We now came to a lake of about two miles in circumference, environed with hills; the water of it is fresh and sweet on the surface, but salt at bottom; some mineral salt conjectured to be the cause, and it is reported of that profunditude in the middle that it is bottomless. The people call it Lago d'Agnano, from the multitude of serpents which, involved together about the spring, fall down from the cliffy hills into it. It has no fish, nor will any live in it. We tried the old experiment on a dog in the Grotto del Cane, or Charon's Cave; it is not above three or four paces deep, and about the height of a man, nor very broad. Whatever having life enters it, presently expires. Of this we made trial with two dogs, one of which we bound to a short pole to guide him the more directly into the further part of the den, where he was no sooner entered, but – without the least noise, or so much as a struggle, except that he panted for breath, lolling out his tongue, his eyes being fixed: – we drew him out dead to all appearance; but immediately plunging him into the adjoining lake, within less than half an hour he recovered, and swimming to shore, ran away from us. We tried the same on another dog, without the application of the water, and left him quite dead. The experiment has been made on men, as on that poor creature whom Peter of Toledo caused to go in; likewise on some Turkish slaves; two soldiers, and other foolhardy persons, who all perished, and could never be recovered by the water of the lake, as are dogs.

John Evelyn
Diary
1645

BAITING WILD BEASTS IN VIENNA

The diversions for the common people of this place are such as seem hardly fit for a civilized and polished nation to allow. Particularly the *combats*, as they are called, or baiting of wild beasts, in a manner much more savage and ferocious than our bull-baiting,

154

throwing at cocks, and prize-fighting of old, to which the legislature has so wisely and humanely put a stop.

These barbarous spectacles are usually attended by two or three thousand people, among whom are a great number of ladies! . . .

This day, by imperial licence, in the great amphitheatre, at five o'clock will begin the following diversions.

1st. A wild Hungarian ox, in full fire (that is, with fire under his tail, and crackers fastened to his ears and horns, and to other parts of his body) will be set upon by dogs.

2nd. A wild boar will in the same manner be baited by dogs.

3rd. A great bear will immediately after be torn by dogs.

4th. A wolf will be hunted by dogs of the fleetest kind.

5th. A very furious and enraged wild bull from Hungary will be attacked by fierce and hungry dogs.

6th. A fresh bear will be attacked by hounds.

7th. Will appear a fierce wild boar, just caught, which will now be baited for the first time by dogs defended with iron armour.

8th. A beautiful African tiger.

9th. This will be changed for a bear.

10th. A fresh and fierce Hungarian ox.

11th. And lastly, a furious and hungry bear, which has had no food for eight days, will attack a young wild bull, and eat him alive upon the spot; and if he is unable to complete the business, a wolf will be ready to help him.

Charles Burney
Continental Travels
1772

THE PAINTER AMAZES THE ITALIANS

The streets of Palizzi, through which no Englishman perhaps had as yet descended, were swarming with perfectly naked, berry-brown children, and before I reached the taverna I could hardly make my way through the gathering crowd of astonished mahogany Cupids. The taverna was but a single dark room, its walls hung with portraits of little saints, and its furniture a very filthy bed with a crimson velvet gold-fringed canopy, containing an unclothed ophthalmic baby, an old cat, and a pointer dog; all the rest of the chamber being loaded with rolls of linen, guns, gourds, pears, hats, glass tumblers, puppies, jugs, sieves, etc.; still it was a better resting place than the hut at Condufóri, inasmuch as it was free from many intruders. Until P– came, and joined with me in despatching a feeble dinner of eggs, figs, and cucumber, wine and snow, I sate exhibited and displayed for the benefit of the landlord, his wife, and family, who regarded me with unmingled amazement, saying perpetually, *'O donde siete?'* – *'O che fai?'* – *'O chi sei?'* And, indeed, the passage of a stranger through these outlandish places is so unusual an occurrence, that on no principle but one can the aborigines account for your appearance. 'Have you *no* rocks, *no* towns, *no* trees in your own country? Are you not rich? Then what *can* you wish *here*? – *here*, in this place of poverty and incommodo? What *are* you doing? Where *are* you going?' You might talk for ever; but you could not convince them you are not a political agent sent to spy out the nakedness of the land, and masking the intentions of your government under the thin veil of pourtraying scenes, in which they see no novelty, and take no delight.

Edward Lear
Journals of a Landscape Painter in Southern Calabria
1852

FURTHER AMAZEMENT AT THE HOUSE OF BARON RIVETTINI

As usual, we rose before sunrise. 'O Dio! *perchè?*' said the diminutive Baron Rivettini, who was waiting outside the door, lest perhaps we might have attempted to pass through the keyhole. A suite of large drawing-rooms was thrown open, and thither *caffè* was brought with the most punctilious ceremony. My suspicions of last night were confirmed by the great precision with which our passports were examined, and by the minute manner in which every particular relating to our eyes, noses, and chins, was written down; nor was it until after endless interrogatories and more *'perchès'* than are imaginable, that we were released. But our usual practice of taking a small piece of bread with our coffee renewed the universal surprise and distrust of our hosts.

'Pane!' said the Baron, *'perchè* pane? O Cielo!'

'I never take sugar,' said P–, as some was offered to him.

'Sant' Antonio, non prendete zucchero? *Perchè?* O Dio! *perchè* mai non prendete zucchero?'*

'We want to make a drawing of your pretty little town,' said I; and, in spite of a perfect hurricane of *'perchès'*, out we rushed, followed by the globular Baron, in the most lively state of alarm, down the streets, across the river on stepping-stones, and up the opposite bank, from the steep cliffs of which, overhung with oak foliage, there is a beautiful view of Gioiosa on its rock.

'O per carità! O Cielo! O San Pietro! cosa mai volete fare?' said the Baron, as I prepared to sit down.

* 'Do you not take sugar?' etc.

156

'I am going to draw for half an hour,' said I.

'Ma – *perchè?*'

And down I sate, working hard for nearly an hour, during all which time the perplexed Baron walked round and round me, occasionally uttering a melancholy –

'O Signore, ma *perchè?*'

'Signore Baron,' said I, when I had done my sketch, 'we have no towns in our country so beautifully situated as Gioiosa!'

'Ma *perchè?*' quoth he.

I walked a little way, and paused to observe the bee-eaters, which were flitting through the air above me, and under the spreading oak branches.

'Per l'amor del Cielo, cosa guardate? Cosa mai osservate?'* said the Baron.

'I am looking at those beautiful blue birds.'

'*Perchè? perchè? perchè?*'

'Because they are so very pretty, and because we have none like them in England.'

'Ma *perchè? perchè?*'

It was evident that do or say what I would, some mystery was connected with each action and word; so that, in spite of the whimsical absurdity of these eternal what fors and whys, it was painful to see that, although our good little host strove to give scope to his hospitable nature, our stay caused more anxiety than pleasure. We then made all ready to start with the faithful Ciccio, and, not unwillingly, took leave of the Palazzo Rivettini, the anxious Baron thrusting his head from a window, and calling out, 'Ma fermatevi, *perchè? Perchè* andatevi? Statevi a pranzo, *perchè* no? *Perchè* ucelli? *Perchè* disegni? *Perchè* confetti? *Perchè, perchè, perchè, perchè?*'** till the last '*perche*' was lost in distance as we passed once more round the rock, and crossed the river Romano.

Edward Lear
Journals of a Landscape Painter in Southern Calabria
1852

SWEDISH SUPERSTITIONS OF CHILDHOOD

A child must first touch a dog and not a cat, 'that its flesh may heal the more readily'.

And should it take pleasure in bathing, 'it will be lasciviously inclined'.

* 'For the love of Heaven, what are you looking at? What do you perceive?'
** 'But stop – *why* do you go? stay to dinner; *why* not? *why* birds? *why* drawings? *why* sugar-plums,' etc.

If a child is to thrive, 'it should not be *"Loused"* on a Sunday, but, in preference, on a Saturday; and that if only loused at the back of one ear, and not of the other, it will be bitten by a dog'.

Should a child be placed on the back of a horse, 'it will be enabled, in after life, to cure the disorders to which that animal is subject by merely laying its hands on it'.

One must not bear water into a room where there is a young child, or take it in one's arms, or pass between it and the fire, without first touching the latter.

On paying a visit to a woman recently 'confined', one must, on entering the house, place one hand on the oven.

When a child has convulsions consequent on 'teething', 'its clothes must be cast into the fire'. Hence its first garments are usually made of coarse and less valuable materials, so that the loss of them may not be great.

If the mother be overburthened with milk, 'a portion of it must be thrown into the fire'.

L. Lloyd
Peasant Life in Sweden
1870

THE WONDER OF LANGUAGE IN ICELAND

It is half-past nine now, and getting dusk, and all men are asleep in the houses of the poor little stead: out they swarm however in a minute or two, like bees out of a hive, and two smart boys help us to pitch our tents handily enough and laughing with joy all the time. We have the smithy handed over to us for our kitchen, as the fire is out in the kitchen proper: thither Magnússon and I take our tools, and smithy soup and stew, while a grey-head big carle, not very right in his wits, a sort of Barnaby Rudge, blows the bellows for us; we talk to him, I taking some share in the conversation, till apropos of something or other Magnússon says:

'This man (meaning me) can talk Icelandic, you see.'

'Does he,' says the carle, 'I have heard him talk a great deal, and I don't know what he has been saying.'

'Don't you understand this?' say I.

'Yes,' says he.

'Isn't it Icelandic then?'

'Well, I don't know,' says he; 'in all tongues there must be some words like other tongues, and perhaps these are some of those.'

Now was dinner served up, and we sat down to it with a close ring of men all round the tent's mouth watching us, stooping down with their hands on their knees, and now and then dropping a sentence one to the other, such as 'Now he's supping the broth': 'What flesh is that?' and so on. They were queer outlandish people, but quite good-tempered and kind, and most willing to do anything we told them.

Magnússon turned in early after dinner, and was soon snoring; but C. J. F. and I lay on our blankets and smoked: while we were at this the tent-flap was drawn aside, and a big carle, surely Wolf the Unwashed again, put in his head and said:

'I am told off to watch your horses' (which were sent down to the out-meadows to graze). I thought this was a hint for liquor, and so handed him a nip of whiskey; he shook hands with me with effusion, and then I found out that he was drunk already. However he took himself off and we thought him gone: but presently back he comes and says as if he were another person:

'I'm told off to watch the horses.'

Therewith he holds out a little bottle empty now of all but dirt, but labelled (in English) 'Essential oil of Almonds'. I was weak enough to put some whiskey in it, and again he shook my hand and again went away, but not so far but that C. J. F. could see him holding his little bottle up against the bright moon to see how much he had got.

William Morris
Journal of Travel in Iceland
1871

'CANTE HONDO' OF ANDALUSIA

The dirty room, lit by one weak and naked electric-light bulb, is full of wretched, ill-looking men; the proprietor wanders round with a bottle of white wine in his hand filling up glasses. In one corner four men are sitting, with their heads close together, and one notices that one of them is strumming quietly on the table and another is murmuring to himself, occasionally glancing up at his friends, who gravely nod. The finger strumming increases and at last the murmurer breaks into one low word, singing it under the breath in the falsetto voice of the gypsies. 'Ay,' he sings. Or 'Leli, Leli,' prolonging the note like a drawn-out sigh, and when he stops, the strumming of the fingers becomes more rapid, building up emotion and tension and obsession, until at last the low voice cries out a few words that are like an exclamation suddenly coming from some unknown person in the dark. What are the words? They are difficult to understand because the gypsies and, indeed, the Andalusians, drop so many consonants from their words that the speech sounds like a mouthful of small pebbles rubbed against one another:

People and Places

Cada vez que considero
Que me tengo que mori

the voice declaims:

'Whenever I remember that I must die – '

wavering on its words and then suddenly ending; and the strumming begins again until the rapid climax of the song,

Tiendo la capa en el suelo
Y me jarto de dormi

'I spread my cloak on the ground
And fling myself to sleep.'

The manners of the thieves' kitchen are correct and unmarred by familiarity. A yellow-haired and drunken prostitute may be annoying a man by rumpling his hair, but otherwise the dejected customers at three in the morning are sober. One night, in a place like this in the middle of Madrid, we sat next to one of these private artists who was murmuring away to his friends. When we nodded our admiration to the whispering singer, he sang a polite love song of delightful conceit to the lady in our party and asked afterwards for 'the loan of a cigarette until next Thursday'. He became obviously impatient of a gypsy singer and guitarist who had smelt us out. He objected, on the usual Spanish grounds, that the young singer – who also danced – was not keeping to the rigid requirements of his art, and was introducing unclassical extravagance and stunts in order to show off to foreigners. The criticism was audible. The gypsy, egged on by criticism, scornfully tried to surpass himself. He had a weak chest and was inclined to be wild and raucous on his top notes, but he was not bad. Finding himself still mocked by the quiet man in the corner, the gypsy decided to silence him by a crushing performance, which meant a display of whirling fury. He moved one or two chairs, to make room to dance in: the customers murmured at this move. They were prepared to put up with it and hold their hand. But when the gypsy started taking off his jacket – the supreme symbol of male respectability in Spain – there was that alarming and general shout of '¡Eso no!' – 'None of that!' – from everyone in the room, and half the men stood up. The proprietor rushed out at him. The gypsy put back his jacket. He knew he had gone too far. . . .

As the singer of *cante flamenco* proceeds, his friends nod and wait for him to reach the few, difficult ornamental notes of the little song, which has been sung entirely for this short crisis of virtuosity. It breaks suddenly, and then the voice flows cleverly away, to the

murmurs of *Olé, Olé,* by his friends. After a long interval, in which
all seem to be savouring the satisfaction the song has given them,
one of the others takes his turn and so, in this low whispering, like
musing aloud or like grief and sobs, they will pass their evenings.

V. S. Pritchett
The Spanish Temper
1954

*One other kind of public show caught the attention. The brutalities
of life, the vendettas, the tortures, the executions forcibly reminded
all of Europe of the uncertainty of existence and the perennial cruelty
of man:*

THE RUSSIAN WAY WITH TREASON

At this time he [the Czar] was very much busied by searching out
a notable treason in practice and purpose against him by Elizius
Bomelius, the bishop of Novgorod, and some others, discovered by
their servants, tortured upon the *pudkie* or rack, letters written in
ciphers, Latin and Greek, sent three manner of ways to the kings
of Poland and Sweden. The bishop upon examination confessed all.
Bomelius denied all, hoping to fare the better by means of some of
his confederates, as it was thought, favourites near about the king,
whom the Emperor had appointed to attend his son, Czarovich Ivan,
to examine the said Bomelius upon the rack; his arms drawn back
disjointed, and his legs stretched from his middle loins, his back
and body cut with wire whips; confessed much and many things
more than was written or willing the Emperor should know. The
Emperor sent word they should roast him. Taken from the *pudkie*,
and bound to a wooden pool or spit, his bloody cut back and body
roasted and scorched till they thought no life in him, cast into a
sled brought through the castle, I pressed among many others to
see him; cast up his eyes naming Christ; cast into a dungeon and
died there. He lived in great favour and pomp; a skilful mathema-
tician, a wicked man and practicer of much mischief. Most of the
nobles were glad of his despatch, for he knew much by them. He
had conveyed great riches and treasure out of the country, to Wesel,
in Westphalia, where he was born, though brought up in Cambridge. An enemy always to our nation. He had deluded the Emper-
or, making him believe the Queen of England was young, and that
it was very feasible for him to marry her; whereof he was now out
of hope. . . .

The bishop of Novgorod was condemned of his treason, and of coining money and sending it and other treasure to the king of Poland and Sweden; of buggery, of keeping witches and boys and beasts, and other horrible crimes. All his goods, horses, money and treasure, was confiscated to the king, which was much; himself to everlasting imprisonment; lived in a cave with irons on his head and legs, made and painted pictures and images, combs and saddles, with bread and water. Eleven of his confederate servants hanged at the palace gate at Moscow, and his women witches shamefully dismembered and burnt.

Sir Jerome Horsey
Travels
1591

AN EXECUTION IN ROME

After a short delay, some monks were seen approaching to the scaffold from this church; and above their heads, coming on slowly and gloomily, the effigy of Christ upon the cross, canopied with black. This was carried round the foot of the scaffold, to the front, and turned towards the criminal, that he might see it to the last. It was hardly in its place, when he appeared on the platform, bare-footed; his hands bound; and with the collar and neck of his shirt cut away, almost to the shoulder. A young man – six-and-twenty – vigorously made, and well-shaped. Face pale; small dark moustache; and dark brown hair.

He had refused to confess, it seemed, without first having his wife brought to see him; and they had sent an escort for her, which had occasioned the delay.

He immediately kneeled down, below the knife. His neck fitting into a hole, made for the purpose, in a cross plank, was shut down, by another plank above; exactly like the pillory. Immediately below him, was a leathern bag. And into it, his head rolled instantly.

The executioner was holding it by the hair, and walking with it round the scaffold, showing it to the people, before one quite knew that the knife had fallen heavily, and with a rattling sound.

When it had travelled round the four sides of the scaffold, it was set upon a pole in front – a little patch of black and white, for the long street to stare at, and the flies to settle on. The eyes were turned upward, as if he had avoided the sight of the leathern bag, and looked to the crucifix. Every tinge and hue of life had left it in that instant. It was dull, cold, livid, wax. The body also.

Nobody cared, or was at all affected. There was no manifestation of disgust, or pity, or indignation, or sorrow. My empty pockets were tried, several times, in the crowd immediately below the scaffold, as the corpse was being put into its coffin. It was an ugly, filthy, careless, sickening spectacle; meaning nothing but butchery beyond the momentary interest, to the one wretched actor. Yes! Such a sight has one meaning and one warning. Let me not forget it. The speculators in the lottery, station themselves at favourable points for counting the gouts of blood that spirt out, here or there; and buy that number. It is pretty sure to have a run upon it.

Charles Dickens
Pictures from Italy
1846

THE ROBBER VENENO MEETS HIS END

When at length the cathedral clock tolled out the fatal hour, a universal stir of tiptoe expectation took place, a pushing forward to get the best situations. Still ten minutes had to elapse, for the clock of the tribunal is purposely set so much later than that of the cathedral, in order to afford the utmost possible chance of a reprieve. When that clock too had rung out its knell, all eyes were turned to the prison-door, from whence the miserable man came forth, attended by some Franciscans. He had chosen that order to assist at his dying moments, a privilege always left to the criminal. He was clad in a coarse yellow baize gown, the colour which denotes the crime of murder, and is appropriated always to Judas Iscariot in Spanish paintings. He walked slowly on his last journey, half supported by those around him, and stopping often, ostensibly to kiss the crucifix held before him by a friar, but rather to prolong existence – sweet life! – even yet a moment. When he arrived reluctantly at the scaffold, he knelt down on the steps, the threshold of death; – the reverend attendants covered him over with their blue robes – his dying confession was listened to unseen. He then mounted the platform attended by a single friar; addressed the crowd in broken sentences, with a gasping breath – told them that he died repentant, that he was justly punished, and that he forgave his executioner. 'Mio delito me mata, y no *ese hombre*,' – my offence puts me to death, and not *this fellow*; as '*Ese hombre*' is a contemptuous expression, and implies insult, the ruling feeling of the Spaniard was displayed in death against the degraded functionary. The criminal then exclaimed, '*Viva la fé! viva la religion! viva el rey! viva el nombre de Jesus!*' All of which met no echo from those who heard him. His dying cry was '*Viva la Virgen Santisima!*' at these words the devotion to the goddess of Spain burst forth in one general acclamation, '*Viva la Santisima!*' So strong is their feeling towards the Virgin, and so lukewarm their comparative indifference towards their king, their faith, and their Saviour! Meanwhile the executioner, a young man dressed in black, was busied in the preparations for death. The fatal instrument is simple: the culprit is placed on a rude seat; his back leans against a strong upright post, to which an iron collar is attached, enclosing his neck, and so contrived as to be drawn home to the post by turning a powerful screw. The executioner bound so tightly the naked legs and arms of Veneno, that they swelled and became black – a precaution not unwise, as the father of this functionary had been killed in the act of executing a struggling criminal. The priest who attended Veneno was a bloated, corpulent man, more occupied in shading the sun from his own face, than in his ghostly office; the robber sat with a writhing look of agony, grinding his clenched teeth. When all was ready, the executioner took the lever of the screw in both hands, gathered himself up for a strong muscular effort, and, at the moment of a preconcerted signal, drew the iron collar tight, while an attendant flung a black handkerchief over the face – a convulsive pressure of the hands and a heaving of the chest were the only visible signs of the passing of the robber's spirit. After a pause of a few moments, the executioner cautiously peeped under the handkerchief, and after having given another turn to the screw, lifted it off, folded it up, carefully put it into his pocket, and then proceeded to light a cigar.

Richard Ford
Gatherings from Spain
1846

Life and Customs
When all allowances had been made for foreigners and their alien habits, the people of the continent did the same things as were done across the Channel. They worked and lived how they could and suffered and died and mourned. And they had the help of family and friends, and the joy of music and entertainment, and entered into the world of the imagination. To dwell on the differences of strangers encouraged the insularity of the English; to see life in stark and familiar terms preserved the sense of humanity:

FREE TOWNS AND RELIGIOUS FOLLIES

I have already passed a large part of Germany, have seen all that is remarkable in Cologn, Frankfort, Wurtsburg, and this place. 'Tis impossible not to observe the difference between the free towns and those under the government of absolute princes, as all the little sovereigns of Germany are. In the first, there appears an air of commerce and plenty. The streets are well built, and full of people, neatly and plainly dressed. The shops are loaded with merchandise, and the commonalty are clean and cheerful. In the other, you see a sort of shabby finery, a number of dirty people of quality tawdered out; narrow nasty streets out of repair, wretchedly thin of inhabitants, and above half of the common sort asking alms. I cannot help fancying one under the figure of a clean Dutch citizen's wife, and the other like a poor town lady of pleasure, painted and ribboned out in her head-dress, with tarnished silver-laced shoes, a ragged under-petticoat, a miserable mixture of vice and poverty.

German street scene

They have sumptuary laws in this town, which distinguish their rank by their dress, prevent the excess which ruins so many other cities, and has a more agreeable effect to the eye of a stranger than our fashions. I think after the Archbishop of Cambray having declared for them, I need not be ashamed to own, that I wish these laws were in force in other parts of the world.

The Lutherans are not quite free from these follies. I have seen here, in the principal church, a large piece of the cross set in jewels, and the point of the spear, which they told me, very gravely, was the same that pierced the side of our Saviour. But I was particularly diverted in a little Roman-catholic church which is permitted here, where the professors of that religion are not very rich, and consequently cannot adorn their images in so rich a manner as their neighbours. For, not to be quite destitute of all finery, they have dressed up an image of our Saviour over the altar, in a fair full-bottomed wig very well powdered.

Lady Mary Wortley Montagu
Travel Letters
1763

AN ARISTOCRATIC FUNERAL

This goodly ceremony began at nine at night, and did not finish till three this morning; for, each church they passed, they stopped for a hymn and holy water. By the by, some of these choice monks, who watched the body while it lay in state, fell asleep one night, and let the tapers catch fire of the rich velvet mantle lined with ermine and powdered with gold flower-de-luces, which melted the lead coffin, and burned off the feet of the deceased before it wakened them. The French love show; but there is a meanness reigns through it all. At the house where I stood to see this procession, the room was hung with crimson damask and gold, and the windows were mended in ten or dozen places with paper. At dinner they give you three courses; but a third of the dishes is patched up with salads, butter, puff-paste, or some such miscarriage of a dish. None, but Germans, wear fine clothes; but their coaches are tawdry enough for the wedding of Cupid and Pysche. You would laugh extremely at their signs: some live at the *Y grec*, some at Venus's Toilette, and some at the Sucking Cat.

Horace Walpole
Letters
1739

EXPENSE AND IDLENESS IN PARIS

Living at Paris, to the best of my recollection, is very near twice as dear as it was fifteen years ago; and, indeed, this is the case in London; a circumstance that must be undoubtedly owing to an increase of taxes; for I don't find, that, in the articles of eating and drinking, the French people are more luxurious than they were heretofore. I am told the *entrées*, or duties paid upon provision imported into Paris, are very heavy. All manner of butcher's meat and poultry are extremely good in this place. The beef is excellent. The wine which is generally drank is a very thin kind of Burgundy. I can by no means relish their cookery; but one breakfasts deliciously upon their *petit pains*, and their *pâtes* of butter, which last is exquisite.

The common people, and even the bourgeois of Paris, live, at this season, chiefly on bread and grapes, which is undoubtedly very wholesome fare. If the same simplicity of diet prevailed in England, we should certainly undersel the French at all foreign markets; for they are very slothful with all their vivacity; and the great number of their holidays not only encourages this lazy disposition, but actually robs them of one half of what their labour would otherwise produce; so that, if our common people were not so expensive in their living, that is, in their eating and drinking, labour might be afforded cheaper in England than in France. There are three young lusty hussies, nieces or daughters of a blacksmith, that lives just opposite to my windows, who do nothing from morning till night. They eat grapes and bread from seven till nine; from nine till twelve they dress their hair, and are all the afternoon gaping at the window to view passengers. I don't perceive that they give themselves the trouble either to make their beds, or clean their apartment. The same spirit of idleness and dissipation I have observed in every part of France, and among every class of people.

Tobias Smollett
Travels through France and Italy
1766

RURAL HARDSHIP IN FRANCE

Walking up a long hill, to ease my mare, I was joined by a poor woman, who complained of the times, and that it was a sad country. Demanding her reasons, she said her husband had but a morsel of land, one cow, and a poor little horse, yet they had a *franchar (42 lb.)* of wheat, and three chickens, to pay as a quit-rent to one seigneur; and four *franchar* of oats, one chicken and 1 *sou* to pay

to another, besides very heavy tailles and other taxes. She had
seven children, and the cow's milk helped to make the soup. But
why, instead of a horse, do not you keep another cow? Oh, her
husband could not carry his produce so well without a horse; and
asses are little used in the country. It was said, at present, that
*something was to be done by some great folks for such poor ones,
but she did not know who nor how,* but God send us better, *car les
tailles et les droits nous écrasent.* This woman, at no great distance,
might have been taken for sixty or seventy, her figure was so bent,
and her face so furrowed and hardened by labour; but she said she
was only twenty-eight. An Englishman who has not travelled
cannot imagine the figure made by infinitely the greater part of the
countrywomen in France; it speaks, at the first sight, of hard and
severe labour. I am inclined to think, that they work harder than
the men, and this, united with the more miserable labour of bringing a new race of slaves into the world, destroys absolutely all
symmetry of person and every feminine appearance. To what are
we to attribute this difference in the manners of the lower people
in the two kingdoms? To government.

Arthur Young
Travels in France
1789

SOCIABILITY IN FRANCE

A green parrot hung in a cage, in a small court under our window,
and received the compliments and caresses of every one who passed.
It is wonderful how fond the French are of holding conversation
with animals of all descriptions, parrots, dogs, monkeys. Is it that
they choose to have all the talk to themselves, to make propositions,
and fancy the answers; that they like this discourse by signs, by
jabbering, and gesticulation, or that the manifestation of the principle of life without thought delights them above all things? The
sociableness of the French seems to expand itself beyond the level
of humanity, and to be unconscious of any descent. Two boys in the
kitchen appeared to have nothing to do but to beat up the white of
eggs into froth for salads. The labour of the French costs them
nothing, so that they readily throw it away in doing nothing or the
merest trifles. A nice-looking girl who officiated as chamber-maid,
brought in a ripe melon after dinner, and offering it with much
grace and good humour as 'un petit cadeau' (a trifling present) was
rather hurt we did not accept of it.

William Hazlitt
Notes of a Journey through France and Italy, 1826

HOT WEATHER IN GENOA

The view, as I have said, is charming; but in the day you must keep the lattice-blinds close shut, or the sun would drive you mad; and when the sun goes down, you must shut up all the windows, or the mosquitoes would tempt you to commit suicide. So at this time of the year, you don't see much of the prospect within doors. As for the flies, you don't mind them. Nor the fleas, whose size is prodigious, and whose name is Legion, and who populate the coachhouse to that extent that I daily expect to see the carriage going off bodily, drawn by myriads of industrious fleas in harness. The rats are kept away, quite comfortably, by scores of lean cats, who roam about the garden for that purpose. The lizards, of course, nobody cares for; they play in the sun, and don't bite. The little scorpions are merely curious. The beetles are rather late, and have not appeared yet. The frogs are company. There is a preserve of them in the grounds of the next villa; and after nightfall, one would think that scores upon scores of women in pattens, were going up and down a wet stone pavement without a moment's cessation. That is exactly the noise they make. . . .

The men, in red caps, and with loose coats hanging on their shoulders (they never put them on), were playing bowls, and buying sweetmeats, immediately outside the church. When half-a-dozen of them finished a game, they came into the aisle, crossed themselves with the holy water, knelt on one knee for an instant, and walked off again, to play another game at bowls.

Charles Dickens
Pictures from Italy
1846

NEAPOLITAN SIGN-LANGUAGE

Why do the beggars rap their chins constantly, with their right hands, when you look at them? Everything is done in pantomime in Naples, and that is the conventional sign for hunger. A man who is quarrelling with another, yonder, lays the palm of his right hand on the back of his left, and shakes the two thumbs – expressive of a donkey's ears – whereat his adversary is goaded to desperation. Two people bargaining for fish, the buyer empties an imaginary waistcoat pocket when he is told the price, and walks away without a word: having thoroughly conveyed to the seller that he considers it too dear. Two people in carriages, meeting, one touches his lips, twice or thrice, holds up the five fingers of his right hand, and gives a horizontal cut in the air with the palm. The other nods briskly, and goes his way. He has been invited to a friendly dinner at half-past five o'clock, and will certainly come.

All over Italy, a peculiar shake of the right hand from the wrist, with the fore-finger stretched out, expresses a negative – the only negative beggars will ever understand. But, in Naples, those five fingers are a copious language.

All this, and every other kind of out-door life and stir, and mac-caroni-eating at Sunset, and flower-selling all day long, and begging and stealing everywhere and at all hours, you see upon the bright sea-shore, where the waves of the Bay sparkle merrily. But, lovers and hunters of the picturesque, let us not keep too studiously out of view, the miserable depravity, degradation, and wretchedness, with which this gay Neapolitan life is inseparably associated! It is not well to find Saint Giles's so repulsive, and the Porta Capuana so attractive. A pair of naked legs and a ragged red scarf, do not make *all* the difference between what is interesting and what is coarse and odious? Painting and poetising for ever, if you will, the beauties of this most beautiful and lovely spot of earth, let us, as our duty, try to associate a new picturesque with some faint recognition of man's destiny and capabilities; more hopeful, I believe, among the ice and snow of the North Pole, than in the sun and bloom of Naples.

Charles Dickens
Pictures from Italy
1846

LIFE ON THE SAMBRE AND OISE CANAL

These little cities by the canal side had a very odd effect upon the mind. They seemed, with their flower-pots and smoking chimneys, their washings and dinners, a rooted piece of nature in the scene; and yet if only the canal below were to open, one junk after another would hoist sail or harness horses and swim away into all parts of France; and the impromptu hamlet would separate, house by house, to the four winds. The children who played together to-day by the Sambre and Oise Canal, each at his own father's threshold, when and where might they next meet? . . .

All this, simmering in my mind, set me wishing to go aboard one of these ideal houses of lounging. I had plenty to choose from, as I coasted one after another and the dogs bayed at me for a vagrant. At last I saw a nice old man and his wife looking at me with some interest, so I gave them good day and pulled up alongside. I began with a remark upon their dog, which had somewhat the look of a pointer; thence I slid into a compliment on Madame's flowers, and thence into a word in praise of their way of life.

If you ventured on such an experiment in England you would get a slap in the face at once. The life would be shown to be a vile one, not without a side shot at your better fortune. Now, what I like so much in France is the clear, unflinching recognition by everybody of his own luck. They all know on which side their bread is buttered, and take a pleasure in showing it to others, which is surely the better part of religion. And they scorn to make a poor mouth over their poverty, which I take to be the better part of manliness. I have heard a woman in quite a better position at home, with a good bit of money in hand, refer to her own child with a horrid whine as 'a poor man's child'. I would not say such a thing to the Duke of Westminster. And the French are full of this spirit of independence. Perhaps it is the result of republican institutions, as they call them. Much more likely it is because there are so few people really poor that the whiners are not enough to keep each other in countenance.

The people on the barge were delighted to hear that I admired their state. They understood perfectly well, they told me, how Monsieur envied them. Without doubt Monsieur was rich, and in that case he might make a canal-boat as pretty as a villa – *joli comme un château.* And with that they invited me on board their own water villa. They apologized for their cabin; they had not been rich enough to make it as it ought to be.

'The fire should have been here, at this side,' explained the husband. 'Then one might have a writing-table in the middle – books – and' (comprehensively) 'all. It would be quite coquettish - *ça serait tout-à-fait coquet.*' And he looked about him as though the improvements were already made. It was plainly not the first time that he had thus beautified his cabin in imagination; and when next he makes a hit, I should expect to see the writing-table in the middle.

Madame had three birds in a cage. They were no great thing, she explained. Fine birds were so dear. They had sought to get a *Hollandais* last winter in Rouen (Rouen? thought I; and is this whole mansion, with its dogs, and birds, and smoking chimneys, so far a traveller as that? and as homely an object among the cliffs and orchards of the Seine as on the green plains of Sambre?) – they had sought to get a *Hollandais* last winter in Rouen; but these cost fifteen francs apiece – picture it – fifteen francs!

'*Pour un tout petit oiseau* – For quite a little bird,' added the husband.

As I continued to admire, the apologetics died away, and the good people began to brag of their barge and their happy condition in life, as if they had been Emperor and Empress of the Indies. It was, in the Scots phrase, a good hearing, and put me in good-humour with the world. If people knew what an inspiriting thing it is to hear a man boasting, so long as he boasts of what he really has, I believe they would do it more freely and with a better grace.

R. L. Stevenson
An Inland Voyage
1873

THE SOUNDS OF SOUTHERN ITALY

One day came a street organ, accompanied by singing, and how glad I was! The first note of music, this, that I had heard at Cotrone. The instrument played only two or three airs, and one of them became a great favourite with the populace; very soon, numerous voices joined with that of the singer, and all this and the following day the melody sounded, near or far. It had the true characteristics of southern song; rising tremolos, and cadences that swept upon a wail of passion; high falsetto notes, and deep tum-tum of infinite melancholy. Scorned by the musician, yet how expressive of a people's temper, how suggestive of its history! At the moment when this strain broke upon my ear, I was thinking ill of Cotrone and its inhabitants; in the first pause of the music I reproached myself bitterly for narrowness and ingratitude. All the faults of the Italian people are whelmed in forgiveness as soon as their music sounds under the Italian sky.

George Gissing
By the Ionian Sea
1901

MISERIA

'What do people do here?' I once asked at a little town between Rome and Naples; and the man with whom I talked, shrugging his shoulders, answered curtly: *'C'è miseria'* – there's nothing but poverty. The same reply would be given in towns and villages without number throughout the length of Italy. I had seen poverty enough, and squalid conditions of life, but the most ugly and repulsive collection of houses I ever came upon was the town of Squillace. I admit the depressing effect of rain and cloud, and of hunger worse than unsatisfied; these things count emphatically in my case; but under no conditions could inhabited Squillace by other than an

Under the southern sun

offence to eye and nostril. The houses are, with one or two exceptions, ground-floor hovels; scarce a weather-tight dwelling is discoverable; the general impression is that of dilapidated squalor. Streets, in the ordinary sense of the word, do not exist; irregular alleys climb about the rugged heights, often so steep as to be difficult of ascent; here and there a few boulders have been thrown together to afford a footing, and in some places the native rock lies bare; but for the most part one walks on the accumulated filth of ages. At the moment of my visit there was in progress the only kind of cleaning which Squillace knows; down every trodden way and every intermural gully poured a flush of rain-water, with occasionally a leaping torrent or small cascade, which all but barred progress. Open doors everywhere allowed me a glimpse of the domestic arrangements, and I saw that my albergo had some reason to pride itself on superiority; life in a country called civilized cannot easily be more primitive than under these crazy roofs. As for the people, they had a dull, heavy aspect; rare as must be the apparition of a foreigner among them, no one showed the slightest curiosity as I passed, and (an honourable feature of the district) no one begged. Women went about in the rain protected by a shawl-like garment of very picturesque colouring; it had broad yellow stripes on a red ground, the tones subdued to a warm richness.

George Gissing
By the Ionian Sea
1901

CAVE-DWELLERS OF DON DIEGO

The hills out of which they are dug are of clay (argillaceous sand-stone) and it takes two men approximately six weeks to cut out a four-roomed dwelling, one doing the hacking, the other wheeling the earth away. All the ceilings must be coved to carry the weight of the hill above them. The floors are often tiled and the walls are always whitewashed annually just as in the structural houses. More often than not the façade is stone-faced and whitewashed and there is a window in each of the front rooms with no glass in it, but iron bars to exclude thieves, not draughts. Further ventilation is provided by the tall wide round chimney which sticks so oddly out of the top of the little hill.

In Don Diego you can buy a ready-excavated cavehouse, with electricity laid on, for £90 to £120 according to its condition and the number of rooms you require. Should you want to dig out a new one you do not have to pay rent to anybody for your bit of hill. Formerly it was the custom to pay a chicken a year to the lord of the village, Don Diego, by whose name the *pueblo* is still locally known though it is different from the one which appears on the map. To either side of your cave you can cut out hen-houses and stables and sties, according to the requirements of your livestock. There are always some bushes handy on which to hang your washing.

I was asked into the living-room of several caves, each one of which was as clean as a new pin and much more spacious and comfortable than those in some of the ordinary houses and inns I had seen. The cooking facilities were identical: a large open hooded fireplace burning twigs and banked up *paja*. I would like above all to make it clear that the word 'cave' is not synonymous with 'slum' as some people in England seem to think. There are poor people and better-off people and some quite well-to-do people living in troglodyte colonies just as in any of our council house estates; and most of the families living in them are of Spanish and not gypsy blood. In point of fact I only saw two gypsies in Don Diego.

Penelope Chetwode
Two Middle-Aged Ladies in Andalusia
1963

Toil was a universal necessity; it was recognizable in every land. But the leisure and entertainments of a country were local matters and often revealed more individuality than the life of work:

IN A VENETIAN PLAYHOUSE

I was at one of their Play-houses where I saw a Comedie acted. The house is very beggarly and base in comparison of our stately Play-houses in England: neyther can their Actors compare with us for apparell, shewes and musicke. Here I observed certaine things that I never saw before. For I saw women acte, a thing that I never saw before, though I have heard that it hath beene sometimes used in London, and they performed it with as good a grace, action, gesture, and whatsoever convenient for a Player, as ever I saw any mascu-line Actor. Also their noble & famous Cortezans came to this Comedy, but so disguised, that a man cannot perceive them. For they wore double maskes upon their faces, to the end they might not be seene: one reaching from the toppe of their forehead to their chinne and under their necke; another with twiskes of downy or woolly stuffe covering their noses. And as for their neckes round about, they were so covered and wrapped with cobweb lawne and other things, that no part of their skin could be discerned. Upon their heads they wore little blacke felt caps very like to those of the Clarissimoes that I will hereafter speake of. Also each of them wore a black short Taffata cloake. They were so graced that they sate on high alone by themselves in the best roome of all the Play-house. If any man should be so resolute to unmaske one of them but in merriment onely to see their faces, it is said that were he never so noble or worthy a personage, he should be cut in pieces before he should come forth of the roome, especially if he were a stranger. I saw some men also in the Play-house, disguised in the same manner with double vizards, those were said to be the favour-ites of the same Cortezans: they sit not here in galleries as we doe in London. For there is but one or two little galleries in the house, wherein the Cortezans only sit. But all the men doe sit beneath in the yard or court, every man upon his severall stoole, for the which hee payeth a gazet.

Thomas Coryat
Crudities
1611

COUNTRY AMUSEMENTS IN CORSICA

The chief satisfaction of these islanders when not engaged in war or in hunting, seemed to be that of lying at their ease in the open air, recounting tales of the bravery of their countrymen, and singing songs in honour of the Corsicans, and against the Genoese. Even

175

in the night they will continue this pastime in the open air, unless rain forces them to retire into their houses.

The *ambasciadore Inglese*, The English ambassadour, as the good peasants and soldiers used to call me, became a great favourite among them. I got a Corsican dress made, in which I walked about with an air of true satisfaction.

Boswell in the dress of a Corsican chief

The Corsican peasants and soldiers were quite free and easy with me. Numbers of them used to come and see me of a morning, and just go out and in as they pleased. I did everything in my power to make them fond of the British, and bid them hope for an alliance with us. They asked me a thousand questions about my country, all which I chearfully answered as well as I could.

One day they would needs hear me play upon my German flute. To have told my honest natural visitants, Really gentlemen I play very ill, and put on such airs as we do in our genteel companies, would have been highly ridiculous. I therefore immediately com-

plied with their request. I gave them one or two Italian airs, and
then some of our beautiful old Scots tunes, Gilderoy, the Lass of
Patie's Mill, Corn riggs are Bonny. The pathetick simplicity and
pastoral gaiety of the Scots musick, will always please those who
have the genuine feelings of nature. The Corsicans were charmed
with the specimens I gave them, though I may now say that they
were very indifferently performed.

My good friends insisted also to have an English song from me.
I endeavoured to please them in this too, and was very lucky in
that which occurred to me. I sung them 'Hearts of oak are our ships,
'Hearts of oak are our men.' I translated it into Italian for them,
and never did I see men so delighted with a song as the Corsicans
were with the Hearts of oak. 'Cuore di quercia,' cried they, 'bravo
Inglese.' It was quite a joyous riot. I fancied myself to be a recruiting
sea officer. I fancied all my chorus of Corsicans aboard the British
fleet.

James Boswell
Journal of a Tour to Corsica
1768

STREET MUSICIANS IN PRAGUE AND THE BOHEMIAN ATTITUDE TO MUSIC

An itinerant band of street musicians came to salute me at the inn,
the 'Einhorn', or Unicorn, during dinner; they played upon the harp,
violin, and horn, several minuets and polonaises, which were, in
themselves very pretty, though their performance of them added
nothing to the beauty of the compositions; and it will, perhaps,
appear strange to some, that this capital of so musical a kingdom,
in which the genius of each inhabitant has a fair trial, should not
more abound with *great* musicians. It is not, however, difficult to
account for this, if we reflect, that music is one of the arts of peace,
leisure, and abundance; and if, according to M. Rousseau, arts have
flourished most in the most corrupt times, those times must, at
least, have been properous and tranquil. Now, the Bohemians are
never tranquil long together; and even in the short intervals of
peace, their first nobility are attached to the court of Vienna, and
seldom reside in their own capital; so that those among the poorer
sort, who are taught music in their infancy, have no encouragement
to pursue it in riper years, and seldom advance further than to
qualify themselves for the street, or for servitude.

Charles Burney
Continental Travels
1772

Kleinseite, Prague

WANDERING ENTERTAINERS

A troop of strollers once came to the inn where I was staying, in the department of Seine et Marne. There were a father and mother; two daughters, brazen, blowsy hussies, who sang and acted, without an idea of how to set about either; and a dark young man, like a

178

tutor, a recalcitrant house-painter, who sang and acted not amiss. The mother was the genius of the party, so far as genius can be spoken of with regard to such a pack of incompetent humbugs; and her husband could not find words to express his admiration for her comic countryman. 'You should see my old woman,' said he, and nodded his beery countenance. One night they performed in the stable yard, with flaring lamps – a wretched exhibition, coldly looked upon by a village audience. Next night, as soon as the lamps were lighted, there came a plump of rain, and they had to sweep away their baggage as fast as possible, and make off to the barn, where they harboured, cold, wet, and supperless. In the morning a dear friend of mine, who has as warm a heart for strollers as I have myself, made a little collection, and sent it by my hands to comfort them for their disappointment. I gave it to the father; he thanked me cordially, and we drank a cup together in the kitchen, talking of roads and audiences, and hard times.

When I was going, up got my old stroller, and off with his hat. 'I am afraid,' said he, 'that Monsieur will think me altogether a beggar; but I have another demand to make upon him.' I began to hate him on the spot. 'We play again to-night,' he went on. 'Of course I shall refuse to accept any more money from Monsieur and his friends, who have been already so liberal. But our programme of to-night is something truly creditable; and I cling to the idea that Monsieur will honour us with his presence.' And then, with a shrug and a smile: 'Monsieur understands, – the vanity of an artist!' Save the mark! The vanity of an artist! That is the kind of thing that reconciles me to life: a ragged, tippling, incompetent old rogue, with the manners of a gentleman and the vanity of an artist, to keep up his self-respect!

R. L. Stevenson
An Inland Voyage
1873

And lastly, there were the occasions when a country was on show – in its institutions, its great public gatherings, its high rituals of state or religion, its festivals, its artistic performances:

THE FRANKFURT FAIR IN THE EARLY 17TH CENTURY

As for the Fayre it is esteemed, and so indeed is the richest meeting of any place of Christendome, which continueth 14 daies together, and is kept in the moneth of March for the Spring, and in September

179

Nuremburg

for the Autumne. This Autumnall Mart it was my chance to see.
Where I met my thrise-honourable countryman the Earle of Essex,
after he had travelled in divers places of France, Switzerland, and

some parts of high Germany. The riches I observed at this Mart were most infinite, especially in one place called Under Den Roemer, where the Goldsmithes kept their shoppes, which made the most glorious shew that ever I saw in my life, especially some of the Citie of Norimberg. This place is divided into divers other roomes that have a great many partitions assigned unto Mercers and such like artificers, for the exposing of their wares. The wealth that I sawe here was incredible, so great that it was unpossible for a man to conceive it in his minde that hath not first seene it with his bodily eies.

After this I went to the Bookesellers streete where I saw such infinite abundance of bookes, that I greatly admired it. For this street farre excelleth Paules Churchyard in London, Saint James streete in Paris, the Merceria of Venice, and all whatsoever else that I sawe in my travels. In so much that it seemeth to be a very epitome of all the principall Libraries of Europe. Neither is that streete famous for selling bookes onely, and that of all manner of artes and disciplines whatsoever, but also for printing of them. For this city hath so flourished within these fewe yeares in the art of printing, that it is not inferiour in that respect to any city in Christendome, no not to Basil it selfe which I have before so much commended for the excellency of that art. Likewise I visited divers Cloysters full of wares and notable commodities, especially the Cloyster of Saint Bartholmewes Church; where amongst other things I saw a world of excellent pictures, inventions of singular curiosity, whereof most were religious, and such as tended to mortification.

Thomas Coryat
Crudities
1611

FEAST OF CORPUS CHRISTI, PARIS, 1740

Thursday 14. This being *Fête Dieu*, or *Corpus Christi* Day, one of the greatest holidays in the whole year, I went to see the processions, and to hear high mass performed at Notre Dame. I had great difficulty to get thither. Coaches are not allowed to stir till all the processions, with which the whole town swarms, are over. The streets through which they are to pass in the way to the churches, are all lined with tapestry; or, for want of that, with bed-curtains and old petticoats: I find the better sort of people (*les gens comme il faut*) all go out of town on these days, to avoid the *embarras* of going to mass, or the *ennui* of staying at home. Whenever the host stops, which frequently happens, the priests sing a psalm, and all the people fall on their knees in the middle of the street, whether dirty or clean. I readily complied with this ceremony rather than give offence or become remarkable. Indeed, when I went out, I determined to do as other people did, in the streets and church, otherwise I had no business there; so that I found it incumbent on me to kneel down twenty times ere I reached Notre Dame. This I was the less hurt at, as I saw it quite general; and many much better dressed people than myself almost prostrated themselves, while I only touched the ground with one knee. At length I reached the church, where I was likewise a *conformist*; though here I walked about frequently, as I saw others do, round the choir and in the great aisle.

Charles Burney
Continental Travels
1770

A BLEAK VIEW OF ITALIAN OPERA

The women in Italy (so far as I have seen hitherto) are detestably ugly. They are not even dark and swarthy, but a mixture of brown and red, coarse, marked with the small pox, with pug-features, awkward, ill-made, fierce, dirty, lazy, neither attempting nor hoping to please. Italian beauty (if there is, as I am credibly informed, such a thing) is retired, conventual, denied to the common gaze. It was and it remains a dream to me, a vision of the brain! I returned to the inn (the *Pension Suisse*) in high spirits, and made a most luxuriant dinner. We had a wild duck equal to what we had in Paris, and the grapes were the finest I ever tasted. Afterwards we went to the Opera, and saw a *ballet of action* (out-heroding Herod) with all the extravagance of incessant dumb-show and noise, the glittering of armour, the burning of castles, the clattering of horses on and off the stage, and heroines like furies in hysterics. Nothing at Bartholomew Fair was ever in worse taste, noisier, or finer. It was as if a whole people had buried their understandings, their imaginations, and their hearts in their senses; and as if the latter were so jaded and worn out, that they required to be inflamed, dazzled, and urged almost to a kind of frenzy-fever, to feel any thing. The house was crowded to excess, and dark, all but the stage, which shed a dim, ghastly light on the gilt boxes and the audience. Milton might easily have taken his idea of Pandemonium from inside of an Italian Theatre, its heat, its gorgeousness, and its gloom. We were at the back of the pit, in which there was only standing room, and leaned against the first row of boxes, full of the Piedmontese Nobility, who talked fast and loud in their harsh guttural dialect, in spite of the repeated admonitions of 'a gentle usher, Authority by name', who every five seconds hissed some lady of quality and high breeding whose voice was heard with an *eclat* above all the rest. No notice whatever was taken of the acting or the singing (which was any thing but Italian, unless Italian at present means a bad imitation of the French) till a comic dance attracted all eyes, and drew forth bursts of enthusiastic approbation. I do not know the performers' names, but a short, squat fellow (a kind of *pollard* of the green-room) dressed in a brown linsey-woolsey doublet and hose, with round head, round shoulders, short arms and short legs, made love to a fine *die-away* lady, dressed up in the hoops, lappets and furbelows of the last age, and stumped, nodded, pulled and tugged at his mistress with laudable perseverance, and in determined opposition to the awkward, mawkish graces of an Adonis of a rival, with flowing locks, pink ribbons, yellow kerseymere breeches, and an insipid expression of the utmost distress. It was an admirable grotesque and fantastic piece of pantomime humour. The little fellow who played the Clown, certainly entered into the part with infinite adroitness and spirit. He merited the *teres et rotundus* of the poet. He bounded over the stage like a foot-ball, rolled himself up like a hedge-hog, stuck his arms in his sides like fins, rolled his eyes in his head like bullets – and the involuntary plaudits of the audience witnessed the success of his efforts at once to electrify and *stultify* them! The only annoyance I found at Turin was the number of beggars who are stuck against the walls like fixtures, and expose their diseased, distorted limbs, with no more remorse or feeling than if they did not belong to them, deafening you with one wearisome cry the whole day long.

William Hazlitt
Notes of a Journey through France and Italy
1826

SPANISH ART AND SPANISH RELIGION

In the mornings in Madrid we used to go to the Prado. The slow walk was like a swim through the sunlight, and it was a preparation for the intense life we should see there. The Spanish streets prepare one for the unabashed records of Spanish painting – a dwarf, an idiot, a deaf and dumb couple laughing, a pair of blind lovers, a beggar or two have their picaresque place in the unpreoccupied crowds. We used to go, for a moment and mainly to get out of the heat for a minute or two, into any church on our way, and we used to notice the difference of worship between Spanish and Italian

183

custom. For whereas in Italy the churches were places for wandering in and camping in, places used by life, which continually flowed into them from outside, and God's familiar market places, the Spanish churches were used by people with a strong sense of purpose and *tenue*. It was on our way to the Prado that I saw an old man kneeling before the crucified Christ in one of the Jesuit churches, a figure splashed by blood specks and with raw wounds, gaping as they would upon the mortuary slab, the face torn by physical pain, the muscles and tendons stretched. One imagined that the sculptor must have copied a crucified model to be so inflexible an anatomist and that the thought of *imagining* the agony of Christ had been beyond him. Before this figure kneeled an old man, and tears ran down his cheeks like the real-seeming tears glazed on the cheeks of the Christ; and, as he prayed, the old man kissed and caressed the toes, the calves, the knees of the figure and held them also with his hands. What grief, what dread or longing the old man was thus transposing one could not know, but one saw how his prayer depended utterly upon the communication of the senses, that he worshipped carnally and conceived of his acquaintance with God as a physical thing. If he described his God, the description would be physical, and the nature of his God would be a minute copy of his own or, if not a copy, a detailed response in the man's own terms.

V. S. Pritchett
The Spanish Temper
1954

Scenes and Landscapes
Travellers who write books are, in the nature of things, word-painters. They strive to give us those distinctive human scenes and those descriptions of landscape which add colour to the dull but necessary monochrome of narrative, observation and statistics. The portrait lives, but only through the words:

ASCENSION WEEK FESTIVITIES IN VENICE

It was now Ascension-week, and the great mart, or fair, of the whole year was kept, every body at liberty and jolly; the noblemen stalking with their ladies on *choppines*. These are high-heeled shoes, particularly affected by these proud dames, or, as some say, invented to keep them at home, it being very difficult to walk with them; whence, one being asked how he liked the Venetian dames, replied, they were *mezzo carne, mezzo legno*, half flesh, half wood, and he would have none of them. The truth is, their garb is very odd, as seeming always in masquerade; their other habits also totally different from all nations. They wear very long crisp hair, of several streaks and colours, which they make so by a wash, dishevelling it on the brims of a broad hat that has no crown, but a hole to put out their heads by; they dry them in the sun, as one may see them at their windows. In their tire, they set silk flowers and sparkling stones, their petticoats coming from their very arm-pits, so that they are near three quarters and a half apron; their sleeves are made exceeding wide, under which their shift-sleeves as wide, and commonly tucked up to the shoulder, showing their naked arms, through false sleeves of tiffany, girt with a bracelet or two, with knots of point richly tagged about their shoulders and other places of their body, which they usually cover with a kind of yellow veil, of lawn, very transparent. Thus attired, they set their hands on the heads of two matron-like servants, or old women, to support them, who are mumbling their beads. It is ridiculous to see how these ladies crawl in and out of their gondolas, by reason of their *choppines*; and what dwarfs they appear, when taken down from their wooden scaffolds; of these I saw near thirty together, stalking half as high again as the rest of the world. For courtezans, or the citizens, may not wear *choppines*, but cover their bodies and faces with a veil of a certain glittering taffeta, or lustrée, out of which they now and then dart a glance of their eye, the whole face being otherwise entirely hid with it: nor may the common misses take this habit; but go abroad barefaced.

John Evelyn
Diary
1645

ARRIVAL AT OSTEND

I am landed in Flanders, smoked with tobacco, and half poisoned with garlic. Were I to remain ten days at Ostend, I should scarcely have one delightful vision; 'tis so unclassic a place! Nothing but preposterous Flemish roofs disgust your eyes when you cast them upwards: swaggering Dutchmen and mungrel barbers are the first objects they meet with below. I should esteem myself in luck, were the woes of this sea-port confined only to two senses; but, alas; the apartment above my head proves a squalling brattery; and the sounds which proceed from it are so loud and frequent, that a person might think himself in limbo without any extravagance. You must know then, since I am resolved to grumble, that, tired with my passage, I went to the Capuchin church, a large solemn building, in search of silence and solitude; but here again I was disappointed: half a dozen squeaking fiddles fugued and flourished away in the galleries, as many paralytic monks gabbled before the altars, whilst a whole posse of devotees, wrapped in long white hoods and flannels, were sweltering on either side. Such piety in warm weather was no very fragrant circumstance; so I sought the open air again as fast as I was able. The serenity of the evening, joined to the desire I had of casting another glance over the ocean, tempted me to the ramparts . . . but it happened, that I had scarcely begun my apostrophe, before out flaunted a whole rank of officers, with ladies and abbés, and puppy dogs, singing, and flirting, and making such a hubbub, that I had not one peaceful moment to observe the bright tints of the western horizon, or enjoy the series of antique ideas with which a calm sun-set never fails to inspire me. Finding therefore no quiet abroad, I returned to my inn, and should have gone immediately to bed, in hopes of relapsing again into the bosom of dreams and delusions, but the limbo, I mentioned before, grew so very outrageous, that I was obliged to postpone my rest till sugar-plumbs and nursery eloquence had hushed it to repose. At length peace was restored, and about eleven o'clock I fell into a slumber.

William Beckford
Dreams, Waking Thoughts and Incidents
1783

HIGH MASS IN ST PETER'S, ROME

On Sunday, the Pope assisted in the performance of High Mass at St. Peter's. The effect of the Cathedral on my mind, on that second visit, was exactly what it was at first, and what it remains after many visits. It is not religiously impressive or affecting. It is an immense edifice, with no one point for the mind to rest upon; and it tires itself with wandering round and round.

A large space behind the altar, was fitted up with boxes, shaped like those at the Italian Opera in England, but in their decoration much more gaudy. In the centre of the kind of theatre thus railed off, was a canopied dais with the Pope's chair upon it. The pavement was covered with a carpet of the brightest green; and what with this green, and the intolerable reds and crimsons, and gold borders of the hangings, the whole concern looked like a stupendous bonbon. On either side of the altar, was a large box for lady strangers. These were filled with ladies in black dresses and black veils. The gentlemen of the Pope's guard, in red coats, leather breeches, and jack-boots, guarded all this reserved space, with drawn swords, that

Rome, with the Castle of St Angelo and Basilica of St Peter's

were very flashy in every sense; and from the altar all down the nave, a broad lane was kept clear by the Pope's Swiss guard, who wear a quaint striped surcoat, and striped tight legs, and carry halberds like those which are usually shouldered by those theatrical supernumeraries, who never *can* get off the stage fast enough, and who may be generally observed to linger in the enemy's camp after the open country, held by the opposite forces, has been split up the middle by a convulsion of Nature.

I got upon the border of the green carpet, in company with a great many other gentlemen, attired in black (no other passport is necessary), and stood there at my ease, during the performance of mass. The singers were in a crib of wire-work (like a large meat-safe or bird-cage) in one corner; and sang most atrociously. All about the green carpet, there was a slowly moving crowd of people: talking to each other: staring at the Pope through eye-glasses: defrauding one another, in moments of partial curiosity, out of precarious seats on the bases of pillars: and grinning hideously at the ladies. Dotted here and there, were little knots of friars (Francescáni, or Cappuccíni, in their coarse brown dresses and peaked hoods) making a strange contrast to the gaudy ecclesiastics of higher degree, and having their humility gratified to the utmost, by being shouldered about, and elbowed right and left, on all sides. Some of these had muddy sandals and umbrellas, and stained garments: having trudged in from the country. The faces of the greater part were as coarse and heavy as their dress; their dogged, stupid,

187

monotonous stare at all the glory and splendour, having something in it, half miserable, and half ridiculous.

Upon the green carpet itself, and gathered round the altar, was a perfect army of cardinals and priests, in red, gold, purple, violet, white, and fine linen. Stragglers from these, went to and fro among the crowd, conversing two and two, or giving and receiving introductions, and exchanging salutations; other functionaries in black gowns, and other functionaries in court-dresses, were similarly engaged.

There was a great pile of candles lying down on the floor near me, which a very old man in a rusty black gown with an open-work tippet, like a summer ornament for a fireplace in tissue-paper, made himself very busy in dispensing to all the ecclesiastics: one apiece. They loitered about with these for some time, under their arms like walking-sticks, or in their hands like truncheons. At a certain period of the ceremony, however, each carried his candle up to the Pope, laid it across his two knees to be blessed, took it back again, and filed off. This was done in a very attenuated procession, as you may suppose, and occupied a long time. Not because it takes long to bless a candle through and through, but because there were so many candles to be blessed. At last they were all blessed; and then they were all lighted; and then the Pope was taken up, chair and all, and carried round the church.

I must say, that I never saw anything, out of November, so like the popular English commemoration of the fifth of that month. A bundle of matches and a lantern, would have made it perfect.

Charles Dickens
Pictures from Italy
1846

THE DAY OF THE BULL-FIGHT

The *plaza* is the focus of a fire, which blood alone can extinguish; what public meetings and dinners are to Britons, reviews and razzias to Gauls, mass or music to Italians, is this one and absorbing bull-fight to Spaniards of all ranks, sexes, ages, for their happiness is quite catching; and yet a thorn peeps amid these rosebuds; when the dazzling glare and fierce African sun calcining the heavens and earth, fires up man and beast to madness, a raging thirst for blood is seen in flashing eyes and the irritable ready knife, then the passion of the Arab triumphs over the coldness of the Goth: the excitement would be terrific were it not on pleasure bent; indeed there is no sacrifice, even of chastity, no denial, even of dinner, which they will not undergo to save money for the bull-fight. It is the birdlime with which the devil catches many a female and male soul. The men go in all their best costume and *majo*-finery; the distinguished ladies wear on these occasions white lace mantillas, and when heated, look, as the Andaluz wag Adrian said, like sausages wrapped up in white paper; a fan, *abanico*, is quite as necessary to all as it was among the Romans. The article is sold outside for a trifle, and is made of rude paper, stuck into a handle of common cane or stick, and the gift of one to his nutbrown *querida* is thought a delicate attention to her complexion from her swarthy swain; at the same time the lower Salamander classes stand fire much better on these occasions than in action, and would rather be roasted fanless alive *á la auto de fe* than miss these hot engagements.

The seats occupied by the mob are filled more rapidly than our shilling galleries, and the 'gods' are equally noisy and impatient. All ranks are now fused into one mass of homogeneous humanity; their good humour is contagious; all leave their cares and sorrows at home, and enter with a gaiety of heart and a determination to be amused, which defies wrinkled care; many and not over-delicate are the quips and quirks bandied to and fro, with an eloquence more energetic than unadorned; things and persons are mentioned to the horror of periphrastic euphuists; the liberty of speech is perfect, and as it is all done quite in a parliamentary way, none take offence. Those only who cannot get in are sad; these rejected ones remain outside grinding their teeth, like the unhappy ghosts on the wrong side of the Styx, and listen anxiously to the joyous shouts of the thrice blessed within.

Richard Ford
Gatherings from Spain
1846

A MACEDONIAN VILLAGE

Lanes, rich in vegetation, and broken ground, animated by every variety of costume, surround the entrance, and conduct you to streets, narrow and flanked with wooden, two-storied houses, galleried and raftered, with broad-tiled eaves overshadowing groups of Turks or Greeks, recumbent and smoking in the upper floor, while loiterers stand at the shop-doors below: in the kennel are geese in crowds, and the remainder of the street is as fully occupied by goats and buffaloes, as by Turks or Christians. Beyond all this are mountains of grandest form, appearing over the high, dark trees, so that altogether no artist need complain of this as a subject.

Curious to know how one would be off for lodgings in Macedonia, I found Giorgio at the postmaster's house, where, in one of the above-noticed wooden galleries (six or eight silent Turks sat puffing around), I was glad of a basin of tea. But it is most difficult to adopt the Oriental mode of sitting; cross-leggism, from first to last, was insupportable to me, and, as chairs exist not, everything must needs be done at full length. Yet it is a great charm of Turkish character that they never stare or wonder at anything; you are not bored by any questions, and I am satisfied that if you chose to take your tea while suspended by your feet from the ceiling, not a word would be said, or a sign of amazement betrayed; in consequence you soon lose the sense of the absurd so nearly akin to shame, on which you are forced to dwell if constantly reminded of your awkwardness by observation or interrogation.

Whatever may be said of the wretchedly 'bare' state of a Turkish house, or khan, that, in my estimation, is its chief virtue. The closet (literally a closet, being about six feet six inches by four, and perfectly guiltless of furniture) in which my mattress was placed, was floored with new deal, and whitewashed all over, so that a few minutes' sweeping made it a clean, respectable habitation, such as you would find but seldom in Italian Locande of greater pretension. One may not, however, always be so lucky; but if all the route has accommodation like this, there will be no great hardship to encounter.

Edward Lear
Journals of a Landscape Painter in Greece and Albania
1851

THE SPIRIT OF CHANGE IN NAPLES

The odours remain; the stalls of sea-fruit are as yet undisturbed, and the jars of the water-sellers; women still comb and bind each other's hair by the wayside, and meals are cooked and eaten *al fresco* as of old. But one can see these things elsewhere, and Santa Lucia was unique. It has become squalid. In the grey light of this sad billowy sky, only its ancient foulness is manifest; there needs the golden sunlight to bring out a suggestion of its ancient charm.

Has Naples grown less noisy, or does it only seem so to me? The men with bullock carts are strangely quiet; their shouts have nothing like the frequency and spirit of former days. In the narrow and thronged Strada di Chiaia I find little tumult; it used to be deafening. Ten years ago a foreigner could not walk here without being assailed by the clamour of *cocchieri*; nay, he was pursued from street to street, until the driver had spent every phrase of importunate invitation; now, one may saunter as one will, with little disturbance. Down on the Piliero, whither I have been to take my passage for Paola, I catch but an echo of the jubilant uproar which used to amaze me. Is Naples really so much quieter? If I had time I would go out to Fuorigrotta, once, it seemed to me, the noisiest village on earth, and see if there also I observed a change. It would not be surprising if the modernisation of the city, together with the state of things throughout Italy, had a subduing effect upon Neapolitan manners. In one respect the streets are assuredly less gay. When I first knew Naples one was never, literally never, out of hearing of a hand-organ; and these organs, which in general had a peculiarly dulcet note, played the brightest of melodies; trivial, vulgar, if you will, but none the less melodious, and dear to Naples. Now the sound of street music is rare, and I understand that some police provision long since interfered with the soft-tongued instruments. I miss them; for, in the matter of music, it is with me as with Sir Thomas Browne. For Italy the change is significant enough; in a few more years spontaneous melody will be as rare at Naples or Venice as on the banks of the Thames.

Happily, the musicians errant still strum their mandoline as you dine. The old trattoria in the Toledo is as good as ever, as bright, as comfortable. I have found my old corner in one of the little rooms, and something of the old gusto for *zuppa di vongole*. The homely wine of Posillipo smacks as in days gone by, and is commended to one's lips by a song of the South.

George Gissing
By the Ionian Sea
1901

TOBOGGANING TO KLOSTERS

The memory of things seen and done in moonlight is like the memory of dreams. It is as a dream that I recall the night of our tobogganing to Klosters, though it was full enough of active energy. The moon was in her second quarter, slightly filmed with very high thin clouds, that disappeared as night advanced, leaving the sky and stars in all their lustre. A sharp frost, sinking to three degrees above zero Fahrenheit, with a fine pure wind, such wind as here they call 'the mountain breath'. We drove to Wolfgang in a two-horse sledge, four of us inside, and our two Christians on the box. Up there, where the Alps of Death descend to join the Lakehorn Alps, above the Wolfswalk, there is a world of whiteness – frozen ridges, engraved like cameos of aërial onyx upon the dark, star-tremulous sky; sculptured buttresses of snow, enclosing hollows filled with diaphanous shadow, and sweeping aloft into the upland fields of pure clear drift. Then came the swift descent, the plunge into the pines, moon-silvered on their frosted tops. The battalions of spruce that climb those hills defined the dazzling snow from which they sprang, like the black tufts upon an ermine robe. At the proper moment we left our sledge, and the big Christian took his reins in hand to follow us. Furs and greatcoats were abandoned. Each stood forth tightly accoutred, with short coat, and clinging cap, and gaitered legs for the toboggan. Off we started in line, with but brief interval between, at first slowly, then glidingly, and when the impetus was gained, with darting, bounding, almost savage swiftness – sweeping round corners, cutting the hard snow-path with keen runners, avoiding the deep ruts, trusting to chance, taking advantage of smooth places, till the rush and swing and downward swoop became mechanical. Space was devoured. Into the massy shadows of the forest, where the pines joined overhead, we pierced without a sound, and felt far more than saw the great rocks with their icicles; and out again, emerging into moonlight, met the valley spread beneath our feet, the mighty peaks of the Silvretta and the vast blue sky. On, on, hurrying, delaying not, the woods and hills rushed by. Crystals upon the snow-banks glittered to the stars. Our souls would fain have stayed to drink these marvels of the moonworld, but our limbs refused. The magic of movement was upon us, and eight minutes swallowed the varying impressions of two musical miles. The village lights drew near and nearer, then the sombre village huts, and soon the speed grew less, and soon we glided to our rest into the sleeping village street.

J. A. Symonds
Sketches and Studies in Italy and Greece
1898

SAND, RAIN AND SOUP IN SOUTH RUSSIA

Each day's progress led where the sand was soft, deep, and unrideable. We generally fell upon a village in a panting and exhausted condition. Several hundred children would sweep down upon us, halloing, screeching, and yelling in the most excited manner. They formed, however, a picturesque guard, so that we usually advanced upon the local inn in some state. Village inns, however, rarely sold anything but vodka, a fiery, throat-scorching spirit made from rye, which the muzjik tossed off as the average Scot disposes of his 'mornin'' of whiskey.

Passing decrepit post-houses, stationed every ten versts or so along the road, we reached Kherson, that goes tumbling down a hill into the river Dnieper. There was no bridge across the Dnieper, so we crossed to Aleschki by a tiny, panting, overcrowded, and much overloaded packet. We wedged our bicycles between some bales, and then sat on a pile of sacks reaching as high as the funnel, while the steamer grunted a way through the swirling water.

We had been told our route beyond Aleschki would be almost impassable. The information was correct. This part of the country must have once been the bed of the sea. It was nothing but a sandy waste, with odd shrivelled bushes to give point to the desolation. Now and then we came across a decent twenty yards of hard soil, but a billow of sand always brought us up sharp. That day the distance we covered was something under twenty miles.

We reached Bolschoi-Kopani dead beat. There wasn't an inn in the place. We had practically to take forcible possession of a cottage. Having pitched our camp we scoured round for food. Luck led us to the police station. There somebody had read about us in a Russian paper. Further, we produced a formidable official document, written in Russian by the Acting British Consul-General at Odessa, stating who and what we were. That cleared the path. We were invited to stay in the police station. Tea, bread, eggs, grapes, and melons were produced in abundance. The village big-wigs came and gazed admiringly as we ate, and probed our muscles as a Yorkshire farmer probes a prize ox. I have since often wondered whether oxen like being probed.

Now a spell of shocking weather set in, and when it rains in South Russia you would think the reservoirs of the heavens had suddenly burst. If anybody has ever attempted to cycle across a clayey, warpy Lincolnshire potato field, he may have a shadowy idea of the sort of ground over which we had to travel. Add to this the fact that for three nights we never removed our clothing, but slept in vile hovels on cold, dank ground, and then, without much exaggeration, the experience may be admitted to be getting near the disagreeable.

We crawled into one village to find we could get nothing to eat but a stale chunk of black bread. As we were forcing our way through the adamant food a shrivelled, spectacled man came into the hut to have a peep at us.

He thought we were French. He dashed to his house and returned with a Russian-French dictionary. He was an astute man. We roamed through those pages till we made him understand we should like soup. '*Da, da!*' (yes, yes) he shouted, wagging his head and beaming. We pulled the book about and roamed up and down its

193

pages. United efforts discovered the Russian for mutton, and ten minutes later we hailed the equivalent for eggs!

'*Da, da!*' yelled our friend, and in an ecstasy of delight he conducted us over the way. We were lucky. He danced about and his wife danced also; and soon we had a lunch of soup, mutton, eggs, and milk, which we consumed while the whole village was pressing its accumulated mass of noses against the window-panes.

That afternoon the rain came down in sheets. We had to walk. The mud clogged the machines, and we often stopped to clear it away. We gathered dirt as quickly as a rolling snowball gathers snow. Our shoes and stockings were caked with muck. It was hard to even lift our feet. So bad, indeed, was the road in places that the bicycles, as a sort of protest, declined to run, and we were obliged to carry them.

J. F. Fraser
Round the World on a Wheel
1899

RAIN ON THE CALABRIAN HILLS

And still it rains. . . .

It will be some time before the picture of this room is effaced from my memory. It is vaulted in the old style and the white walls are adorned with American calendars and advertisements; under foot, a richly tinted pavement of Vietri tiles, broken yellows and blues, dating from the days ere the modern Neapolitan ware, with its undignified patterns and anæmic coloration, was exported hitherward. The massive furniture gives an air of well-being to the place; upon a commodious wardrobe stands the inevitable *lar familiaris* – the infant Jesus – under a glass case, and a fine selection of *caccia-cavallo* cheeses, suspended from iron hooks in the ceiling, reminds me of the dinner awaiting me at home.

Pazienza!

The good folk have retired into the kitchen region, leaving me in sole possession here; the rain seems to have chilled their wonted communicativeness; an uncle, too, has lately arrived from over the sea and certain family questions, I understand, are likely to become acute. Every ten minutes a polite young girl thrusts her head within the doorway to ask if I am comfortable. Incomparably more comfortable, I reply, than out of doors. Perhaps the signore would prefer to write with a *calamaio*? No, the signore will continue to use his pencil, having learned long ago that neither pens, ink, nor blotting-paper can be procured in the kingdom of Italy.

194

'A long letter,' she ventures to remark.

'To my *sposa* – at Naples.'

'My bridegroom,' she informs me, 'is twenty-two and has been twice to New York. The last time he returned with three thousand francs, and the next time we go together.'

'Is that your engagement ring?'

'Yes; it cost him thirty-five francs. And this watch and chain, a hundred and fifteen francs. And now he has bought me twenty pairs of silk stockings and says I must put them on, all twenty, when we go through the American custom-house, else the officials will steal them. I think it will be difficult.'

'The *sposo* might wear half of them.'

'Oh, he! He could wear forty, but he won't.'

Of course she will marry him; they all do; the old maid, so familiar to lovers of English landscape, is practically unknown in Siren land. But the husbands seldom take them to America, contenting themselves with sending money home and returning every now and then. Like the women of Lemnos, these sit manless among their rocks, doing a little laundry work and an infinity of chattering.

The Italian field-labourers wash their clothes but never their bodies; the Russian, their bodies but never their clothes; ours – neither. . . .

Dirty clothes, says Saint Jerome, are a sign of a clean mind. Saint Bernard, if I remember rightly, lays down a contrary maxim. . . .

'Perhaps the signore would like to read? I have brought a book.'

Ariosto!

God forgive me; I cannot read Ariosto on a rainy day, and when the sun shines, he always contrives to make himself invisible. A most retiring disposition these heroic poets have.

Norman Douglas
Siren Land
1911

LIFE OF THE SPANISH 'MESTA'

The traveller who goes by the Extremadura road into Andalusia, through Trujillo, where Cortés was born, and on to Plasencia, pretty Cáceres with its garrison, and Badajoz, has a sight of the real army that Castile sent out to attack the economy of southern Spain. He will see the survival of the *mesta*, the large migratory flocks of sheep slowly moving south or north according to the season. One sits under the cork trees of the wilderness talking to the shepherds. Spare, austere men, they wear tooled leather aprons over their trouser legs and carry the crook and the horn slung on their shoul-

ders. Formed by the lonely life, they speak with majestic yet simple
courtliness to strangers in a clear sagacious Castilian of complete
purity. It is delivered slowly.

'Man! How are you? And how are your family? Is your wife well?
Are your children well? I am glad. You are right to rest in the heat.
If God does not want to send the rain, one may complain above,
below, everywhere, but that will not make the rain come.'

'What do you think of life?'

'Nothing.'

'Nothing?'

'Nothing. When one eats well, good. When one eats badly – well,
good too. One remains living until one is put into the ground. Then
nothing, man – nothing.'

The white dust of the flocks clouds on the roads, and before the
motor-car came in, whenever one saw a cloud of dust on the Castilian tracks it was made by the flocks of sheep. The flocks of the
mesta, the great enemies of the dying farmer, and the enemies of
Andalusia, were the sheep charged by Don Quixote when he
thought they were an army led by hostile knights. In his madness,
Don Quixote was right. When wool ousted silk as the profitable
product – and the Arabs introduced the merino sheep into Spain –
the famous wool monopoly of the *mesta* was founded in Castile, and
Andalusian ruin was complete.

V. S. Pritchett
The Spanish Temper
1954

CAMPAIGNING IN CRETE

The villages through which we stalked with our guns cocked were
silent and unreal as fictions of snow and ivory. We tiptoed under
their arches and down lanes that twisted round the corners in paper
fans of steps. Sometimes we stopped with circumspection at the
shutter of a friend's house, and after a brief entry and whispered
confabulation, continued on our way. Metallic chestnut woods gleamed; the oleanders and poplars were doubly silver by the beds of
shrunk streams. The water had dwindled to a net of quicksilver in
a waste of boulders that Venetian or Turkish bridgebuilders had
spanned with pale arcs of masonry. At a loop in a valley, hundreds
of frogs drowned the nightingales, the drilling of crickets and the
little owl's hesitant note. We heard dogs in the villages and brief
jangles as flocks woke and fell asleep again in folds half-way to the
sky. These sounds strung a thread of urgency and collusion through
the peace of the night. Sometimes we would lie flat with held breath

in a cactus clump or among the rocks or flattened against a wall under an archway till the footfalls of an enemy patrol died away; noticing that the boulders, the dust and the white plaster were still warm from the daylight hours of midsummer basking. The smell of many herbs filled the air. (A fragrance so powerful that it surrounds the island with a halo of sweet smells several miles in radius; it told us when we were stealthily approaching Crete by sea on moonless nights from the stinking desert, and long before we could descry the great silhouette, that we were getting near.) Advancing through the warm night, we had the sleeping island to ourselves and a thousand charms hung in the air. We reached our rendezvous before dawn; a broken-down water mill, a small monastery thinly monked by warlike brethren, a solitary chapel, a circular threshing floor, or a lonely goat-fold on a high ledge. There would be challenge and answer, a scrape of hobnails on rock and a clinking of arms as dark figures rose gleaming from the shadows into the moonlight; then salutations and fifty whiskery embraces. When the moon set, the sky lifted a wing of radiance at the other end of the heavens. The shafts of the sun sloped up into the air from many clefts between the eastern vertebrae of the island. When the beams fell horizontal, our meeting place was anchored like a flying carpet in the line of their advance. We killed the microbe of the night with swigs of raki and watched these massed prisms of light shooting beyond us for overlapping leagues until they hit and ignited the white ibex-haunts in the west. The peaks all round us sent darker volleys of shadow along their path, all of them streaming westwards and tilting down into the canyons until the whole intervening labyrinth was filled with early light.

Patrick Leigh Fermor
Roumeli: Travels in Northern Greece
1966

ESCAPING THE HEAT IN VENICE

The heats were so excessive in the night, that I thought myself several times on the point of suffocation, tossed about like a wounded fish, and dreamt of the devil and Senegal. Towards sunrise, a faint breeze restored me to life and reason. I slumbered till late in the day; and, the moment I was fairly awake, ordered my gondolier to row out to the main ocean, that I might plunge into its waves, and hear and see nothing but waters round me. We shot off, wound amongst a number of sheds, shops, churches, casinos, and palaces, growing immediately out of the canals, without any apparent foundation. No quay, no terrace, not even a slab is to be seen before the doors; one step brings you from the hall into the bark, and the vestibules of the stateliest structures lie open to the waters, and level with them. I observed several, as I glided along, supported by rows of well-proportioned pillars, adorned with terms and vases, beyond which the eye generally discovers a grand court, and sometimes a garden. In about half an hour, we had left the thickest cluster of isles behind, and, coasting the palace of St Mark opposite to San Giorgio Maggiore, whose elegant frontispiece was painted on the calm waters, launched into the blue expanse of sea. I ran to the smooth sands, extending to both sides out of sight, cast off my clothes, and dashed into the waves; which were coursing one another with a gentle motion, and breaking lightly on the shores. The tide rolled over me as I lay floating about, buoyed up by the water, and carried me wheresoever it listed. My ears filled with murmuring undecided sounds; my limbs stretched languidly on the surf, rose, or sunk, just as it swelled or subsided. In this passive, senseless state I remained, till the sun cast a less intolerable light, and the fishing vessels, lying out in the bay at great distance, spread their sails and were coming home.

William Beckford
Dreams, Waking Thoughts and Incidents
1783

THE APPROACH TO ROME

Dreary flats thinly scattered over the ilex, and barren hillocks crowned by solitary towers, were the only objects we perceived for several miles. Now and then, we passed a flock of black, ill-favoured sheep feeding by the way's side, near a ruined sepulchre; just such animals as an antient would have sacrificed to the Manes. Sometimes we crossed a brook, whose riplings were the only sounds which broke the general stillness, and observed the shepherds' huts on its banks, propped up with broken pedestals and marble friezes. I entered one of them, whose owner was abroad, tending his herds, and began writing upon the sand, and murmuring a melancholy song. Perhaps, the dead listened to me from their narrow cells. The living I can answer for; they were far enough removed. You will not be surprized at the dark tone of my musings in so sad a scene; especially, as the weather lowered; and you are well acquainted how greatly I depend upon skies and sunshine. To-day I had no blue firmament to revive my spirits; no genial gales, no aromatic plants to irritate my nerves, and give at least a momentary animation. Heath and furze were the sole vegetation which covers this endless wilderness. Every slope is strewed with the relics of a happier period; trunks of trees, shattered columns, cedar beams, helmets of bronze, skulls, and coins, are frequently dug up together. I cannot boast of having made any discoveries, nor of sending you any novel intelligence. You knew before how perfectly the environs of Rome were desolate, and how completely the papal government contrives to make its subjects miserable. But, who knows that they were not just as wretched, in those boasted times we are so fond celebrating? I could have spent the whole day by the rivulet, lost in dreams and meditations; but recollecting my vow, I ran back to the carriage, and drove on. The road, not having been mended, I believe, since the days of the Cæsars, would not allow our motions to be very precipitate. When you gain the summit of yonder hill, you will discover Rome, said one of the postillions: up we dragged; no city appeared. From the next, cried out a second; and so on, from height to height, did they amuse my expectations. I thought Rome fled before us, such was my impatience; till, at last, we perceived a cluster of hills, with green pastures on their summits, inclosed by thickets, and shaded by flourishing ilex. Here and there, a white house, built in the antient style, with open porticos, that received a faint gleam of the evening sun, just emerged from the clouds and tinting the meads below. Now, domes and towers began to discover themselves in the valley, and St Peter's to rise above the magnificent roofs of the Vatican. Every step we advanced, the scene extended; till, winding suddenly round the hill, all Rome opened to our view. A spring flowed opportunely into a marble cistern close by the way; two cypresses and a pine waved over it. I leaped out, poured water upon my hands, and then, lifting them up to the sylvan Genii of the place, implored their protection.

William Beckford
Dreams, Waking Thoughts and Incidents
1783

PARIS

In winter, you are splashed all over with the mud; in summer, you are knocked down with the smells. If you pass along the middle of the street, you are hurried out of breath; if on one side, you must pick your way no less cautiously. Paris is a vast pile of tall and dirty alleys, of slaughter-houses and barbers' shops – an immense suburb huddled together within the walls so close, that you cannot see the loftiness of the buildings for the narrowness of the streets, and where all that is fit to live in, and best worth looking at, is turned out upon the quays, the boulevards, and their immediate vicinity.

Paris, where you can get a sight of it, is really fine. The view from the bridges is even more imposing and picturesque than ours, though the bridges themselves and the river are not to compare with the Thames, or with the bridges that cross it. The mass of public buildings and houses, as seen from the Pont Neuf, rises around you on either hand, whether you look up or down the river, in huge, aspiring, tortuous ridges, and produces a solidity of impression and a fantastic confusion not easy to reconcile. The clearness of the air, the glittering sunshine, and the cool shadows add to the enchantment of the scene. In a bright day, it dazzles the eye like a steel mirror. The view of London is more open and extensive; it lies lower, and stretches out in a lengthened line of dusky magnificence. After all, it is an ordinary town, a place of trade and business. Paris is a splendid vision, a fabric dug out of the earth, and hanging over it. The stately, old-fashioned shapes and jutting angles of the houses give it the venerable appearance of antiquity, while their texture and colour clothe it in a robe of modern splendour. It looks like a collection of palaces, or of ruins!

William Hazlitt
Notes of a Journey through France and Italy
1826

GOING TOWARDS THE MOUNTAINS

For the last two days, we had seen great sullen hills, the first indications of the Alps, lowering in the distance. Now, we were rushing on beside them: sometimes close beside them: sometimes with an intervening slope, covered with vineyards. Villages and small towns hanging in mid-air, with great woods of olives seen through the light open towers of their churches, and clouds moving slowly on, upon the steep acclivity behind them; ruined castles perched on every eminence; and scattered houses in the clefts and gullies of the hills; made it very beautiful. The great height of these, too, making the buildings look so tiny, that they had all the charm of elegant models; their excessive whiteness, as contrasted with the brown rocks, or the sombre, deep, dull, heavy green of the olive-tree; and the puny size, and little slow walk of the Lilliputian men and women on the bank; made a charming picture. There were ferries out of number too; bridges; the famous Pont d'Esprit, with I don't know who many arches; towns where memorable wines are made; Vallence, where Napoleon studied; and the noble river, bringing at every winding turn new beauties into view.

A mountain vista

There lay before us, that same afternoon, the broken bridge of Avignon, and all the city baking in the sun; yet with an under-done-pie-crust, battlemented wall, that never will be brown, though it bake for centuries.

Charles Dickens
Pictures from Italy
1846

THE ROMAN CAMPAGNA

A short ride from this lake, brought us to Ronciglione; a little town like a large pig-sty, where we passed the night. Next morning at seven o'clock, we started for Rome.

As soon as we were out of the pig-sty, we entered on the Campagna Romana; an undulating flat (as you know) where few people can live; and where, for miles and miles, there is nothing to relieve the terrible monotony and gloom. Of all kinds of country that could, by possibility, lie outside the gates of Rome, this is the aptest and fittest burial-ground for the Dead City. So sad, so quiet, so sullen; so secret in its covering up of great masses of ruin, and hiding them; so like the waste places into which the men possessed with devils used to go and howl, and rend themselves, in the old days of Jerusalem. We had to traverse thirty miles of this Campagna; and for two-and-twenty we went on and on, seeing nothing but now and then a lonely house, or a villanous-looking shepherd: with matted hair all over his face, and himself wrapped to the chin in a frowsy brown mantle: tending his sheep. At the end of that distance, we stopped to refresh the horses, and to get some lunch, in a common malaria-shaken, despondent little public-house, whose every inch of wall and beam, inside, was (according to custom) painted and decorated in a way so miserable that every room looked like the wrong side of another room, and, with its wretched imitation of drapery, and lop-sided little daubs of lyres, seemed to have been plundered from behind the scenes of some travelling circus.

Charles Dickens
Pictures from Italy
1846

A MACEDONIAN PROSPECT

The village, composed of scattered wooden houses, is full of prettiness; but fierce dogs, when the rain ceases, prevent my going near any of the buildings, as much as a multitude of wasps do my eating a peaceful dinner on the khan platform. Yet, spite of dogs, wasps, and wet, distances veiled over by cloud, and all other hindrances, there is opportunity to remark in the scene before me a subject somewhat ready-made to the pencil of a painter, which is marvellous: it is not easy to say why it is so, but a picture it is. Copy what you see before you, and you have a picture full of good qualities, in its way – a small way, we grant – a mere village landscape in a classic land. Blocks of old stone – squared and cut long ago in other ages – overgrown with very long grass, clustering lentisk, and glossy leaves of arum, form your nearest foreground; among them sit and lie three Soorudgís, white-kilted, red, brown, and orange-jacketed, red-capped, piped, moustached, blue-gaitered, bare-footed. Your next distance is a flat bit of sandy ground, with a winding road, and on it one white-capoted shepherd: beyond, yet still near the eye, is a tract of gray earth, something between common and quarry, broken into miniature ravines, and tufted with short herbage: here, lie some fifty white and black sheep, and a pair of slumbering dogs, while near them two shepherd-boys are playing on a simple reed-like flute, such as Praxiteles might have put in a statue's hands. A little farther on you see two pale stone and wooden houses, with tiled roofs, mud walls, and long galleries hung with many a coloured bit of carpet. Close by, in gardens, dark-cloaked women are gathering gourds, and placing them on the roofs to dry. Gray, tall willows, and spreading planes overshade these houses, and between the trees you catch a line of pale lilac plain, with faint blue hills of exquisite shapes – the last link in the landscape betwixt earth and heaven.

Edward Lear
Journals of a Landscape Painter in Greece and Albania
1851

A JOURNEY THROUGH THE CORSICAN FOREST

At 3 the top of the pass, or Bocca di Larone, is reached; and here the real forest of Bavella commences, lying in deep cup-like hollow between this and the opposite ridge, the north and south side of the valley being formed by the tremendous columns and peaks of granite (or porphyry?), the summits of which are seen above the hills from Sarténe, and which stand up like two gigantic portions of a vast amphitheatre, the whole centre of which is filled with a thick forest of pine. These crags, often as I have drawn their upper outline from the pass I have been ascending to-day, are doubly awful and magnificent now that one is close to them, and, excepting the heights of Serbal and Sinai, they exceed in grandeur anything of the kind I have ever seen, the more so that at present the distance is half hidden with dark cloud, heavily curtaining all this singular valley; and the tops of the huge rock buttresses being hidden, they seem as if they connected heaven and earth. At times the mist is suddenly lifted like a veil, and discloses the whole forest – as it were in the pit of an immense theatre confined between towering rock-wall, and filling up with its thousands of pines all the great hollow (for it is hardly to be called a valley in the ordinary sense

of the term) between those two screens of stupendous precipices. As
I contemplate the glory of this astonishing amphitheatre, I decide
to stay at least another day within its limits, and I confess that a
journey to Corsica is worth any amount of expense and trouble, if
but to look on this scene alone. At length I have seen that of which
I have heard so much – a Corsican forest.

Edward Lear
Journal of a Landscape Painter in Corsica
1868

RAIN ON THE TREES

The whole day was showery, with occasional drenching plumps.
We were soaked to the skin, then partially dried in the sun, then
soaked once more. But there were some calm intervals, and one
notably, when we were skirting the forest of Mormal, a sinister
name to the ear, but a place most gratifying to sight and smell. It
looked solemn along the river-side, drooping its boughs into the
water, and piling them up aloft into a wall of leaves. What is a
forest but a city of nature's own, full of hardy and innocuous living
things, where there is nothing dead and nothing made with the
hands, but the citizens themselves are the houses and public monuments? There is nothing so much alive, and yet so quiet, as a
woodland; and a pair of people, swinging past in canoes, feel very
small and bustling by comparison.

And surely, of all smells in the world, the smell of many trees is
the sweetest and most fortifying. The sea has a rude pistolling sort
of odour, that takes you in the nostrils like snuff, and carries with
it a fine sentiment of open water and tall ships; but the smell of a
forest, which comes nearest to this in tonic quality, surpasses it by
many degrees in the quality of softness. Again, the smell of the sea
has little variety, but the smell of a forest is infinitely changeful;
it varies with the hour of the day, not in strength merely, but in
character; and the different sorts of trees, as you go from one zone
of the wood to another, seem to live among different kinds of atmosphere. Usually the rosin of the fir predominates. But some woods
are more coquettish in their habits; and the breath of the forest of
Mormal, as it came aboard upon us that showery afternoon, was
perfumed with nothing less delicate than sweetbriar.

R. L. Stevenson
An Inland Voyage
1873

'GREAT, DREARY RUSSIA'

And now at last we were in a land without roads – great dreary
Russia. There were only cart tracks across wide stretches of uninter-
esting steppes, spreading like billows for weary miles and seeming
to have no end; tracks, indeed, with nothing definite about them,
fifty yards wide, and every driver selecting his own course.

One night, when about three or four miles from our halting place,
we lost our way. Darkness overtook us quickly; there was nothing
but desolateness on either side, and some of the paths we followed
as experiments simply led to a hill and there stopped. Opening a
map and trying to find a way by the light of some rapidly ignited
matches, while one argued one route was our road and another was
certain it was nothing of the sort, generally ended in burning a
hole in the map, followed by a prodigious waste of temper.

We trundled our machines over rough ground to the summit of
a mound, and there we found nothing but three disconsolate and
decrepit windmills that creaked mockery at us. Far down in the
valley was heard the yelping of dogs. Slowly we wended forward;
at last we saw a cottage. Could they tell us the way? The cottagers
were in a fright; the children screamed, the door was hastily bolted,
and through the window could be seen the whole family huddled
in a corner shaking with terror. So we went on.

We laid hold of a man who, happily, did not think us from another
world. He knew what we wanted, and led us down a precipitous
path, so steep that at times we had to carry the bicycles and cautiously feel our way through the blackness with our heels. At last,
panting and exhausted, we reached a shanty that served the village
as hotel.

We did not find this region attractive. Squalidness, dejection,
and hopelessness were everywhere. The houses were dirty hovels,
thatched with black twigs, and in front was generally a sickening
pool of slime in which grunting hogs wallowed. The people were
sullen, as though they knew their lot was misery and semi-
starvation, and recognized the futility of attempting to put things
straight.

J. F. Fraser
Round the World on a Wheel
1899

THE ALTIPIANO DI POLLINO

I was glad to descend once more, and to reach the *Altipiano di
Pollino* – an Alpine meadow with a little lake (the merest puddle),

bright with rare and beautiful flowers. It lies 1780 metres above sea-level, and no one who visits these regions should omit to see this exquisite tract encircled by mountain peaks, though it lies a little off the usual paths. Strawberries, which I had eaten at Rossano, had not yet opened their flowers here; the flora, boreal in parts, has been studied by Terracciano and other Italian botanists.

It was on this verdant, flower-enamelled mead that, fatigued with the climb, I thought to try the powers of my riding mule. But the beast proved vicious; there was no staying on her back. A piece of string attached to her nose by way of guiding-rope was useless as a rein; she had no mane wherewith I might have steadied myself in moments of danger, and as to seizing her ears for that purpose, it was out of the question, for hardly was I in the saddle before her head descended to the ground and there remained, while her hinder feet essayed to touch the stars. After a succession of ignominious and painful flights to earth, I complained to her owner, who had been watching the proceedings with quiet interest.

'That lady-mule,' he said, 'is good at carrying loads. But she has never had a Christian on her back till now. I was rather curious to see how she would behave.'

'*Santo Dio!* And do you expect me to pay four francs a day for having my bones broken in this fashion?'

'What would you, sir? She is still young – barely four years old. Only wait! Wait till she is ten or twelve.'

To do him justice, however, he tried to make amends in other ways. And he certainly knew the tracks. But he was a returned emigrant, and when an Italian has once crossed the ocean he is useless for my purposes, he has lost his savour – the virtue has gone out of him. True Italians will soon be rare as the dodo in these parts. These *americani* cast off their ancient animistic traits and patriarchal disposition with the ease of a serpent; a new creature emerges, of a wholly different character – sophisticated, extortionate at times, often practical and in so far useful; scorner of every tradition, infernally wide awake and curiously deficient in what the Germans call 'Gemüt' (one of those words which we sadly need in our own language). Instead of being regaled with tales of Saint Venus and fairies with the Evil Eye, I learnt a good deal about the price of food in the Brazilian highlands.

The only piece of local information I was able to draw from him concerned a mysterious plant in the forest that 'shines by night'. I dare say he meant the *dictamnus fraxinella*, which is sometimes luminous.

Norman Douglas
Old Calabria, 1915

A SPANISH CHAOS

At Guadix one looks out upon one of those panoramas of rock and mountain which are the delight of the peninsula. It is a land for the connoisseur of landscape, for in no other European country is there such variety and originality. Here Nature has had vast space, stupendous means, and no restraint of fancy. One might pass a lifetime gazing at the architecture of rock and its strange colouring, especially the colouring of iron, blue steel, violet and ochreous ores, metallic purples, and all the burned, vegetable pigments. These landscapes frighten by their scale and by the suggestion of furrowed age, geological madness, malevolence, and grandeur. One is looking out on a perspective of causeways, going up step by step, for miles at a time to the steeper walls of the horizon, and each step worn into short vertical furrows. The colours, gold, brown, violet, and slate by turns, the aspect that of a wrinkled face, the scale gigantic. One is entering upon those mountains that seem like the coarse, plated hides of the rhinoceros. The sight appals. Once pine forests were here, but now the only pines one sees are a few 'trees', no more than a foot high, planted in the stones of the roadside. Rain is a mere memory. Worse appears if one goes down to Almería by way of Vera. These lumpish mountains open at one point into an enormous amphitheatre, twenty or thirty miles across, perhaps more. Range after range surrounds it until the farthest are a faint ring of tossing flames. One can only say that Nature has died and that only its spectre, geology, remains. It is simply chaos. Ravines are gashed out, sudden pinnacles of rock shoot up five hundred feet into the air; their tops seem to have been twisted by whirlwind, the Ice Age has eaten into their sides, the Great Flood has broken their splitting foundations into gullies. This amphitheatre is the abandoned home of fire and water, for only wind lives there now; the colours are of the rusted knife, the bruised body, the bleached bone. For miles the road follows a watercourse which lies in a deep and ragged ravine, but it is simply a shingle bed with no water in it. There has not been water for years. It is rare to see a human being; and if one does, it will be a man making a fire in the bed, burning, I suppose, the soda plant. Or one will pass the solitary lime-burner.

V. S. Pritchett
The Spanish Temper
1954

207

Destinations

From the Renaissance onwards, the great goal of English travellers
was Italy. Less fortunate men and women might whirl about to the
fringes of Europe – even as far as Russia, or Albania, or Iceland.
But the mass gravitated slowly towards the sun of Italy – towards a
classical past and a present intellectual curiosity, towards a land of
broken statues and wine and intrigue and art and political insta-
bility. From the Channel ports the travellers spread out by many
routes. Wandering steps took them to many destinations. But on the
large scale of history all these seemed but punctuation marks on the
road to Italy:

CHEAP PICTURES AND RARE BEASTS IN ROTTERDAM

We arrived late at Rotterdam, where was their annual mart or fair,
so furnished with pictures (especially landscapes and drolleries, as
they call those clownish representations), that I was amazed. Some
of these I bought, and sent into England. The reason of this store
of pictures, and their cheapness, proceeds from their want of land
to employ their stock, so that it is an ordinary thing to find a
common farmer lay out two or three thousand pounds in this commodity. Their houses are full of them, and they vend them at their
fairs to very great gains. Here I first saw an elephant, who was
extremely well disciplined and obedient. It was a beast of a monstrous size, yet as flexible and nimble in the joints, contrary to the
vulgar tradition, as could be imagined from so prodigious a bulk
and strange fabric; but I most of all admired the dexterity and
strength of its proboscis, on which it was able to support two or
three men, and by which it took and reached whatever was offered
to it; its teeth were but short, being a female, and not old. I was
also shown a pelican, or *onocratulas* of Pliny, with its large gullets,
in which he kept his reserve of fish; the plumage was white, legs
red, flat, and film-footed: likewise a cock with four legs, two rumps
and vents: also a hen which had two large spurs growing out of her
sides, penetrating the feathers of her wings.

John Evelyn
Diary
1641

OVERCROWDING AND LUXURY IN VIENNA

This town, which has the honour of being the emperor's residence,
did not at all answer my ideas of it, being much less than I expected

to find it; the streets are very close, and so narrow, one cannot observe the fine fronts of the palaces, though many of them very well deserve observation, being truly magnificent. They are built of fine white stone, and are excessively high. For as the town is too little for the number of the people that desire to live in it, the builders seem to have projected to repair that misfortune, by clapping one town on the top of another, most of the houses being of five, and some of them six stories. You may easily imagine, that the streets being so narrow, the rooms are extremely dark; and, what is an inconveniency much more intolerable, in my opinion, there is no house that has so few as five or six families in it. The apartments of the greatest ladies, and even of the ministers of state, are divided, but by a partition, from that of a taylor or shoemaker; and I know nobody that has above two floors in any house, one for their own use, and one higher for their servants. Those that have houses of their own, let out the rest of them to whoever will take them; and thus the great stairs (which are all of stone) are as common and as dirty as the street. 'Tis true, when you have once travelled through them, nothing can be more surprisingly magnificent than the apartments. They are commonly a *suite* of eight or ten large rooms, all inlaid, the doors and windows richly carved and gilt, and the furniture, such as is seldom seen in the palaces of sovereign princes in other countries. Their apartments are adorned with hangings of the finest tapestry of Brussels, prodigious large looking-glasses in silver frames, fine japan tables, beds, chairs, canopies, and window curtains of the richest Genoa damask or velvet, almost covered with gold lace or embroidery. The whole is made gay by pictures, and vast jars of japan china, and in almost every room large lustres of rock crystal.

Lady Mary Wortley Montagu
Travel Letters
1763

A BAD CASE OF MISERY

I arrived at Utrecht on a Saturday evening. I went to the Nouveau Château d'Anvers. I was shown up to a high bedroom with old furniture, where I had to sit and be fed by myself. At every hour the bells of the great tower played a dreary psalm tune. A deep melancholy seized upon me. I groaned with the idea of living all winter in so shocking a place. I thought myself old and wretched and forlorn. I was worse and worse next day. All the horrid ideas that you can imagine, recurred upon me. I was quite unemployed and had not a soul to speak to but the clerk of the English meeting, who could do me no good. I sunk quite into despair. I thought that at length the time was come that I should grow mad. I actually believed myself so. I went out to the streets, and even in public could not refrain from groaning and weeping bitterly. I said always, 'Poor Boswell! is it come to this? Miserable wretch that I am! what shall I do?' – O my friend, pause here a little and figure to yourself what I endured. I took general speculative views of things; all seemed full of darkness and woe. Tortured in this manner, I determined to leave Utrecht, and next day returned to Rotterdam in a condition that I shudder to recollect.

James Boswell
Boswell in Holland
1763

CATHOLIC COLOGNE

Clouds of dust hindered my making any remarks on the exterior of this celebrated city. But, of what avail are stately palaces, broad streets, or airy markets, to a town which can boast of such a treasure, as the bodies of those three wise sovereigns, who were star-led to Bethlehem? Is not this circumstance enough to procure it every respect? I really believe so, from the pious and dignified contentment of its inhabitants. They care not a hair of an ass's ear, whether their houses be gloomy, and ill contrived; their pavements overgrown with weeds, and their shops with filthiness; provided the carcases of Gaspar, Melchior, and Balthazar might be preserved with proper decorum. Nothing, to be sure, can be richer, than the shrine which contains these precious relics. I payed my devotions before it, the moment I arrived; this step was inevitable; had I omitted it, not a soul in Cologne but would have cursed me for a Pagan. Do you not wonder at hearing of these venerable bodies, so far from their native country? I thought them snug in some Arabian pyramid, ten feet deep in spice; but, you see, one can never tell what is to become of one, a few ages hence . . . Very well; I think I had better stop in time, to tell you, without further excursion, that we set off after dinner for Bonn. Our road-side was lined with beggarly children, high convent-walls, and scarecrow crucifixes; lubberly monks, dejected peasants, and all the delights of Catholicism. Such scenery not engaging a great share of my attention, I kept gazing at the azure, irregular mountains, which bounded our view; and, in thought, was already transported to their summits.

William Beckford
Dreams, Waking Thoughts and Incidents
1783

The ports of the French coast were the main gates of entry for English travellers visiting the south of Europe. Crossing France, they did not forget to take in the city of Paris, the one place outside Italy which rivalled the fame of Venice and Rome:

PARISIAN DISADVANTAGES

This great city appears to be in many respects the most ineligible and inconvenient for the residence of a person of small fortune of any that I have seen; and vastly inferior to London. The streets are very narrow, and many of them crowded, nine-tenths dirty, and all without foot pavements. Walking, which in London is so pleasant and so clean, that ladies do it every day, is here a toil and a fatigue to a man, and an impossibility to a well-dressed woman. The coaches are numerous, and, what are much worse, there are an infinity of one horse cabriolets, which are driven by young men of fashion and their imitators, alike fools, with such rapidity as to be real nuisances, and render the streets exceedingly dangerous, without an incessant caution. I saw a poor child run over and probably killed, and have been myself many times blackened with the mud of the kennels. The beggarly practice, of driving a one horse booby hutch about the streets of a great capital, flows either from poverty or a wretched and despicable economy; nor is it possible to speak of it with too much severity. If young noblemen at London were to drive their chaises in streets without footways, as their brethren do at Paris, they would speedily and justly get very well thrashed, or rolled in the kennel. This circumstance renders Paris an ineligible residence for persons, particularly families that cannot afford to keep a coach; a convenience which is as dear as at London. The *fiacres* (hackney coaches) are much worse than at that city; and chairs there are none, for they would be driven down in the streets. To this circumstance also it is owing, that all persons of small or moderate fortune are forced to dress in black, with black stockings; the dusky hue of this in company is not so disagreeable a circumstance as being too great a distinction; too clear a line drawn in company between a man that has a good fortune, and another that has not. With the pride, arrogance, and ill temper of English wealth this could not be borne; but the prevailing good humour of the French eases all such untoward circumstances. Lodgings are not half so good as at London, yet considerably dearer. If you do not hire a whole suite of rooms at an hotel, you must probably mount three, four, or five pair of stairs, and in general have nothing but a bedchamber. After the horrid fatigue of the streets, such an

211

elevation is a delectable circumstance. You must search with trouble before you will be lodged in a private family, as gentlemen usually are at London, and pay a higher price. Servants' wages are about the same as at that city. It is to be regretted that Paris should have these disadvantages, for in other respects I take it to be a most eligible residence for such as prefer a great city.

Arthur Young
Travels in France
1787

STREET SCENES OF PARIS

Paris, 28. – What said the witty Frenchwoman? – *Paris est le lieu du monde où l'on peut le mieux se passer de bonheur;* – in that case it will suit me admirably.

29. – We walked and drove about all day: I was amused. I marvel at my own versatility when I think how soon my quick spirits were excited by this gay, gaudy, noisy, idle place. The different appearance of the streets of London and Paris is the first thing to strike a stranger. In the gayest and most crowded streets of London the people move steadily and rapidly along, with a grave collected air, as if all had some business in view; *here*, as a little girl observed the other day, all the people walk about 'like ladies and gentlemen going a visiting': the women well-dressed and smiling, and with a certain jaunty air, trip along with their peculiar mincing step, and appear as if their sole object was but to show themselves; the men ill-dressed, slovenly, and in general ill-looking, lounge indolently, and stare as if they had no other purpose in life but to look about them.

July 12 – *Quel est à Paris le suprême talent? celui d'amuser: et quel est le suprême bonheur? l'amusement.*

Then *le suprême bonheur* may be found every evening from nine to ten, in a walk along the Boulevards, or a ramble through the Champs Elysées, and from ten to twelve in a salon at Tortoni's.

What an extraordinary scene was that I witnessed to-night! how truly *French!* Spite of myself and all my melancholy musings, and all my philosophic allowances for the difference of national character, I was irresistibly compelled to smile at some of the farcical groups we encountered. In the most crowded parts of the Champs Elysées this evening,(Sunday), there sat an old lady with a wrinkled yellow face and sharp features, dressed in a flounced gown of dirty white muslin, a pink sash and a Leghorn hat and feathers. In one hand she held a small tray for the contribution of amateurs, and in the other an Italian bravura, which she sung or rather screamed out with a thousand indescribable shruggings, contortions, and grimaces, and in a voice to which a cracked tea-kettle, or a 'brazen candlestick turned', had seemed the music of the spheres. A little farther on we found two elderly gentlemen playing at see-saw; one an immense corpulent man of fifteen stone at least, the other a thin dwarfish animal with grey mustachios, who held before him what I thought was a child, but on approaching, it proved to be a large stone strapped before him, to render his weight a counterpoise to that of his huge companion. We passed on, and returning about half an hour afterwards down the same walk, we found the same venerable pair pursuing their edifying amusement with as much enthusiasm as before.

Before the revolution, sacrilege became one of the most frequent crimes. I was told of a man who, having stolen from a church the silver box containing the consecrated wafers, returned the wafers next day in a letter to the Curé of the parish, *having used one of them to seal his envelope.*

Anna Jameson
Diary of an Ennuyée
1826

The main stream of travellers in Europe went by the river valleys of the Rhine and Danube, or across France to the Alps and the Mediterranean. The large, harsh land of Spain stood apart from these well-trodden routes. Conservative, Moorish, proud, ultra-Catholic, centre of a failed empire, Spain was and remained the oddity of the European powers. Hardly any place in Europe felt more strange:

THE FIRST IMPACT OF SPAIN

For myself, the passage through Pancorbo is the moment of conversion. Now one meets Spain, the indifferent enemy. Out of this clear, rare air the sun seems to strike, the senses become sharper, the heart and mind are excited, the spirit itself seems to clear itself of dreams and to dry out like the crumbling soil; one feels oneself invaded by the monotonous particularity of Spanish speech. It is a dry, harsh, stone-cracking tongue, a sort of desert Latin chipped off at the edges by its lisped consonants and dry-throated gutturals, its energetic 'r's,' but opened by its strong emphatic vowels. It is a noble tongue with a cynical parrot-like sound as it is spoken around one, but breaking out of this mutter

The Escorial, Spain

into splendid emphasis. It is a language in which one hears each word, at any rate in Castile – in Andalusia whole sentences wash down the throat like the sound of water coming out of a bottle – and each word is as distinct and hard as a pebble. Castilian is above all a language which suggests masculinity, or at any rate it is more suited to the male voice than to the feminine voice, which, in Spain, shocks one by its lack of melody. Spaniards tell one that when they return from northern Europe, where the voices of women are melodious and sweet, they are shocked by the hard, metallic, or gritty, nasal voices of their Spanish women, and by the shouting pitch all Spaniards use.

On the steppe one is electrified, and one can feel one's life burn faster. Like the Spaniards, one sinks into torpor in the heat and one wakes out of it in flashes of intensity. So clear is the air, so hard the hard line of the horizon, that when the sun goes down, it seems to drop suddenly like a golden stone. The sun seems to be a separate thing, the sky a thing, the air a thing that can be felt in particular grains in the fingers or that can be caught, as even on windless days it keeps up its continual hard, wing-like flutter under the nose. In the green north all sights are bound together by mist, by the damp, and by greenness itself, and our minds dream on from one thing to another in a delicious vagueness, a compassionate blur; but in the south, and in Spain especially, there is no misting of the sights, everything is separate, everything is exposed, and there is no mercy extended from one sight to another. There is

214

no illusion, no feeding of the imagination, and, in this sense, no perspective. The tree, the house, the tower, the wall stand equal in sight.

V. S. Pritchett
The Spanish Temper
1954

If Spain was the unknown close at hand, the further unknown was the historical borderland between Europe and Asia Minor. Here the famous antiquity of Greece had become submerged beneath Turkish rule. After the fall of Constantinople in 1453, the famous places retained their names and a debased Greek culture, but the reality was Asian and Moslem and as alien to most Englishmen as the economy of the moon:

CONSTANTINOPLE

Truly I may say of Constantinople,

A painted Whoore, the maske of deadly sin,
Sweet faire without, and stinking foule within.

For indeed outwardly it hath the fairest show, and inwardly in the streets being narrow, and most part covered, the filthiest & deformed buildings in the world; the reason of its beauty, is, because being situate on moderate prospective heights, the universall textures, a farre off, yeeld a delectable show, the covertures being erected like the backe of a Coach after the Italian fashion with guttered tyle. But being entred within, there is nothing but a stinking deformity, and a loathsome contrived place; without either internall domesticke furniture, or externall decorements of fabricks palatiatly extended. Notwithstanding that for its situation, the delicious wines, & fruits, the temperate climat, the fertile circumjacent fields, and for the Sea Marmora, and pleasant Asia on the other side: it may truely be called the Paradice of the earth.

William Lithgow
Rare Adventures and Painful Peregrinations
1632

INFIDEL SMYRNA

Smyrna, I think, may be called the chief town and capital of that Grecian race against which you will be cautioned so carefully as soon as you touch the Levant. You will say that I ought not to confound as one people the Greeks living under a constitutional government with the unfortunate Rayahs who 'groan under the Turkish yoke', but I can't see that political events have hitherto produced any strongly marked difference of character. If I could venture to rely (this I feel that I cannot at all do) upon my own observation, I should tell you that there were more heartiness and strength in the Greeks of the Ottoman Empire than in those of the new kingdom: the truth is that there is a greater field for commercial enterprise, and even for Greek ambition, under the Ottoman sceptre than is to be found in the dominions of Otho. Indeed the people, by their frequent migrations from the limits of the constitutional kingdom, to the territories of the Porte, seem to show, that, on the whole, they prefer 'groaning under the Turkish yoke', to the honour of 'being the only true source of legitimate power', in their own land.

For myself I love the race; in spite of all their vices, and even in spite of all their meannesses, I remember the blood that is in them, and still love the Greeks. The Osmanlees are, of course, by nature, by religion, and by politics, the strong foes of the Hellenic people; and as the Greeks, poor fellows! happen to be a little deficient in some of the virtues which facilitate the transaction of commercial business (such as veracity, fidelity, etc.), it naturally follows that they are highly unpopular with the European merchants. Now these are the persons through whom, either directly or indirectly, is derived the greater part of the information which you gather in the Levant, and therefore you must make up in your mind to hear an almost universal and unbroken testimony against the character of the people, whose ancestors invented Virtue. And strange to say, the Greeks themselves do not attempt to disturb this general unanimity of opinion by any dissent on their part. Question a Greek on the subject, and he will tell you at once that the people are 'traditori', and will then, perhaps, endeavour to shake off his fair share of the imputation, by asserting that his father had been dragoman to some foreign embassy, and that he (the son), therefore, by the law of nations, had ceased to be Greek.

Alexander Kinglake
Eothen
1844

ARRIVING IN SALONIKI

Instantly the wildest confusion seized all the passive human freight.
The polychromatic hareem arose, and moved like a bed of tulips in
a breeze; the packed Wallachians, and Bosniacs, and Jews started
crampfully from the deck, and disentangled themselves into numerous boats; the Consular Esiliati departed; and lastly, I and my
dragoman prepared to go, and were soon at shore, though it was
not so easy to be upon it. Saloníki is inhabited by a very great
proportion of Jews; nearly all the porters in the city are of that
nation, and now that the cholera had rendered employment scarce,
there were literally crowds of black-turbaned Hebrews at the
water's edge, speculating on the possible share of each in the conveyance of luggage from the steamer. The enthusiastic Israelites
rushed into the water, and seizing my arms and legs, tore me out
of the boat, and up a narrow board, with the most unsatisfactory
zeal; immediately after which they fell upon my enraged dragoman
in the same mode, and finally throwing themselves on my luggage,
each portion of it was claimed by ten or twelve frenzied agitators,
who pulled this way and that way, till I who stood apart, resigned
to whatever might happen, confidently awaited the total destruction
of my *roba*. From yells and pullings to and fro, the scene changed
in a few minutes to a real fight, and the whole community fell to
the most furious hair-pulling, turban-clenching, and robe-tearing,
till the luggage was forgotten, and all the party was involved in
one terrific combat. How this exhibition would have ended I cannot
tell, for in the heat of the conflict my man came running with a
half-score of Government Kawási, or police; and the way in which
they fell to belabouring the enraged Hebrews was a thing never to
be forgotten. They took a deal of severe beating from sticks and
whips before they gave way, and eventually some six or eight were
selected to carry the packages of the Ingliz, which I followed into
the city, not unvexed at being the indirect cause of so much strife.

In Saloníki there is a Locanda – a kind of hotel – the last dim
shadow of European 'accommodation' between Stamboul and Cát-
taro: it is kept by the politest of Tuscans, and the hostess is the
most corpulent and blackest of negresses.

Edward Lear
Journals of a Landscape Painter in Greece and Albania
1851

ATHENS

Athens is in a state of headlong flux.

On every return, I discover that a fresh crop of cafés, taverns, restaurants and bookshops, all of which had seemed as firm as the pyramids, has vanished, and the reshuffle of landmarks sends me careering from street to street like a fox with all his earths stopped. A few years ago, after only six months' absence, I arrived from Piraeus and headed for a corner of the Syntagma – Constitution Square, the agora of modern Athens – intending to alight at my old refuge, the oddly named Hotel New Angleterre. (This was a dilapidated yellow building in the engaging neo-classical style of the reign of King Otho, at the pillared and pedimented door of which Victorian travellers would assemble on horseback for the journeys to Sunium, Marathon and Delphi. Flaking plaster cary-atids supported the balcony, a stubborn lift groaned within, the hall ceiling was frescoed with centaurs, and along cobwebby vistas eccentric plumbing ran wild.) But it had gone, vanished as com-pletely as if djinns had whisked it away, and there stood a gleaming cube of concrete and a brand-new café full of tubular chairs whose backs were strung like harps with plastic thongs:

> Thank God, thank God that I wasn't there
> When they blew off the roof of the New Angleterre . . .

I crossed the blazing Syntagma to the Hotel Grande Bretagne thirsting for a consolation drink. Nothing would have changed there, I thought. But I was wrong. The old hall had acquired the vast and aseptic impersonality of an airport lounge. (Greek archi-tects have forgotten the saying of their ancestor Isocrates about man being the measure of all things.) Beyond it, the bar, the noisy and delightful meeting place of many years, had become a silent waste dotted with lost and furtively murmuring customers dwarfed by their habitat into air-conditioned skaters on a rink of marble. Only the old barmen were unchanged. They looked puzzled and wistful. . . . (At the moment of writing, this bar is closed yet again for its fifth alteration in the last three decades. I wonder what Babylonian phoenix will emerge.)

It is the same everywhere. The Athenians look on this constant change with a mixture of abstract pride and private bewilderment. Much of this architectural restlessness may spring from the sudden boom in tourism. One's first reaction to this new windfall is delight: Greek economy needs these revenues; one's second is sorrow. Econ-omists rejoice, but many an old Athenian, aware of the havoc that tourism has spread in Spain and France and Italy, lament that this

The Acropolis at Athens

gregarious passion, which destroys the object of its love, should have chosen Greece as its most recent, most beautiful, perhaps its most fragile victim. They know that in a few years it has turned dignified islands and serene coasts into pullulating hells. In Athens itself, many a delightful old tavern has become an alien nightmare of bastard folklore and bad wine. Docile flocks converge on them, herded by button-eyed guides, Mentors and Stentors too, with all Manchester, all Lyons, all Cologne and half the Middle-West at heel. The Athenians who ate there for generations have long since fled. (Fortunately, many inns survive unpolluted; but for how long? The works of writers mentioning these places by name should be publicly burnt by the common hangman.) Greece is suffering its most dangerous invasion since the time of Xerxes. Bad money may drive out good, but good money, in this case, drives out everything.

Patrick Leigh Fermor
Roumeli: Travels in Northern Greece
1966

And at last our English traveller sets foot in Italy. By reason of history and religion, Rome was the chief magnet, at least to the imagination. But most travellers found, in fact, that Venice was the greater attraction, and in that faithless, beautiful and improbable city they found an epitome of European achievement:

WHAT TO EXPECT IN ITALY

And being now in *Italy that great limbique of working braines*, he must be very circumspect in his cariage, for she is able to turne a *Saint* into a *Devill*, and deprave the best natures, if one will abandon himselfe [to pleasure], and become a prey to dissolut courses and wantonnesse.

The *Italian*, being the *greatest embracer of pleasures*, [and] the *greatest Courtier of Ladies* of any other. Here he shall find Vertue and Vice, Love and Hatred, Atheisme and Religion in their extremes; being a witty contemplative people; and *Corruptio optimi est pessima. Of the best wines you make your tartest vinegar.*

Italy hath beene alwayes accounted the Nurse of *Policy, Learning, Musque, Architecture*, and *Limining*, with other perfections, which she disperseth to the rest of *Europe*, nor was the *Spaniard* but a dunce, till he had taken footing in her, and so grew subtilized by co-alition with her people. *She is the prime climat of Complement, which oftentimes puts such a large distance 'twixt the tongue and the heart, that they are seldome relatives, but they often give the lye one to another; some will offer to kisse the hands, which they wish were cut off, and would be content to light a candle to the Devill, so they may compasse their owne ends: He is not accounted essentially wise, who openeth all the boxes of his breast to any.*

The *Italians* are for the most part of a speculative complexion (as I have discovered more amply in another *Discours*) and *he is accounted little lesse than a foole, who is not melancholy once a day; they are only bountifull to their betters, from whom they may expect a greater benefit; To others the purse is closest shut, when the mouth openeth widest, nor are you like to get a cup of wine there, unlesse your grapes be known to be in the wine-presse.*

James Howell
Instructions for Forraine Travell
1642

THE SAD STATE OF ROME

I am very glad that I see Rome while it yet exists; before a great number of years are elapsed, I question whether it will be worth seeing. Between the ignorance and poverty of the present Romans, every thing is neglected and falling to decay; the villas are entirely out of repair, and the palaces so ill kept, that half the pictures are spoiled by damp. At the villa Ludovisi is a large oracular head of red marble, colossal, and with vast foramina for the eyes and mouth:

– the man that showed the palace said it was *un ritratto della famiglia?* The Cardinal Corsini has so thoroughly pushed on the misery of Rome by impoverishing it, that there is no money but paper to be seen. He is reckoned to have amassed three millions of crowns. You may judge of the affluence the nobility live in, when I assure you, that what the chief princes allow for their own eating is a testoon a day: eighteenpence; there are some extend their expense to five pauls, or half a crown: Cardinal Albani is called extravagant for laying out ten pauls for his dinner and supper. You may imagine they never have any entertainments: so far from it, they never have any company. The princesses and duchesses particularly lead the dismallest of lives. Being the posterity of popes, though of worse families than the ancient nobililty, they expect greater respect than my ladies the countesses and marquises will pay them; consequently they consort not, but mope in a vast palace with two miserable tapers, and two or three monsignori, whom they are forced to court and humour, that they may not be entirely deserted. Sundays they do issue forth in a vast unwieldy coach to the Corso.

Horace Walpole
Letters
1740

PISA – BATTERED BUT PLEASANT

Pisa is a fine old city that strikes you with the same veneration you would feel at sight of an antient temple which bears the marks of decay without being absolutely dilapidated. The houses are well built, the streets open, straight, and well paved, the shops well furnished, and the markets well supplied; there are some elegant palaces, designed by great masters. The churches are built with taste, and tolerably ornamented. There is a beautiful wharf of freestone on each side of the river Arno, which runs through the city, and three bridges thrown over it, of which that in the middle is of marble, a pretty piece of architecture; but the number of inhabitants is very inconsiderable; and this very circumstance gives it an air of majestic solitude, which is far from being unpleasant to a man of a contemplative turn of mind; for my part, I cannot bear the tumult of a populous commercial city, and the solitude that reigns in Pisa would with me be a strong motive to choose it as a place of residence; not that this would be the only inducement for living at Pisa. Here is some good company, and even a few men of taste and learning. The people in general are counted sociable and polite, and there is a great plenty of provisions at a very reasonable rate.

Tobias Smollett
Travels through France and Italy
1766

ROME AND THE COLISEUM BY MOONLIGHT

Last night we took advantage of a brilliant full moon to visit the Coliseum by moonlight; and if I came away disappointed of the pleasure I had expected, the fault was not in me nor in the scene around me. In its sublime and heart-stirring beauty, it more than equalled, it surpassed all I had anticipated – but – (there must always be a *but!* always in the realities of this world something to disgust) it happened that one or two gentlemen joined our party – young men too, and classical scholars, who perhaps thought it fine to affect a well-bred *nonchalance*, a fashionable disdaine for all romance and enthusiasm, and amused themselves with *quizzing* our guide, insulting the gloom, the grandeur, and the silence around them, with loud impertinent laughter at their own poor jokes; and I was obliged to listen, sad and disgusted, to their empty and taste-less and misplaced flippancy. The young barefooted friar, with his dark lanthorn, and his black eyes flashing from under his cowl, who acted as our cicerone, was in picturesque unison with the scene; but – more than one murder having lately been committed among the labyrinthine recesses of the ruin, the government has given orders that every person entering after dusk should be attended by a guard of two soldiers. These fellows therefore necessarily walked close after your heels, smoking, spitting, and spluttering German. Such were my companions, and such was my *cortège*. I returned home vowing that while I remained at Rome, nothing should induce me to visit the Coliseum by moonlight again.

Anna Jameson
Diary of an Ennuyée
1826

THE PECULIARITY OF VENICE

Genoa stands *on* the sea, this *in* it. The effect is certainly magical, dazzling, perplexing. You feel at first a little giddy: you are not quite sure of your footing as on the deck of a vessel. You enter its narrow, cheerful canals, and find that instead of their being scooped out of earth, you are gliding amidst rows of palaces and under broad-arched bridges, piled on the sea-green wave. You begin to

The Bridge of Sighs, Venice

think that you must cut your liquid way in this manner through the whole city, and use oars instead of feet. You land, and visit quays, squares, market-places, theatres, churches, halls, palaces; ascend tall towers, and stroll through shady gardens, without being once reminded that you are not on *terra firma*. Venice is loaded with ornament, like a rich city-heiress with jewels. It seems the natural order of things. Her origin was a wonder: her end is to surprise. The strong, implanted tendency of her genius must be to the showy, the singular, the fantastic. Herself an anomaly, she reconciles contradictions, liberty with aristocracy, commerce with nobililty, the want of titles with the pride of birth and heraldry. A violent birth in nature, she lays greedy, perhaps ill-advised, hands on all the artificial advantages that can supply her original defects. Use turns to gaudy beauty; extreme hardship to intemperance in pleasure. From the level uniform expanse that forever encircles her, she would obviously affect the aspiring in forms, the quaint, the complicated, relief and projection. The richness and foppery of her architecture arise from this: its stability and excellence pro-bably from another circumstance counteracting this tendency to the buoyant and fluttering, *viz.*, the necessity of raising solid edifices on such slippery foundations, and of not playing tricks with stone-walls upon the water. Her eye for colours and costume she would bring with conquest from the East. The spirit, intelligence, and activity of her men, she would derive from their ancestors: the grace, the glowing animation and bounding step of her women, from the sun and mountain-breeze! The want of simplicity and severity in Venetian taste seems owing to this, that all here is factitious and the work of art: redundancy again is an attribute of commerce, whose eye is gross and large, and does not admit of the *too much*; and as to irregularity and want of fixed principles, we may account by analogy at least for these, from that element of which Venice is the nominal bride, to which she owes her all, and the very essence of which is caprice, uncertainty, and vicissitude!

William Hazlitt
Notes of a Journey through France and Italy
1826

A CITY TO LIVE IN

We walked out in the evening, and found Ferrara enchanting. Of all the places I have seen in Italy, it is the one by far I should most covet to live in. It is the *ideal* of an Italian city, once great, now a shadow of itself. Whichever way you turn, you are struck with picturesque beauty and faded splendours, but with nothing squalid,

mean, or vulgar. The grass grows in the well-paved streets. You
look down long avenues of buildings, or of garden walls, with sum-
merhouses or fruit-trees projecting over them, and airy palaces with
dark portraits gleaming through the grated windows – you turn,
and a chapel bounds your view one way, a broken arch another, at
the end of the vacant, glimmering, fairy perspective. You are in a
dream, in the heart of a romance; you enjoy the most perfect solitude, that of a city which was once filled with 'the busy hum of
men', and of which the tremulous fragments at every step strike
the sense, and call up reflection. In short, nothing is to be seen of
Ferrara, but the remains, graceful and romantic, of what it was –
no sordid object intercepts or sullies the retrospect of the past – it
is not degraded and patched up like Rome, with upstart improvements, with earthenware and oil-shops; it is a classic vestige of
antiquity, drooping into peaceful decay, a sylvan suburb.

William Hazlitt
Notes of a Journey through France and Italy
1826

A CITY OF COMMON-PLACES

'As London is to the meanest country town, so is Rome to every
other city in the world.'

So said an old friend of mine, and I believed him till I saw it.
This is not the Rome I expected to see. No one from being in it
would know he was in the place that had been twice mistress of
the world. In London there is a look of wealth and populousness
which is to be found nowhere else. In Rome you are for the most
part lost in a mass of tawdry, fulsome *common-places*. It is not the
contrast of pig-styes and palaces that I complain of, the distinction
between the old and new; what I object to is the want of any such
striking contrast, but an almost uninterrupted succession of narrow,
vulgar-looking streets, where the smell of garlick prevails over the
odour of antiquity, with the dingy, melancholy flat fronts of modern-
built houses, that seem in search of an owner. A dunghill, an
outhouse, the weeds growing under an imperial arch offend me
not; but what has a green-grocer's stall, a stupid English china
warehouse, a putrid *trattoria*, a barber's sign, an old clothes or old
picture shop or a Gothic palace, with two or three lacqueys in
modern liveries lounging at the gate, to do with ancient Rome? No!
this is not the wall that Romulus leaped over: this is not the Capitol
where Julius Cæsar fell: instead of standing on seven hills, it is
situated in a low valley: the golden Tiber is a muddy stream: St.
Peter's is not equal to St. Paul's: the Vatican falls short of the

225

Louvre, as it was in my time; but I thought that here were works immoveable, immortal, inimitable on earth, and lifting the soul half way to heaven. I find them not, or only what I had seen before in different ways: the Stanzas of Raphael are faded, or no better than the prints; and the mind of Michael Angelo's figures, of which no traces are to be found in the copies, is equally absent from the walls of the Sistine Chapel. Rome is great only in ruins: the Coliseum, the Pantheon, the Arch of Constantine fully answered my expectations; and an air breathes round her stately avenues, serene, blissful, like the mingled breath of spring and winter, betwixt life and death, betwixt hope and despair. The country about Rome is cheerless and barren. There is little verdure, nor are any trees planted, on account of their bad effects on the air. Happy climate! in which shade and sunshine are alike fatal.

William Hazlitt

Notes of a Journey through France and Italy

1826

A SHORT TOUR OF MANTUA

'Well!' said I, when I was ready, 'shall we go out now?'

'If the gentleman pleases. It is a beautiful day. A little fresh, but charming; altogether charming. The gentleman will allow me to open the door. This is the Inn Yard. The court-yard of the Golden Lion! The gentleman will please to mind his footing on the stairs.'

We are now in the street.

'This is the street of the Golden Lion. This, the outside of the Golden Lion. The interesting window up there, on the first Piano, where the pane of glass is broken, is the window of the gentleman's chamber!'

Having viewed all these remarkable objects, I inquired if there were much to see in Mantua.

'Well! Truly, no. Not much! So, so,' he said, shrugging his shoulders apologetically.

'Many churches?'

'No. Nearly all suppressed by the French.'

'Monasteries or convents?'

'No. The French again! Nearly all suppressed by Napoleon.'

'Much business?'

'Very little business.'

'Many strangers?'

'Ah Heaven!'

1 thought he would have fainted.

226

'Then, when we have seen the two large Churches yonder, what shall we do next?' said I.

He looked up the street, and down the street, and rubbed his chin timidly; and then said, glancing in my face as if a light had broken on his mind, yet with a humble appeal to my forbearance that was perfectly irresistible:

'We can take a little turn about the town, Signore! (Sipuò far 'un píccolo gíro della citta.)

It was impossible to be anything but delighted with the proposal, so we set off together in great good-humour. In the relief of his mind, he opened his heart, and gave up as much of Mantua as a Cicerone could.

'One must eat,' he said; 'but, bah! it was a dull place, without doubt!'

Charles Dickens
Pictures from Italy
1846

REPUTATION AND REALITY IN VENICE

It is easy to feel and to say something obvious about Venice. The influence of this sea-city is unique, immediate, and unmistakable. But to express the sober truth of those impressions which remain when the first astonishment of the Venetian revelation has subsided, when the spirit of the place has been harmonized through familiarity with our habitual mood, is difficult.

I have escaped from the hotels with their bustle of tourists and crowded *tables-d'hôte*. My garden stretches down to the Grand Canal, closed at the end with a pavilion, where I lounge and smoke and watch the cornice of the Prefettura fretted with gold in sunset light. My sitting-room and bedroom face the southern sun. There is a canal below, crowded with gondolas, and across its bridge the good folk of San Vio come and go the whole day long – men in blue shirts with enormous hats, and jackets slung on their left shoulder; women in kerchiefs of orange and crimson. Barelegged boys sit upon the parapet, dangling their feet above the rising tide. A hawker passes, balancing a basket full of live and crawling crabs. Barges filled with Brenta water or Mirano wine take up their station at the neighbouring steps, and then ensues a mighty splashing and hurrying to and fro of men with tubs upon their heads. The brawny fellows in the wine-barge are red from brows to breast with drippings of the vat. And now there is a bustle in the quarter. A *barca* has arrived from S. Erasmo, the island of the market-gardens. It is piled with gourds and pumpkins, cabbages and tomatoes, pomegranates and pears – a pyramid of gold and green and scarlet. Brown men lift the fruit aloft, and women bending from the pathway bargain for it. A clatter of chattering tongues, a ring of coppers, a Babel of hoarse sea-voices, proclaim the sharpness of the struggle. When the quarter has been served, the boat sheers off diminished in its burden. Boys and girls are left seasoning their polenta with a slice of *zucca*, while the mothers of a score of families go pattering up yonder courtyard with the material for their husbands' supper in their handkerchiefs. Across the canal, or more correctly the *Rio*, opens a wide grass-grown court. It is lined on the right hand by a row of poor dwellings, swarming with gondoliers' children. A garden wall runs along the other side, over which I can see pomegranate-trees in fruit and pergolas of vines. Far beyond are more low houses, and then the sky, swept with sea-breezes, and the masts of an ocean-going ship against the dome and turrets of Palladio's Redentore.

This is my home. By day it is as lively as a scene in *Masaniello*. By night, after nine o'clock, the whole stir of the quarter has subsided. Far away I hear the bell of some church tell the hours. But no noise disturbs my rest, unless perhaps a belated gondolier moors his boat beneath the window. My one maid, Catina, sings at her work the whole day through. My gondolier, Francesco, acts as valet. He wakes me in the morning, opens the shutters, brings sea-water for my bath, and takes his orders for the day. 'Will it do for Chioggia, Francesco?' '*Sissignore*! The Signorino has set off in his *sandolo* already with Antonio. The Signora is to go with us in the gondola.' 'Then get three more men, Francesco, and see that all of them can sing.'

J. A. Symonds
Sketches and Studies in Italy and Greece
1898

THE SOUTH

Lucky the mortal who arrives on the summit of San Costanzo during one of those bewitching moments when the atmosphere is permeated with a glittering haze of floating particles, like powdered gold-dust. The view over the Gulf of Naples, at such times, with its contours framed in a luminous aureole rather than limned, is not easily forgotten. They are rare, and their glory of brief duration. On other occasions this fairy-like effect is atoned for by the clarity; not only Siren land, but half Campania, lies at our feet. Far away, the sinuous outlines of Tyrrhenian shores with the headland of Circe and the Ponza islets that call up grim memories of Roman

Land and the people of the South

banishments; the complex and serrated Apennines whose peaks are visible into the far Abruzzi country; nearer at hand, Elysian Fields, Tartarus and Cimmerian gloom, and the smoking head of Vesuvius decked with a coral necklace of towns and villages. Not an inch of all this landscape but has its associations. Capua and Hannibal; the Caudine Forks; Misenum and Virgil; Nisida, the retreat of a true Siren-worshipper, Lucullus; the venerable acropolis of Cumæ; Pompeii; yonder Puteoli, where the apostle of the gentiles touched land; here the Amalfitan coast, Pæstum, and the Calabrian hills.

And everywhere the unharvested sea. The sea, with its intense restfulness, is the dominant note of Siren land. There is no escaping from it. Incessant gleams of light flash from that mirror-like expanse; even when unperceived by the senses, among squalid tenements of leafy uplands, they will find you out and follow, like some all-pervading, inevitable melody.

Norman Douglas
Siren Land
1911

CHAPTER 4

Judgements

The English and the Natives

Travel has always been tiring and stressful, and it was far more so before the advent of trains and cars and planes. A traveller was (and to some extent still is) an alien in a puzzling world, battered by strange sounds, strange country, strange people. It is an unsettling world of mental and physical discomfort. In these circumstances, it is not unexpected that the traveller retreats into familiar prejudice. Foreigners are suspect; their ways are not our ways. They demonstrate that most worrying of human qualities – a certain otherness. So though there are many virtues and wonders abroad, the message of the traveller is, on the whole, 'Let Englishmen beware!'

AFFECTATIONS AND FANTASIES

Every one knowes the *Tale* of him, *who reported hee had seen a Cabbage under whose leafes a Regiment of Souldiers were sheltred from a shower of raine:* Another who was n *Traveller* (yet the wiser man) said, *hee had passed by a place where there were* 400 *brasiers making of a Cauldron,* 200 *within, and* 200 *without, beating the nayles in;* the *Traveller asking for what use that huge Cauldron was?* he told him, *Sir it was to boyle your cabbage.*

Such another was the *Spanish Traveller*, who was so habituated to *hyperbolize*, and related wonders, that he became ridiculous in al[l] companies, so that he was forced at last to give order to his man, when he fell into any *excesse this way*, and report any thing improbable, he should pul him by the sleeve: The Master falling into his wonted *hyperboles*, spoke *of a Church in China, that was ten thousand yards long;* his man standing behind and pulling him by the sleeve, made him stop suddenly: the company asking, I pray Sir, how broad might that Church be? he replyed, *but a yard broad, and you may thanke my man for pulling me by the sleeve, else I had made it fouresquare for you.*

Others have another kind of *hyperbolizing* vaine, as they will say, *there's not a woman in Italy, but weares an Iron girdle next her skin in the absence of her husband, that for a pistoll one may be master of any mans life there; That there is not a Gentleman in*

230

*France but hath his box of playsters about him; That in Germany
every one hath a rouse in his pate, once a day; That there are [a]
few Dons in Spaine that eat flesh once a week, or that hath not a
Mistresse besides his wife; That Paris hath more Courtizans than
London honest Women* (which may admit a double sense;) *That
Sevill is like a chessebord table, having as many Moriscos as Spaniards; That Venice hath more Maquerelles, than Marchands; Portu-
gall more Jews than Christians:* whereas it is sarre otherwise, *for
the Devill is not so black as he is painted,* no more are these Noble
Nations and *Townes* as they are tainted.

James Howell
Instructions for Forraine Travell
1642

BARBARISM BEYOND

This I made the *non ultra* of my travels, sufficiently sated with
rolling up and down, and resolving within myself to be no longer
an *individuum vagum*, if ever I got home again; since, from the
report of divers experienced and curious persons, I had been assured
there was little more to be seen in the rest of the civil world
after Italy, France, Flanders, and the Low Countries, but plain and
prodigious barbarism.

John Evelyn
Diary
1645

ROMAN SNARES SET FOR THE ENGLISH

Our young gentlemen who go to Rome will do well to be upon their
guard against a set of sharpers (some of them of our own country),
who deal in pictures and antiques, and very often impose upon the
uninformed stranger by selling him trash, as the productions of
the most celebrated artists. The English are more than any other
foreigners exposed to this imposition. They are supposed to have
more money to throw away; and therefore a greater number of
snares are laid for them. This opinion of their superior wealth they
take a pride in confirming, by launching out in all manner of
unnecessary expense. But what is still more dangerous, the moment they set foot in Italy, they are seized with the ambition of
becoming connoisseurs in painting, music, statuary, and architecture; and the adventurers of this country do not fail to flatter this
weakness for their own advantage. I have seen in different parts of
Italy, a number of raw boys, whom Britain seemed to have poured

forth on purpose to bring her national character into contempt. Ignorant, petulant, rash, and profligate, without any knowledge or experience or their own, without any director to improve their understanding, or superintend their conduct. One engages in play with an infamous gamester, and is stripped, perhaps, in the very first party: another is poxed and pillaged by an antiquated canta-trice. A third is bubbled by a knavish antiquarian; and a fourth is laid under contribution by a dealer in pictures. Some turn fiddlers, and pretend to compose. But all of them talk familiarly of the arts, and return finished connoisseurs and coxcombs to their own country. The most remarkable phænomenon of this kind which I have seen, is a boy of seventy-two, now actually travelling through Italy, for improvement, under the auspices of another boy of twenty-two. When you arrive at Rome, you receive cards from all your country-folks in that city. They expect to have the visit returned next day, when they give orders not to be at home; and you never speak to one another in the sequel. This is a refinement in hospi-tality and politeness which the English have invented by the strength of their own genius, without any assistance either from France, Italy, or Lapland. No Englishman above the degree of a painter or cicerone frequents any coffee-house at Rome; and as there are no public diversions except in carnival time, the only chance you have for seeing your compatriots, is either in visiting the curi-osities, or at a conversazione.

Tobias Smollett
Travels through France and Italy
1766

ENGLISH SIMPLICITY AND FRENCH FASHION

What is the consequence? when an Englishman comes to Paris, he cannot appear until he has undergone a total metamorphosis. At his first arrival, he finds it necessary to send for the tailor, peru-quier, hatter, shoemaker, and every other tradesman concerned in the equipment of the human body. He must even change his buckles, and the form of his ruffles; and, though at the risque of his life, suit his clothes to the mode of his season. For example, though the weather should be never so cold, he must wear his *habit d'été*, or *demi-saison*, without presuming to put on a warm dress before the day which fashion has fixed for that purpose; and neither old age nor infirmity will excuse a man for wearing his hat upon his head, either at home or abroad. Females are, if possible, still more subject to the caprices of fashion; and as the articles of their dress are more manifold, it is enough to make a man's heart ache to see his wife surrounded by a multitude of *cotturières*, milliners, and tire-women. All her sacks and negligees must be altered and new trimmed. She must have new caps, new laces, new shoes, and her hair new cut. She must have her taffaties for the summer, her flowered silks for the spring and autumn, her satins and damasks for winter. The good man who used to wear the *beau drap d'Angleterre*, quite plain all the year round, with a long bob, or tie perriwig, must here provide himself with a camblet suit trimmed with silver for spring and autumn, with silk cloaths for summer, and cloth laced with gold or velvet for winter; and he must wear his bag-wig *à la pigeon*. This variety of dress is absolutely indispensable for all those who pretend to any rank above the mere bourgeois. On his return to his own country, all this frippery is useless. He cannot appear in London until he has undergone another thorough metamorphosis: so that he will have some reason to think, that the tradesmen of Paris and London have combined to lay him under contribution. And they, no doubt, are the directors who regulate the fashions in both capitals; the English, however, in a subordinate capacity: for the puppets of their making will not pass at Paris, nor indeed in any other part of Europe; whereas, a French *petit-maître* is reckoned a complete figure every where, London not excepted. Since it is so much the humour of the English to run abroad, I wish they had antigallican spirit enough to produce themselves in their own genuine English dress.

Tobias Smollett
Travels through France and Italy
1766

THE FRENCH AND THE ENGLISH

One of the most amusing circumstances of travelling into other countries is the opportunity of remarking the difference of customs amongst different nations in the common occurrences of life. In the art of living, the French have generally been esteemed by the rest of Europe to have made the greatest proficiency, and their manners have been accordingly more imitated, and their customs more adopted than those of any other nation. Of their cookery, there is but one opinion; for every man in Europe, that can afford a great table, either keeps a French cook, or one instructed in the same manner. That it is far beyond our own, I have no doubt in asserting. We have about half-a-dozen real English dishes, that exceed anything, in my opinion, to be met with in France; by English dishes I mean, a turbot and lobster sauce; ham and chicken; turtle; a haunch of venison; a turkey and oysters; and after these, there is an end of an English table. It is an idle prejudice, to class roast beef among them; for there is not better beef in the world than at Paris. Large handsome pieces were almost constantly on the considerable tables I have dined at. The variety given by their cooks, to the same thing, is astonishing; they dress an hundred dishes in an hundred different ways, and most of them excellent; and all sorts of vegetables have a savouriness and flavour, from rich sauces, that are absolutely wanted to our greens boiled in water. This variety is not striking, in the comparison of a great table in France with another in England; but it is manifest in an instant, between the tables of a French and English family of small fortune. The English dinner, of a joint of meat and a pudding, as it is called, or *pot luck*, with a neighbour, is bad luck in England; the same fortune in France gives, by means of cookery only, at least four dishes to one among us, and spreads a small table incomparably better. A regular dessert with us is expected, at a considerable table only, or at a moderate one, when a formal entertainment is given; in France it is as essential to the smallest dinner as to the largest; if it consists only of a bunch of dried grapes, or an apple, it will be as regularly served as the soup. I have met with persons in England who imagine the sobriety of a French table carried to such a length, that one or two glasses of wine are all that a man can get at dinner; this is an error; your servant mixes the wine and water in what proportion you please; and large bowls of clean glasses are set before the master of the house, and some friends of the family, at different parts of the table, for serving the richer and rarer sorts of wines, which are drunk in this manner freely enough. The whole nation are scrupulously neat in refusing to drink out of glasses used by other people. At the house of a carpenter or blacksmith, a tumbler is set to every cover. This results from the common beverage being wine and water; but if at a large table, as in England, there were porter, beer, cyder, and perry, it would be impossible for three or four tumblers or goblets to stand by every plate; and equally so for the servants to keep such a number separate and distinct. In table-linen, they are, I think, cleaner and wiser than the English; that the change may be incessant, it is everywhere coarse. The idea of dining without a napkin seems ridiculous to a Frenchman, but in England we dine at the tables of people of tolerable fortune without them. A journeyman carpenter in France has his napkin as regularly as his fork; and at an inn, the *fille* always lays a clean one to every cover that is spread in the kitchen, for the lowest order of pedestrian travellers. The expense of linen in England is enormous, from its fineness; surely a great change of that which is coarse would be much more rational.

In point of cleanliness, I think the merit of the two nations is divided; the French are cleaner in their persons, and the English in their houses; I speak of the mass of the people, and not of individuals of considerable fortune. A *bidet* in France is as universally in every apartment as a basin to wash your hands, which is a trait of personal cleanliness I wish more common in England; on the other hand, their necessary houses are temples of abomination; and the practice of spitting about a room, which is amongst the highest as well as the lowest ranks, is detestable. I have seen a gentleman spit so near the clothes of a duchess, that I have stared at his unconcern.

In everything that concerns the stables, the English far exceed the French; horses, grooms, harness, and change of equipage; in the provinces you see cabriolets undoubtedly of the last century; an Englishman, however small his fortune may be, will not be seen in a carriage of the fashion of forty years past; if he cannot have another, he will walk on foot. It is not true that there are no complete equipages at Paris, I have seen many; the carriage, horses, harness, and attendance, without fault or blemish; but the number is certainly very much inferior to what are seen at London. English horses, grooms, and carriages, have been of late years largely imported.

In the blended idea I had formed of the French character from reading, I am disappointed from three circumstances, which I expected to find predominant. On comparison with the English, I looked for great talkativeness, volatile spirits, and universal politeness. I think, on the contrary, that they are not so talkative as the English; have not equally good spirits, and are not a jot more polite; nor do I speak of certain classes of people, but of the general mass. I think them, however, incomparably better tempered; and I propose it as a question, whether good temper be not more reasonably expected under an arbitrary, than under a free government?

> Arthur Young
> *Travels in France*
> 1790

THE ENGLISHMAN IN BRESCIA

But Brescia ought to be immortalized in the history of our travels: for there, stalking down the Corso – *le nez en l'air* – we met our acquaintance L–, from whom we had parted last on the pavé of Piccadilly. I remember that in London I used to think him not remarkable for wisdom, – and his travels have infinitely improved him – in folly. He boasted to us triumphantly that he had run over sixteen thousand miles in sixteen months: that he had bowed at the levée of the Emperor Alexander, – been slapped on the shoulder by the Archduke Constantine, – shaken hands with a Lapland witch, – and been presented in full volunteer uniform at every court between Stockholm and Milan. Yet is he not one particle wiser than if he had spent the same time in walking up and down the Strand. He has contrived, however, to pick up on his tour, strange odds and ends of foreign follies, which stick upon the coarse-grained materials of his own John Bull character like tinfoil upon sackcloth: so that I see little difference between what he was, and what he is, except that from a *simple goose*, – he has become a compound one.

Anna Jameson
Diary of an Ennuyée
1826

THE ENGLISHMAN IN VENICE

The public gardens are the work of the French, and occupy the extremity of one of the islands. They contain the only trees I have seen at Venice: – a few rows of dwarfish unhappy-looking shrubs, parched by the sea breezes, and are little frequented. We found here a solitary gentleman, who was sauntering up and down with his hands in his pockets, and a look at once stupid and disconsolate. Sometimes he paused, looked vacantly over the waters, whistled, yawned, and turned away to resume his solemn walk. On a trifling remark addressed to him by one of our party, he entered into conversation, with all the eagerness of a man, whose tongue had long been kept in most unnatural bondage. He congratulated himself on having met with some one who would speak English; adding contemptuously, that 'he understood none of the outlandish tongues the people spoke hereabouts:' he inquired what was to be seen here, for though he had been four days in Venice, he had spent every day precisely in the same manner; viz. walking up and down the public gardens. We told him Venice was famous for fine buildings and pictures; he knew nothing of *them* things. And that it contained also, 'some fine statues and antiques' – he cared nothing about them neither – he should set off for Florence the next morning, and begged to know what was to be seen there? Mr. R– told him, with enthusiasm, 'the most splendid gallery of pictures and statues in the world!' He looked very blank and disappointed. 'Nothing else?' then he should certainly not waste his time at Florence, he should

The Great Briton on the Rhine

go direct to Rome; he had put down the name of that *town* in his
pocket-book, for he understood it was a very *convenient* place.

Anna Jameson
Diary of an Ennuyée
1826

WHAT THE ENGLISH EXPECT ABROAD

A French gentleman, a man of sense and wit, expressed his wonder
that all the English did not go and live in the South of France,
where they would have a beautiful country, a fine climate, and
every comfort almost for nothing. He did not perceive that they
would go back in shoals from this scene of fancied contentment to

their fogs and sea-coal fires, and that no Englishman can live without something to complain of. Some persons are sorry to see our countrymen abroad cheated, laughed at, quarrelling at all the inns they stop at: – while they are in *hot water*, while they think themselves ill-used and have but the spirit to resent it, they are happy. As long as they can swear, they are excused from being complimentary: if they have to fight, they need not think: while they are provoked beyond measure, they are released from the dreadful obligation of being pleased. Leave them to themselves, and they are dull: introduce them into company, and they are worse. It is the incapacity of enjoyment that makes them sullen and ridiculous; the mortification they feel at not having their own way in everything, and at seeing others delighted without asking their leave, that makes them haughty and distant. An Englishman is silent abroad from having nothing to say; and he looks stupid, because he is so.

William Hazlitt
Notes of a Journey through France and Italy
1826

'AN ASSEMBLY FOR WITS AND PHILOSOPHERS'

I spent an hour one evening at the principal café, where a pianist of great pretensions and small achievement made rather painful music. Watching and listening to the company (all men, of course, though the Oriental system regarding women is not so strict at Catanzaro as elsewhere in the South), I could not but fall into a comparison of this scene with any similar gathering of middle-class English folk. The contrast was very greatly in favour of the Italians. One has had the same thought a hundred times in the same circumstances, but it is worth dwelling upon. Among these representative men, young and old, of Catanzaro, the tone of conversation was incomparably better than that which would rule in a cluster of English provincials met to enjoy their evening leisure. They did, in fact, converse – a word rarely applicable to English talk under such conditions; mere personal gossip was the exception; they exchanged genuine thoughts, reasoned lucidly on the surface of abstract subjects. I say on the surface; no remark that I heard could be called original or striking; but the choice of topics and the mode of viewing them was distinctly intellectual. Phrases often occurred such as have no equivalent on the lips of everyday people in our own country. For instance, a young fellow in no way distinguished from his companions, fell to talking about a leading townsman, and praised

him for his *ingenio simpatico*, his *bella intelligenza*, with exclamations of approval from those who listened. No, it is not merely the
difference between homely Anglo-Saxon and a language of classic
origin; there is a radical distinction of thought. These people have
an innate respect for things of the mind, which is wholly lacking
to a typical Englishman. One need not dwell upon the point that
their animation was supported by a tiny cup of coffee or a glass of
lemonade; this is a matter of climate and racial constitution; but I
noticed the entire absence of a certain kind of jocoseness which is
so naturally associated with spirituous liquors; no talk could have
been less offensive. From many a bar-parlour in English country
towns I have gone away heavy with tedium and disgust; the café
at Catanzaro seemed, in comparison, a place of assembly for wits
and philosophers.

George Gissing
By the Ionian Sea
1901

WHAT ITALY TEACHES THE ENGLISH

Even so, in Italy, the domesticated Englishman is amazed to find
that he possesses a sense hitherto unrevealed, opening up a new
horizon, a new zest in life – the sense of law-breaking. At first,
being an honest man, he is shocked at the thought of such a thing;
next, like a sensible person, reconciled to the inevitable; lastly, as
befits his virile race, he learns to play the game so well that the
horrified officials grudgingly admit (and it is their highest praise):

> *Inglese italianizzato –*
> *Diavolo incarnato.*

Yes; slowly the charm of law-breaking grows upon the Italianated
Saxon; slowly, but surely. There is a neo-barbarism not only in
matters of art ...

And yet – how seriously we take this nation! Almost as seriously
as we take ourselves. The reason is that most of us come to Italy
too undiscerning, too reverent; in the pre-critical and pre-humorous
stages. We arrive here, stuffed with Renaissance ideals or classical
lore, and viewing the present through coloured spectacles. We
arrive here, above all things, too young; for youth loves to lean on
tradition and to draw inspiration from what has gone before; youth
finds nothing more difficult than to follow Goethe's advice about
grasping that living life which shifts and fluctuates about us. Few
writers are sufficiently detached to laugh at these people as they,

together with ourselves, so often and so richly deserve. I spoke of
the buffoonery of Italian law; I might have called it a burlesque.

Norman Douglas
Old Calabria
1915

WEEDS AND MODERNITY

It amounts almost to a national characteristic, this hatred of growing things among the works of men. I have often, in old Italian
towns, seen workmen laboriously weeding the less frequented
streets and squares. The Colosseum, mantled till thirty or forty
years ago with a romantic, Piranesian growth of shrubs, grasses
and flowers, was officially weeded with such extraordinary energy
that its ruinousness was sensibly increased. More stones were
brought down in those few months of weeding than had fallen of
their own accord in the previous thousand years. But the Italians
were pleased; which is, after all, the chief thing that matters. Their
hatred of weeds is fostered by their national pride; a great country,
and one which specially piques itself on being modern, cannot allow
weeds to grow even among its ruins. I entirely understand and
sympathize with the Italian point of view. If Mr. Ruskin and his
disciples had talked about my house and me as they talked about
Italy and the Italians, I too should pique myself on being up-to-
date; I should put in bathrooms, central heating and a lift, I should
have all the moss scratched off the walls, I should lay cork lino on
the marble floors. Indeed, I think that I should probably, in my
irritation, pull down the whole house and build a new one. Considering the provocation they have received, it seems to me that the
Italians have been remarkably moderate in the matter of weeding,
destroying and rebuilding. Their moderation is due in part, no
doubt, to their comparative poverty. Their ancestors built with such
prodigious solidity that it would cost as much to pull down one
of their old houses as to build a new one. Imagine, for example,
demolishing the Palazzo Strozzi in Florence. It would be about as
easy to demolish the Matterhorn. In Rome, which is predominantly
a baroque, seventeenth-century city, the houses are made of flimsier
stuff. Consequently, modernization progresses there much more
rapidly than in most other Italian towns. In wealthier England
very little antiquity has been permitted to stand. Thus, most of the
great country houses of England were rebuilt during the eighteenth
century. If Italy had preserved her independence and her prosperity
during the seventeenth, eighteenth and nineteenth centuries, there
would probably be very much less mediaeval or renaissance work

240

now surviving than is actually the case. Money, then, is lacking to modernize completely. Weeding has the merit of being cheap and, at the same time, richly symbolic. When you say of a town that the grass grows in its streets, you mean that it is utterly dead. Conversely, if there is no grass in its streets, it must be alive. No doubt the mayor and corporation of Siena did not put the argument quite so explicitly. But that the argument was put, somehow, obscurely and below the surface of the mind, I do not doubt. The weeding was symbolic of modernity.

Aldous Huxley
Along the Road
1925

'THE OTHERS'

The city is dominated by the mountain called Tibidabo and the repellent church that is being built on its summit. One would a thousand times sooner have Gaudí's work than this religious Odéon. The building has been going on for a generation, and a terrible figure of the Christ stands in the courtyard waiting to be heaved on top, where its halo will be electrically lit. The collapse of Spanish religious art has this awful monument, which is one of the jokes of the city.

One of the world-shakers who showed me round Barcelona again stopped in the street and pointed to this horror. 'Through that building,' he said, 'I lost my religious faith. For it was announced on a public notice when I was young that by Divine Promise the church would be completed by a certain date that was named. It was not completed, and I complained to one of the fathers, who explained that by completion was meant that the roof would be on. That was too much for me.' Oh blessed, pagan, literal Mediterranean. With worldly eye you regard those offers of indulgences inscribed on the walls of Tibidabo. Childishly you take your families for a joy ride at the Amusement Park, which has been placed beside the church on the precipice overlooking the city. Savagely you drove your political prisoners there, only fifteen years ago, on the last ride of their lives, gave them the last cigarette, and shot them.

Long before we reached the city, at a second crossing of the Ebro by some bad mountain road, we came to a new steel bridge across this superb river. Green and smooth as marble, or thick blood-colour, according to the season, it is a river that flows a good deal in profound ravines, as indeed do most of the Spanish rivers. We crossed the bridge and stopped for a glass of beer on the other side.

There were four men in the café playing cards, and I asked the proprietor which side had destroyed the bridge in the Civil War. He was a dusty, thin-haired, sly-faced man in his fifties.

'The others,' he said.

'But who are the others?' I said. 'Fascists or the Reds?'

'The others,' he said. 'In a civil war,' he said, 'it is always "the others" – and whoever wins is right.'

And saying this, he rubbed his forefinger lightly down his nose and let it rest at the tip – the gesture of innuendo, the gesture of Sancho Panza. One will find the correlative passage in almost any chapter of that book, which contains all other books on Spain.

V. S. Pritchett
The Spanish Temper
1954

The Point of it all

When the irritation was past and the discomfort forgotten, there were lessons to be learnt from travelling. The wide world was a richer place than any homeland. No man learnt except by experiment, and the world was the great laboratory of human experience. But travel, which was for pleasure and instruction, contained a warning also. And excess of it – when it becomes the mass movement of a giant tourist industry – produces not variety but sameness, not the richness of foreign experience but the impoverishment of popular commercial culture. The traveller today stands at an interesting point: does the road lead to a modest personal enlightenment, refreshed by the example of strangers? or does it descend into the brackish swamp of sub-Hollywood pleasure-seeking, where we wallow together in universal forgetfulness?

CITIZENS OF THE WORLD

For my part, I thinke variety to be the most pleasing thing in the World, and the best life to be, neither contemplative alone, nor active altogether, but mixed of both. God would have made eternall spring, had he not knowne, that the divers seasons would be not onely most profitable to the workes of nature, but also most plesant to his creatures, while the cold Winter makes the temperate Spring more wished. Such is the delight of visiting forraigne Countreys, charming all our sences with most sweet variety.

Let us imitate the Storkes, Swallowes, and Cranes, which like the Nomades yeerely fetch their circuits, and follow the Sunne, without suffering any distemper of the seasons: The fixed Starres have not such power over inferiour bodies, as the wandring Planets. Running water is sweet, but standing pooles stinke: Take away Idlenes, and the bate of all vice is taken away. Men were created to move, as birds to flie; what they learne by nature, that reason joined to nature teacheth us.

In one word, I will say what can be said upon this subject; Every soyle is to a valiant man his owne Countrey, as the Sea to the Fishes. We are Citizens of the whole World, yea, not of this World, but of that to come: All our life is a Pilgrimage. God for his onely begotten Sonnes sake, (the true Mercury of Travellers) bring us that are here strangers safely into our true Countrey.

Fynes Moryson
Itinerary
1605–17

LESSONS FROM EUROPE

If any Forrainer be to be imitated in his manner of *Discours* and *Comportement*, it is the *Italian*, who may be said to be a *medium* 'twixt the *Gravity* of the *Spaniard*, the *Heavinesse* of the *Dutch*, and *Levity* of our next Neighbours, for he seemes to allay the one, and quicken the other two; to serve as a *bouy* to the one, and a *ballast* to th'other.

France useth to work one good effect upon the *English*, she useth to take away the mothers milk (as they say), that blush and bashfull tincture, which useth to rise up in the face upon sudden salutes, and enter-change of Complement, and to enharden one with confidence; For the Gentry of *France* have a kind of loose becomming boldnes, and forward vivacity in their cariage, whereby [as] they seeme to draw respect from the *Superiours* and *Equals*, and [so they] make their *Inferiours* [and all kind of mechaniques to] keepe a fitting distance.

In *Italy* amongst other morall cautions, one may learne *not to be over prodigall of speech* when there is no need, for with a *nod* with a *shake of the head*, and *shrug of the shoulder*, they will answer to many queftions.

One shall learne besides there not to *interrupt* one in the relation of his tale, or to *feed* it with odde *interlocutions*: One shall learne also not to *laugh at his own jest*, as too many use to do, *like a Hen, which cannot lay an egge but she must cackle.*

James Howell
Instructions for Forraine Travell
1642

'LET THEM ALONE'

The English are too apt to take every opportunity, and to seize on every pretext for treating the rest of the world as wretches – a tone of feeling which does not exactly tend to enhance our zeal in the cause either of liberty or humanity. If people are wretches, the next impression is that they deserve to be so; and we are thus prepared to lend a helping hand to make them what we say they are. The Northern Italians are as fine a race of people as walk the earth; and all that they want, to be what they once were, or that any people is capable of becoming, is neither English abuse nor English assistance, but three words spoken to the other powers; 'Let them alone!'

William Hazlitt
Notes of a Journey through France and Italy
1826

REALITY AND THE DREAM

I confess, London looked to me on my return like a long, straggling, dirty country-town; nor do the names of Liverpool, Manchester, Birmingham, Leeds or Coventry, sound like a trumpet in the ears, or invite our pilgrim steps like those of Sienna, of Cortona, Perugia, Arezzo, Pisa and Ferrara. I am not sorry, however, that I have got back. There is an old saying, *Home is home, be it never so homely.* However delightful or striking the objects may be abroad, they do not take the same hold of you, nor can you identify yourself with them as at home. Not only is the language an insuperable obstacle; other things as well as men speak a language new and strange to you. You live comparatively in a dream, though a brilliant and a waking one. It is in vain to urge that you learn the language; that you are familiarized with manners and scenery. No other language can ever become our mother-tongue. We may learn the words; but they do not convey the same feelings, nor is it possible they should do so, unless we could begin our lives over again, and divide our conscious being into two different selves. Not only can we not attach the same meaning to words, but we cannot see objects with the same eyes, or form new loves and friendships after a certain period of our lives. The pictures that most delighted me in Italy were those I had before seen in the Louvre 'with eyes of youth'. I could revive this feeling of enthusiasm, but not transfer it. Neither would I recommend the going abroad when young, to become a mongrel being, half French, half English. It is better to be something than nothing. It is well to see foreign countries to enlarge one's speculat-

244

ive knowledge, and dispel false prejudices and libellous views of human nature; but our affections must settle at home. Besides though a dream, it is a splendid one. It is fine to see the white Alps rise in the horizon of fancy at the distance of a thousand miles; or the imagination may wing its thoughtful flight among the castellated Apennines, roaming from city to city over cypress and olive grove, viewing the inhabitants as they crawl about mouldering palaces or temples, which no hand has touched for the last three hundred years, and see the genius of Italy brooding over the remains of virtue, glory and liberty, with Despair at the gates, an English Minister handing the keys to a foreign Despot, and stupid Members of Parliament wondering what is the matter!

William Hazlitt
Notes of a Journey through France and Italy
1826

A LIGHT SHED UPON THE WORLD

What light is shed upon the world, at this day, from amidst these rugged Palaces of Florence! Here, open to all comers, in their beautiful and calm retreats, the ancient Sculptors are immortal, side by side with Michael Angelo, Canova, Titian, Rembrandt, Raphael, Poets, Historians, Philosophers – those illustrious men of history, beside whom its crowned heads and harnessed warriors shew so poor and small, and are so soon forgotten. Here, the imperishable part of noble minds survives, placid and equal, when strongholds of assault and defence are overthrown; when the tyranny of the many, or the few, or both, is but a tale; when Pride and Power are so much cloistered dust. The fire within the stern streets, and among the massive Palaces and Towers, kindled by rays from Heaven, is still burning brightly, when the flickering of war is extinguished and the household fires of generations have decayed; as thousands upon thousands of faces, rigid with the strife and passion of the hour, have faded out of the old Squares and public haunts, while the nameless Florentine Lady, preserved from oblivion by a Painter's hand, yet lives on, in enduring grace and youth.

Let us look back on Florence while we may, and when its shining Dome is seen no more, go travelling through cheerful Tuscany, with a bright remembrance of it; for Italy will be the fairer for the recollection. The summer time being come: and Genoa, and Milan, and the Lake of Como lying far behind us: and we resting at Faido, a Swiss village, near the awful rocks and mountains, the everlasting snows and roaring cataracts, of the Great Saint Gothard: hearing the Italian tongue for the last time on this journey: let us part

245

from Italy, with all its miseries and wrongs, affectionately, in our admiration of the beauties, natural and artificial, of which it is full to overflowing, and in our tenderness towards a people, naturally well disposed, and patient, and sweet tempered. Years of neglect, oppression, and misrule, have been at work, to change their nature and reduce their spirit; miserable jealousies, fomented by petty Princes to whom union was destruction, and division strength, have been a canker at the root of their nationality, and have barbarized their language; but the good that was in them ever, is in them yet, and a noble people may be, one day, raised up from these ashes. Let us entertain that hope! And let us not remember Italy the less regardfully, because, in every fragment of her fallen Temples, and every stone of her deserted palaces and prisons, she helps to inculcate the lesson that the wheel of Time is rolling for an end, and that the world is, in all great essentials, better, gentler, more forbearing, and more hopeful, as it rolls!

Charles Dickens
Pictures from Italy
1846

A REASON FOR TRAVELLING

Why anyone should desire to visit either Luc or Cheylard is more than my much-inventing spirit can suppose. For my part, I travel not to go anywhere, but to go. I travel for travel's sake. The great affair is to move; to feel the needs and hitches of our life more nearly; to come down off this feather-bed of civilisation, and find the globe granite underfoot and strewn with cutting flints. Alas, as we get up in life, and are more preoccupied with our affairs, even a holiday is a thing that must be worked for. To hold a pack upon a pack-saddle against a gale out of the freezing north is no high industry, but it is one that serves to occupy and compose the mind. And when the present is so exacting, who can annoy himself about the future?

R. L. Stevenson
Travels with a Donkey
1879

DREAMS OF THE PAST

Every man has his intellectual desire; mine is to escape life as I know it and dream myself into that old world which was the imaginative delight of my boyhood. The names of Greece and Italy draw me as no others; they make me young again, and restore the keen

246

impressions of that time when every new page of Greek or Latin was a new perception of things beautiful. The world of the Greeks and Romans is my land of romance; a quotation in either language thrills me strangely, and there are passages of Greek and Latin verse which I cannot read without a dimming of the eyes, which I cannot repeat aloud because my voice fails me. In Magna Græcia the waters of two fountains mingle and flow together; how exquisite will be the draught!

George Gissing
By the Ionian Sea
1901

A DEAD WITNESS FOR LIBERTY

An interesting feature of the streets is the frequency of carved inscriptions, commemorating citizens who died in their struggle for liberty. Amid quiet byways, for instance, I discovered a tablet with the name of a young soldier who fell at that spot, fighting against the Bourbon, in 1860: '*offerse per l'unità della patria sua vita quadri-lustre.*' The very insignificance of this young life makes the fact more touching; one thinks of the unnumbered lives sacrificed upon this soil, age after age, to the wild-beast instinct of mankind, and how pathetic the attempt to preserve the memory of one boy, so soon to become a meaningless name! His own voice seems to plead with us for a regretful thought, to speak from the stone in sad arraignment of tyranny and bloodshed. A voice which has no accent of hope. In the days to come, as through all time that is past, man will lord it over his fellow, and earth will be stained red from veins of young and old. That sweet and sounding name of *patria* becomes an illusion and a curse; linked with the pretentious modernism, *civilisation*, it serves as plea to the latter-day barbarian, ravening and reckless under his civil garb. How can one greatly wish for the consolidation and prosperity of Italy, knowing that national vigour tends more and more to international fear and hatred? They who perished that Italy might be born again, dreamt of other things than old savagery clanging in new weapons. In our day there is but one Italian patriot; he who tills the soil, and sows, and reaps, ignorant or careless of all beyond his furrowed field.

George Gissing
By the Ionian Sea
1901

A FREEMAN OF THE WORLD

It may seem a lazy way of living, but have the wisdom to enjoy your life in your own way. To be master of your time is a great step on the road to happiness; and, after all, there is a good deal of hard work in the life of a poor traveller. At any rate he lives in warm and observant touch with his fellow-men. He has a passion for seeing how the world is made, and is more interested in human beings than in art; what their houses are like and what clothes they wear; what money do they have; what food they eat; what do they love and hate; what do they see of the surrounding world; and what are the ideals which fill the spaces of their active lives. And his pleasures, though simple, are satisfying – constant change of scene; hunger and the satisfaction of a good meal; the pleasant languor of tiredness; sea-bathing; sunrises and sunsets. If I am in a little town, I go outside the walls to see the sun set and do not return until I can count three stars; then back to my inn through the darkling streets, which are never so interesting as at the hour when the lights are being lit and you can see the inside of the shops through the windows.

My instincts are those of a solitary and so I travel alone, but I pick up acquaintances everywhere and chance companionship is the best of all. I carry a trout rod, not seeking out fishing but taking it as it comes, and, if possible, I spend my occasional lazy week fishing. Indeed, even if you do not care for angling, you might strap a light rod to your umbrella. The sight of it is an open sesame to the confidence of the country-folk, accounting for your presence in out-of-the-way places, for the primitive suspicion of the stranger is by no means dead. If you get tired of carrying it, you can sell it with advantage anywhere abroad, foreign anglers having a just admiration for English tackle.

Life is short and the world is wide, but, moving thus about the countries as a freeman of the world, the time seems endless. Even after a week abroad, it seems a long time since home was left; surely a noteworthy hint of the way to increase the enjoyment got out of living.

Realize, then, that the true fun in life consists in doing things not in having them; and that, though comparatively poor, a man can be accounted rich who has the means to get what he wants and does get it. Indeed, the success of your journey depends less on the heaviness of your purse than on your lightness of heart. A healthy man is very much a vagabond in his soul, scorning the conventions, viewing life from a broad standpoint and never so happy as when in old clothes, lightly burdened, and with no watch but his belly.

It is something of an advantage to be one of the world's poor men, though you are unkempt and your travel-stained coat meets glances of disfavour. Your sense of humour is quickened and you no longer believe that rich men are bad any more than that poor men are virtuous. You are willing to associate with poor people, and not ashamed to visit ignorant people, no, nor afraid to be seen with 'wicked' people. You have self-reliance and are ready to laugh at the many discomforts and absurdities of life.

Frank Tatchell
The Happy Traveller
1923

EQUALITY

One feels lonely and free in the vast space of Castile, and the few roads suggest long, monotonous journeys. The eye picks up the green of the rare acacias or poplars which mark the metalled roads. On some mule track we mark the figure of some peasant riding away on a mule: miles between that figure and ourselves – who is he? What is the solitary insect thinking? What peasant with skin incised by wind and sun? We become absorbed, in these dawdling hours, in the task of overtaking a man who would greet one openly, talk in a pure, almost Biblical tongue, and who will speak his business straight out and expect to hear all yours.

'Good day. I am going to Santa X with this corn. I am from that village. There I have my family, my so many brothers, my so many sisters. Where do you come from? What country, what village? Where is England? Is that in France? Are you married? How many children have you? If you have, good; if you have not, bad. God has not granted them. What is your employment? How much do you earn? In your country' – the final deciding question – 'is there plenty to eat?' And after that – some string of proverbs, a page of Don Quixote, a page of Sancho Panza. And then that lordly Spanish sentence of farewell and one's impression that one has been talking as a nobleman to a nobleman – as the Aragonese say, 'We are as noble as the King but not as rich.'

The egalitarianism of the Spaniards is not like the citizenship of the French, nor the anonymity of the English or American democracy, where we seek the lowest common denominator and try to hide our distinctions. The Spanish live in castes, but not in classes, and their equality – the only real equality I have met anywhere in the world – is in the sense of nobility or, rather, in the sense of the absolute quality of the person. One will hear this sentence spoken of people living in the lowest wretchedness: 'They are noble people.' These words are not especially a compliment, nor do they convey resignation, pity, or regret; they are meant almost conventionally, to describe the normal condition of man.

V. S. Pritchett
The Spanish Temper
1954

A VISION OF THE FUTURE

In dark moments I see bay after lonely bay and island after island as they are today and as they may become. The present vision is familiar enough: rough slabs with bollards and capstans, crescents of sand or white pebbles where the fishermen toil barefoot at their nets, caulk and careen their boats, repair their tridents and weave complex fishtraps of wicker and twine. The ribs of caïques assemble above the froth of shavings like whales' skeletons. Humorous, sardonic, self-reliant men live there, lean from their war with the elements, ready to share their wine with any stranger. At nightfall they assemble under the branches outside the single ramshackle taverna. Now and then, after a good catch, if musicians are handy, one of them performs a slow and solitary dance for his own pleasure, and then rejoins the singing and the talk. Sponge fishing and storms and far travel and shipwrecks and half-a-dozen wars, and sometimes smuggling, play a great part in their conversation; laughter often interrupts it. After dark, beyond the caïque masts, the water a mile or two out is scattered with constellations where other sailors are laying their nets from little acetylene-lit fleets or craning overboard to lunge with their long fish-spears. Behind them the alleyways descend the hillside in rivulets of cobbles between archways and escalading whitewash. The smell of basil and rosemary fills these lanes, competing with the salt, tar, sweat, resin, fish scales and sawdust of the waterfront. Their life is rigorous to the point of austerity and sometimes of hardship; but there are a hundred things to make it worth while. There is no trace of depression or wage-slavery in the brine-cured and weather-beaten faces under those threadbare caps. The expression is wary, energetic, amused and friendly and their demeanour is a marine compound of masculinity, independence and easy-going dignity.

Then the second vision assembles. The shore is enlivened with fifty jukeboxes and a thousand transistor wirelesses. Each house is now an artistic bar, a boutique or a curio shop; new hotels tower and concrete villas multiply. Battalions of holidaymakers agleam with lotion relax under striped umbrellas. The roar of the speed-boats sometimes drowns the transistors, sirens announce fresh steamerloads, helicopters clatter. The caïque-building yard has long been cleared away to make room for a row of bathing huts and a concrete lavatory; the spotless Tourist Police stroll past in couples. Somewhere at the edge of this scene, round a table of tubular metal, the old fishermen sit; they approve of the boom but they are slightly at a loss to know why they are not enjoying themselves any more. The Tourist Police tell them that last week's directive from the ministry forbidding bare feet and narghilé-smoking has been reversed: the tourists find them more picturesque. The mayor observes that his new hygiene-order is being enforced: no donkey is unequipped with the regulation net under its tail to catch the droppings; when the new and unnecessary road is finished and the first blasts of exhaust-smoke and klaxon set the final stamp of civilization on the place those obsolete animals will have to go. The struggle for life is over. The old fishermen's sons have jobs as waiters, knick-knack-salesmen and guides. The more personable fulfil a pliant role similar to that of gondoliers or Capri boatmen, while alms keep the little ones supplied with bubble-gum.

No tubular tables in the old taverna. One of a score now, the *boîte* is redecorated with old ships' timbers. Here, by neonrise, candles in bottles gleam from barrels turned into tables, each with its painted skull-and-crossbones; nets are draped from anchors and tridents, the bulbs hang in lobster pots, while another old fisherman's son in fancy dress twirls on the dance floor in an arranged and stepped-up dance based on the *zeibekiko*. Beaming and sweating in carefree clothes, conducted tours accompany the simplified beat with massed clapping and their own electric guitars and accordions. Cameras flash; Westphalia and the Midlands send up their acclaim.

But all is not well. Bronzed by long sojourn and gazing sadly into their highballs and away from the freckled and steaming influx, the older settlers are at bay. Who could have foreseen all this three summers ago; when their yachts first dropped anchor here; when the first village houses were bought and converted, the earliest cocktail cabinets borne ashore, the first property acquired and developed? The gloom of the fifth century AD weighs on them; the dismay of Gothic patricians, long-Romanized, at the sight of their kinsmen fresh from Illyricum swarming through the Aurelian walls. It is time to weigh anchor again and seek remoter islands and farther shores and pray for another three years' reprieve.

This vision of the future is coming true. But only a few places are affected and the islanders have so far withstood the impact with considerable dignity. Perhaps they will take it in their stride. If they do, it will call for heroic qualities. It would be sad if Greece went the way of Italy and the South of France. She deserves a nobler destiny. Let those who are responsible see what five years have done to the south coast of Spain, and tremble.

Patrick Leigh Fermor
Roumeli: Travels in Northern Greece
1966

ACKNOWLEDGEMENTS

Penelope Chetwode, *Two Middle Aged Ladies in Andalusia*, 1963. Reprinted by kind permission of John Murray (Publishers) Ltd.

Norman Douglas, *Old Calabria*, 1915. Reprinted by kind permission of The Society of Authors as the literary representative of the Estate of Norman Douglas.

Norman Douglas, *Siren Land*, 1911. Reprinted by kind permission of Martin Secker & Warburg Ltd.

Aldous Huxley, *Along the Road*, 1925. Reprinted by kind permission of Chatto & Windus Ltd and The Hogarth Press Ltd and Mrs Laura Huxley.

Patrick Leigh Fermor, *Roumeli: Travels in Northern Greece*, 1966. Reprinted by kind permission of John Murray (Publishers) Ltd.

V. S. Pritchett, *The Spanish Temper*, 1954. Reprinted by kind permission of the Peters Fraser & Dunlop Group Ltd.

Frank Tatchell, *The Happy Traveller*, 1923. Reprinted by kind permission of Methuen & Co.

INDEX